Building a Culture of Peace

Building a Culture of Peace

Baptist Peace Fellowship of North America,
the First Seventy Years

PAUL R. DEKAR

☙PICKWICK *Publications* · Eugene, Oregon

BUILDING A CULTURE OF PEACE
Baptist Peace Fellowship of North America, the First Seventy Years

Pickwick Publications
An Imprint of Wipf and Stock Publishers
199 W. 8th Ave., Suite 3
Eugene, OR 97401

www.wipfandstock.com

ISBN 13: 978-1-60608-228-7

Cataloging-in-Publication data:

Dekar, Paul R.

Building a culture of peace : Baptist Peace Fellowship of North America, the first seventy years / Paul R. Dekar.

xiv + 278 p. ; 23 cm. Includes bibliographical references.

ISBN 13: 978-1-60608-228-7

1. Peace — Societies, etc. 2. Peace — Religious aspects — Christianity. 3. War — Religious aspects — Christianity. 4. Pacifism — Religious aspects — Christianity. I. Title.

BT376.4 .D34 2010

Manufactured in the U.S.A.

With Gandhi, I believe that to teach real peace in this world, and carry on a real war against war, we must begin with creating a sustainable future for Emma Jessamine Dekar (now aged five), Abigail Jack-Ellen Dekar (now aged eight), and all children of the next generation.

Contents

Contents

Abbreviations

ABCUSA	American Baptist Churches in the United States of America
AFSC	American Friends Service Committee
BCOQ	Baptist Convention of Ontario and Quebec
BPF	Baptist Pacifist Fellowship
BPFNA	Baptist Peace Fellowship of North America
BP	*Baptist Peacemaker*
BWA	Baptist World Alliance
BNM	Board of National Ministries of the American Baptist Churches USA
CBF	Canadian Baptist Federation
CDC	Centers for Disease Control
CDF	Children's Defense Fund
CSC	Churches Supporting Churches
CPS	Civilian Public Service
CBPPR	*Conferencía Bautísta de la Paz de Puerto Rico*
CEPAD	*Comité Evangélico Pro-Ayuda al Desarrollo*
CO	Conscientious objector
CICEM	*Consejo Indígena Campesino Evangélico de México*
CoBF	Cooperative Baptist Fellowship
CCF	Co-operative Commonwealth Federation
EPMG	Ethics and Public Ministry Group
FMLN	*Frente Farabundo Martí para la Liberación Nacional*
FOR	Fellowship of Reconciliation
GLBT	Gay, Lesbian, Bisexual, and Transgender
HPC	Historic Peace Churches

Abbreviations

HMS	Home Mission Society
IFOR	International Fellowship of Reconciliation
IFCO	Interreligious Foundation for Community Organization
MPF	Muslim Peace Fellowship
OBPF	Ohio Baptist Peace Fellowship
OBC	Ohio Baptist Convention
OBIPP	Olive Branch Interfaith Peace Partnership
PW	*PeaceWork*
ROTC	Reserve Officers' Training Corps
SSS	Selective Service System
SERPAJ-México	*Servicio Paz y Justicia-México*
SIPAZ	*Servicio Internacional para la Paz*
SLORC	State Law and Order Restoration Commission
SBC	Southern Baptist Convention
SCPC	Swarthmore College Peace Collection
TNG	The Next Generation
USSR	Union of Soviet Socialist Republics
UNICEF	United Nations Children's Fund
UBC	University Baptist Church, Minneapolis, Minnesota
WWI	World War I
WWII	World War II
YMCA, YWCA	Young Men's [Women's] Christian Association

Acknowledgments

I HAVE DONE MY best to get permission to use copyrighted material and to check findings with others. I am aware of the need for additional research and am accountable for the final text.

In the introduction I allude to a phrase of Antonio Machado y Ruiz (1875–1939), "caminante, no hay camino, se hace camino al andar." Often cited in Latin America, it reads in English, "Wayfarer, there is no way, you make the way as you go."[1]

In chapter 6, I allude to a poem by Daniel Berrigan, read on a poster gifted to the Open Door Community in Atlanta, Georgia, by Bartimaeus Community Ministry.[2]

> For every 10,000 words
> There's a deed
> Floating somewhere
> head down, unborn
> Words can't make it happen
> They only wave it away
> Unwanted
> Yet Child, necessary One
> Unless you come home to my hands
> why hands at all?
> Your season—your cries
> are their skill
> their reason.

Chapter 1 draws from my article "The 'Good War' and Baptists Who Refused to Fight It," which first appeared in *Peace and Change*. I am grateful for permission to use it.

Chapters 2 through 6 draw on research for an earlier book, *For the Healing of the Nations*, conducted at the Swarthmore College Peace

1 Machado, "Proverbs and Song-Verse," *Selected Poems*, 143.

2 Email, February 2, 2009 from Heather McVoy, Support Services Coordinator, Open Door.

Collection (SCPC) and at the headquarters of the American Baptist Churches USA in Valley Forge, Pennsylvania. In 2008, I did further research at the Baptist Peace Fellowship of North America (BPFNA) archives in Nashville, Tennessee and BPFNA offices in Charlotte, North Carolina. As well, having served from 1984 to 2001 on the steering committee, now called the board of directors, I have a significant personal collection of books and records.

Anyone undertaking further investigation of BPFNA peace work will encounter several names of the organization. The Baptist Pacifist Fellowship formed in 1940 and became in 1963 the Baptist Peace Fellowship. In 1970, it took the name Baptist Fellowship for Peace. In 1974, the group became the American Baptist Peace Fellowship. The newsletter's name also changed, as follows: *Baptist Pacifist Fellowship Newsletter* (1955–1956); *Baptist Peace News* (1957–1973); *Newsletter of the Baptist Fellowship for Peace* (1974–1981); *PeaceWork* (1981–1983). In addition, there were corresponding changes of the organization's logo. The present symbol first appeared on the November 1982 issue of *PeaceWork*.

The BPFNA has had four "homes." After Ken Sehested was hired as Executive Director, Oakhurst Baptist Church in Decatur, Georgia, provided the original office from September 1, 1984 until January 1988 followed by Prescott Memorial Baptist Church in Memphis, Tennessee, until January 1996 when the office moved to the Providence Lodge retreat center at Lake Junaluska, North Carolina, just west of Asheville. In February 1999, the main office moved to Wedgewood Baptist Church in Charlotte, North Carolina. Historically Southern Baptist, now affiliated with the American Baptist Churches USA, this congregation has provided office space for many of the BPFNA staff until the present writing.

In terms of contemporary English usage, I seek to write inclusively but do not change the text when quoting authors who use male language to express inclusive ideas. To avoid possible association of the words "old" as dated or "new" as better, I refer to the First Testament and Second Testament. Citations are from the New Revised Standard Version. Used by Permission. All rights reserved. Unless otherwise indicated, the photographs are from the BPFNA offices and are used with permission.

Foreword

MARY LIN HUDSON

PEACEMAKING IS NOT FOR the faint of heart. It demands commitment and courage, energy and effort. Peacemaking is, at its best, hard work. And yet, when the stories of peacemaking are passed along, they tend to focus attention toward one person of influence who embodies the ideology of a group or on certain pivotal events that symbolize a hope fulfilled. Behind each of these kinds of stories, however, lies a longer narrative in which countless people, conversations, and contributions have come together to give shape to the person or event that is remembered.

Paul Dekar is a historian. He values the stories that shape the consciousness of communities. Paul's view of history, however, has been shaped by a life that challenges conventional assumptions about war and self-interest. Paul Dekar is a peacemaker. He knows first hand the demanding work of faith and action born out of love of God and neighbor. His life's work testifies to the ideals of love and justice, to the extent that, the contours of a historic movement could be revealed in his own autobiography. And yet, Paul knows the faces, the places, the programs and the publications that have all played a part in shaping the efforts of a community of Baptists to stand for peace in the face of violence, from the early part of the twentieth century through the present day. He knows that change comes through the endless efforts of countless persons in community working in love toward a shared ideal. He writes history through the broader lens that recognizes the contributions of many efforts over a lengthy period time that have worked to build and form of a movement of influence in the world, nations, church, families, and in individual lives. In an effort to honor the tradition and understand its significance, Paul Dekar writes history as an act peacemaking itself.

This history of the Baptist Peace Fellowship of North America reveals more than a simple record of all the various leaders, programs, and decisions made by an organized group. As the historical record takes shape, the reader can glimpse a larger story of faith set in the background of American religious history. Like the continuous movement of a river that etches its way through the geographical landscape of a specific location, this movement of non-violent resistance and reconciliation left its mark on a unique landscape of American history and on a distinctive church that had its own political issues and agendas. Without the story of the BPFNA, the Baptist tradition would miss one of its finest testimonies to its own historical ideals of counter-cultural witness to the prevailing popular culture of the day. The story of the BPFNA adds one more important perspective to the wider witness of Christian peacemaking within the larger history of the American church.

At the same time, this history is told from the perspective of one who lived it. Participants in a movement seldom have the luxury of culling through years of records, documents, and memories in order to reflect on the influence of that movement over time. Here, readers find themselves witnessing tense moments on the floor of a convention, to children's poetry read in open air gatherings, to wine glasses clinking over kitchen tables in the wee hours of the night. A movement comes alive in those moments when people risked themselves for the sake of new possibilities. Members of the BPFNA who supported its work for decades can step back with Paul and survey their own amazing journey with an increasing sense of the overarching importance of what has taken place. Looking back, one can see that what may have seemed to be a solitary effort of the moment was really part of something more than simply the sum of its parts. Paul helps us see the bigger picture and understanding its place in both the past and the future.

Stories help us remember. Is remembering simply an exercise in playing old home movies on the closet door of fleeting human consciousness? Or does remembering actually allow the energy, vitality, and spirit of the past to flow into the conscious present and reform it with a power beyond the self? As a historian, liturgist, and preacher, I believe that memory through story rekindles the human desire to look ahead and anticipate a future ending. Thank you, Paul, for remembering well, and offering this story to others for the sake of future endings.

Introduction

T HIS BOOK OPENS A window into a culture of peaceful and coopera- tive life ways. Imagine peace. Imagine being peace. Imagine being peace as a member of nurturing families where feelings are shared hon- estly, anger can be expressed safely, and everyone works cooperatively to resolve problems. Imagine being peace as a member of a worshipping congregation in which disagreement is understood to be a natural and normal opportunity to search together for resourceful solutions to con- flicts. Imagine being peace as a student in schools where no one bullies anyone and everyone feels safe. Imagine being peace in communities that respond to crime by working to find ways creatively and appropriately to restore what has been damaged or destroyed. Imagine being peace as a member of a nation in which everyone has enough. Imagine being peace as a member of a culture in which it has become second nature to consid- er the impact one's lifestyle and decisions will have on the earth. Imagine living in a world in which all people are respected, loved and realize their identity as beloved of God. Imagine being part of a culture of peace.[1]

The Baptist Peace Fellowship of North America (BPFNA) is a grass- roots movement of people who imagine and work actively to build a culture of peace rooted in justice. A culture of peace is a set of values, at- titudes, modes of behavior, and ways of life. Individuals, groups, and com- munities can form cultures of peace. Members seek to address problems through dialogue and negotiation. They seek to identify the root causes of conflict by anticipating, addressing and thus averting them. They reject violence as a way to affect change. Nonviolent peacemakers do not seek to defeat or humiliate opponents. Rather, they seek to win their friendship and understanding.[2]

The roots of twentieth-century Christian pacifism may be found in the peace teachings of the Bible and the witness of early Christians.

1. Polaski, "Learning to See."
2. Boulding, *Cultures of Peace*, 1.

With antecedents in medieval monasticism and several sectarian movements, adherents of various streams of Anabaptists, the Religious Society of Friends, and the Church of the Brethren—the historic peace churches (HPC)—have brought to North America a tradition of peacemaking that concentrates on compassionate service, loving even one's enemy, and nonresistance.

The latter term derives from Jesus' instruction to "resist not evil" (Matt 5:39 KJV) or "evildoers" (RSV), part of his Sermon on the Mount (Matthew 5–7) or Plain (Luke 6:17 KJV). Looking to these biblical passages as a realistic guide to living rather than an impossible ideal, Christian pacifists seek "the things that make for peace" (Luke 19:42).

On November 18, 1939, Laurence T. Hosie, Fellowship of Reconciliation (FOR) Field and Industrial Secretary and a Baptist pastor, opened his home in Leonia, New Jersey, for a gathering of several Baptist pacifists. They were part of the Northern Baptist Convention. In 1950, the denomination took the name American Baptist Convention and, after reorganization in 1972, the American Baptist Churches in the United States of America.

The group discussed the likelihood that conflicts which were at the time still limited to parts of Europe and Asia would widen into a second world war and that the United States would be involved. They recalled circumstances of 1917 when the United States instituted a draft without providing adequately for conscientious objectors (COs), persons who by reason of deeply held moral, ethical, or religious beliefs are opposed to participating in the armed forces.

The threat of a national system of military conscription and of the entry of the United States into the war intensified. On May 24, 1940, some of the founding group gathered with others during the annual convention of the denomination. Taking a positive stand for Christ's way of redemptive love in all the individual and social relationships of life, they organized the Baptist Pacifist Fellowship (BPF) and affiliated with FOR.

On September 14, 1940, the Congress of the United States enacted the Selective Training and Service Act (STSA). Men between the ages of twenty-one and thirty had to register with local draft boards. After the December 7, 1941 bombing of Pearl Harbor the United States entered World War II. All men aged eighteen to sixty-five were required to register and all men aged eighteen to forty-five were made liable for military service.

During the ensuing years, BPF members encouraged other Baptists in the Northern Baptist Convention to recognize the freedom of conscience of COs and to provide financial assistance to those who did noncombatant service within the military and those in Civilian Public Service (CPS). They continued these needed activities through the Korean and Vietnam wars until 1973 when Congress ended conscription and instituted in its place an all-volunteer army.

Use of nuclear weapons against Hiroshima and Nagasaki in 1945 and the threat of nuclear war after August 29, 1949, when the Soviet Union became a nuclear power, led some Christians who had not previously been active in the peace movement to adopt a stance of nuclear pacifism. These were people who considered the impersonal annihilation of large numbers of defenseless civilians through the use of nuclear weapons to be so contrary to the spirit of Christ that they could not in conscience participate in a system which threatened to bring the superpower alliances to the brink of nuclear war. They found themselves at home in the BPF, perhaps more so as the organization began occasionally to use the alternative title, Baptist Peace Fellowship. Formal adoption of the name in 1963 enabled BPF members to undertake a wider range of peace initiatives.

Baptist peacemaking groups developed in other parts of the Baptist family. During World War II, the Southern Baptist Convention formally and officially recognized the legitimacy of conscientious objection to war. The denomination created a mechanism whereby those so persuaded could register their dissent. Some did. For the duration of the war and through the Korean and Vietnamese conflicts, some Southern Baptists sought CO status. In 1980, Southern Baptists re-formed a Committee for Conscientious Objection. Also that year, a group of faculty and students at Southern Baptist Theological Seminary in Louisville, Kentucky began publishing *Baptist Peacemaker*, a journal which has remained for thirty years a voice for radical Baptists.

In 1980 Mary Cosby of the Church of the Saviour in Washington DC, addressed delegates to assemblies of the Baptist Convention of Ontario and Quebec and Baptist Women's Missionary Society. Responding to her challenge to make Christian peacemaking a priority for prayer, study, and action, fifty people formed Baptists of Ontario and Quebec for Peace and Justice. A steering committee organized the first of what would become for twenty years an annual event. In December 1981, Cosby returned to the first retreat at Ganaraska Woods, a farm owned by Calvary Baptist

Church of Toronto. She addressed thirty-five Baptists from a number of different congregations. A few months later, the first issue of *Baptist Peace Link,* the group's newsletter appeared.

In 1983 a group composed of clergy, church members, and the general public organized the *Conferencía Bautísta de la Paz de Puerto Rico.* Members recognized the need to address concerns of local significance, such as the presence of nuclear arms in Puerto Rico, the future status of the "commonwealth," and the use by the United States Navy of its base on Vieques, an island municipality just off the northeast coast of Puerto Rico, for bombing target practice.

During the Second World War, FOR member Devere Allen (1891–1955) was based in *México,* where he began publishing and distributing literature throughout Latin America. More recently, Baptists have been part of an IFOR affiliate founded in 1987, *Servicio Paz y Justicia-México (SERPAJ-México),* and a program which had its beginning in 1995, following the Zapatista uprising in 1994, *Servicio Internacional para la Paz* (SIPAZ). Baptists helped form the latter to monitor the conflict and to promote a culture of peace in Chiapas. Increasingly, it has worked in Oaxaca, Guerrero, or other states in *México.* Mexican law has required all males between eighteen and forty-five years of age to perform military service.

The early 1980s were perilous years. Many questioned if the world would survive the confrontation of two superpowers armed with nuclear weapons. Writing three decades later, I cannot understate just how visionary was the initiative of BPF board president Richard Newell Myers to organize a friendship tour by Baptists from the United States to the former Soviet Union.

The trip took place during May 5–19, 1983 at the peak of the Cold War. Forty-nine Southern, American, and National Baptists participated in the tour. They had two goals: contacting Baptists in the USSR and sharing their concern for world peace. Arriving at the Moscow airport, the group was tested. Soviet authorities seized their Bibles and threatened to confiscate 350 copies of an issue of *Baptist Peacemaker.* One of its founders, Robert C. Broome, stood his ground. He stalwartly defended the publication and announced to the customs officials that group members were bringing gifts for members of the Soviet Peace Committee. The Evangelical Union intervened. Officials returned all of the materials. Group members subsequently delivered the literature to Baptist congregations.

The delegation worshipped in sanctuaries near where silos with Soviet missiles pointed at targets in the north central United States, whose missiles were pointed at the Soviet locations. In spite of this, a sense of hope prevailed. In the words of tour member Tom Walsh, an attorney and member of Prescott Memorial Baptist Church in Memphis, Tennessee, "When we looked at one another with this weighing on our minds, we could only embrace and pray that somehow, each nation could see the human face of the other. Then, surely, the nuclear madness would end."[3]

Hope came in another form. Some of the participants in the 1983 friendship tour met from August 27–28 in Washington DC, where they marked the twentieth anniversary of the March on Washington.[4] This in turn fueled efforts to arrange a meeting of American and Southern Baptists. The desire was to explore making peace between two parts of a divided family as well as joining together in common efforts in the nation and the world at large. Organizers also sought to extricate peacemaking from an association, for some people, with passivity.

Participants met March 30–31, 1984 at Deer Park Baptist Church in Louisville, Kentucky. At the end of the weekend, the group took the name Baptist Peace Fellowship of North America, appointed officers, and formulated goals. It was *kairos,* "fullness of time," and tongues of fire, the confluence of Dixie, Midwestern, and Yankee drawls. In just thirty-six hours, infant BPFNA was born. The phrase "North America" in BPFNA was tacked on in good faith. BPFNA founders promised to address two concerns: first, Baptists in the United States desperately needed an international perspective. Second, the continent's millions of Baptists, most numerous after the Catholics among Christians, needed peace and justice in their heart.

BPFNA has miraculously addressed both needs. Having begun without any guarantee of success, a Baptist peace network exists with several thousand members, regional groups, over eighty partner congregations from the North America Baptist family, and covenant relationships with myriad organizations. From around the continent, Baptist peacemakers come together for peace camps, friendship tours, training programs, and other activities. Baptist peacemakers around the world have discovered

3. Walsh, "Baptist Peace Mission to Russia."

4. Email, Richard Myers, April 13, 2008. What follows draws on Rachel Gill's talk in Ottawa, Ontario, July 6, 1990 at the fifth peace camp; Sehested, "The Road to Rome"; Williamson, "Twenty-five Jubilees."

one another at four international Baptist peace conferences held in Sjövik, Sweden (1988), La Boquita, Nicaragua (1992), Melbourne, Australia (2000), and Rome, Italy (2009). There have been regional gatherings as well in Chiang Mai, Thailand (1996) and in Birmingham, England (2005) during the nineteenth Baptist World Alliance (BWA) congress.

BPFNA members think globally and act locally while trying to build a culture of peace in societies marred by violence. In reality, the world is a configuration of neighborhoods and communities with populations and problems not over there but right here, wherever here may be. In such a diverse world, it is a sign of hope that a few Baptists living in Canada, Mexico, Puerto Rico, and the United States have claimed an identity which transcends specific nationalities and is enriched by all of the world's cultures. Baptist peacemakers have committed themselves to building a culture of peace rooted in justice for not only themselves, but all people.

WHY THIS BOOK?

This book is not primarily an exercise in historical introspection. We live in a world in which evil persists and technology assaults human dignity. Intolerance, poverty, war, so-called scientific progress and other forces engender opportunities to be involved in social change movements. Struggles in these arenas are making the Civil Rights Movement of the 1950s and 1960s look like a picnic Dr. Bernice Johnson Reagon, activist and lead singer with Sweet Honey in the Rock, made this point twenty years ago by in an interview with journalist Bill Moyers.[5]

In the novel *Ceremony*, Leslie Marmon Silko explores the deep connections between healing and peacemaking in her Laguna Pueblo culture. Emphasizing the importance of story, Silko writes, "I will tell you something about stories . . . They aren't just for entertainment. Don't be fooled. They are all we have, you see, all we have to fight off illness and death. You don't have anything if you don't have stories."[6]

Telling the BPF-BPFNA story has arisen from my own. I am the son of parents who fled to North America in the 1920s out of their experiences of war, revolution, and genocide. As a student at the University of California, Berkeley from 1961–1965, I became involved in the civil

---

5. In Farley and Jones, *Liberating Eschatology,* 224, Joan M. Martin cites Reagon, "The Songs Are Free."

6. Silko, *Ceremony,* 2.

rights and anti-war movements of the day. Subsequently, from September 1965 through May 1967, I studied at Colgate Rochester Divinity School in Rochester, New York. I was wrestling with accepting pacifism and sought the advice of Gene Bartlett, seminary president at the time. Dr. Bartlett encouraged me, as he did others working against the Vietnam War. He suggested that I contact the Baptist Peace Fellowship and Fellowship of Reconciliation. I joined both organizations.

At the time I did not know of Dr. Bartlett's earlier involvement with these organizations. Later I learned from his son David Bartlett that his father "was very supportive of those of us who worked against the Vietnam War."[7]

At a crucial moment in my discernment process, a speech by Dr. Martin Luther King, Jr., confirmed the direction my emerging pacifist convictions were taking me. On April 4, 1967 at The Riverside Church in New York City, Dr. King warned that "a nation that continues year after year to spend more money on military defense than on programs of social uplift is approaching spiritual death." Dr. King urged ministers to give up their ministerial immunity from conscription and to seek status as conscientious objectors.[8]

After I read Dr. King's speech, I decided to give up my seminary exemption. With needed support from my future wife Nancy and others, I went before my draft board and offered to do alternative service as a conscientious objector. This led to my work for three years with the United States government, after which I returned to Colgate Rochester Divinity School. On May 28, 1971, I received the Master of Divinity degree.

Writing for readers in varied contexts, I am struck by the ongoing significance of Dr. King in my life as well as in the lives of many members of the BPFNA and its predecessor organizations. In a war-wearied, war-worried world, Dr. King asks questions as germane today as forty years ago or earlier.

How for example does a good neighbor think or behave? Dr. King reflected on this question in his Riverside Church address. He used a story in Luke 10:29–37. A lawyer asked Jesus, "Who is my neighbor?" Jesus responded by telling of a man mugged and left for dead on the road between Jericho and Jerusalem. A priest and a Levite passed by the man

7. Email, January 3, 2006.
8. Washington, *Testament of Hope*, 240–41.

on their way to religious services. A foreigner not expected to show sympathy to Jews came along. The "good Samaritan" was moved with pity and helped the man at the side of the road. Jesus asked the lawyer, "Which of these three . . . was a neighbor to the man who fell into the hands of the robbers?" The lawyer answered, "The one who showed him mercy." Jesus replied, "Go and do likewise."

In his discussion of this story, Dr. King observed that the merciful response to the plight of the man left for dead on the road between Jericho and Jerusalem was needed. However, it was "only an initial act. One day we must come to see that the whole Jericho road must be transformed so that men and women will not be constantly beaten and robbed as they make their journey on life's highway. True compassion is more than flinging a coin to a beggar; it is not haphazard and superficial."[9]

A year later, on April 3, 1968, Dr. King was in Memphis, Tennessee, to support striking sanitation workers. Dr. King stressed the importance of their struggle as part of a wider challenge to white society in the United States. Dr. King stressed that the movement must "always anchor our external direct action with the power of economic withdrawal." Dr. King called for "a kind of dangerous unselfishness." As an example, he returned to the story of the good Samaritan. Dr. King asked people to imagine why the priest and Levite failed to stop. Dr. King then considered some plausible thoughts which might have stirred in the minds of the two religious leaders when they saw the man at the side of the road. Perhaps they were late for a church meeting. Perhaps they were on the way to organize a "Jericho Road Improvement Association" and felt it was better to deal with the problem from the causal root, rather than to get bogged down with an individual effort. Perhaps they felt that the man on the ground was merely faking. For whatever reason, the first question which went through their mind was this, "If I stop to help this man in need, what will happen to me?" Dr. King re-framed and contextualized the problem by asking, "If I do not stop to help the sanitation workers, what will happen to them?"

Dr. King urged that everyone who had packed into Mason Temple to hear him stand with a greater determination. Consistent with his rhetoric over many years, Dr. King acknowledged that the United States was deeply flawed. He challenged his audience to rise to the challenge of making

9. Ibid., 241.

the United States what it ought to be. "We have an opportunity to make America a better nation." Dr. King thanked God for allowing him to carry on. "Whenever men and women straighten their backs up, they are going somewhere, because a man can't ride your back unless it is bent."

Dr. King concluded his April 3, 1968 speech by affirming that he would not give up in the face of threats on his life.

> Well, I don't know what will happen now. We've got some difficult days ahead. But it doesn't matter with me now. Because I've been to the mountaintop. And I don't mind. Like anybody, I would like to live a long life. Longevity has its place. But I'm not concerned about that now. I just want to do God's will. And He's allowed me to go up to the mountain. And I've looked over. And I've seen the promised land. I may not get there with you. But I want you to know tonight, that we, as a people will get to the promised land. And I'm happy tonight. I'm not worried about anything. I'm not fearing any man. Mine eyes have seen the glory of the coming of the Lord.[10]

Less than twenty-four hours later, Dr. King was dead. His dream of a beloved community and of a world house—his phrases for a culture of peace—did not die with him. He never considered his dream as utopian. He saw it as a realistic goal which could be attained by a critical mass of people committed to and trained in nonviolence. This was evident as early as December 3, 1956 when Dr. King addressed the First Institute on Nonviolence and Social Change at Holt Street Baptist Church in Montgomery, Alabama,

> . . . love might well be the salvation of our civilization. This is why I am so impressed with our motto "Freedom and Justice through Love." Not through violence; not through hate; no, not even through boycotts; but through love. It is true that as we struggle for freedom in America [and the world] we will have to boycott at times. But we must remember as we boycott that a boycott is not an end within itself; it is merely a means to awaken a sense of shame within the oppressor and challenge his false sense of superiority. But the end is reconciliation; the end is redemption; the end is the creation of the beloved community.[11]

Dr. King first used the world house metaphor in a lecture given at the Auditorium of the University of Oslo on December 11, 1964, the

10. Ibid., 282–86. In his original manuscript Dr. King gave the speech no title.
11. Ibid., 140.

day after he received the Nobel Peace Prize. Unlike Dr. King's speech of acceptance delivered the day before in the same place, Dr. King's lecture has largely been forgotten. In my view this has reflected a tendency to treat Dr. King as an icon rather than a prophet whose radical ideas and actions should continue to engage us in the unfinished work of freedom, justice, and peace.

Speaking in Norway, Dr. King told of a deceased novelist among whose papers was an idea for a future story of a widely separated family which inherits a house in which they must live together. For Dr. King, this communicated a great new problem of humankind. "We have inherited a large house, a great world house in which we have to live together—black and white, easterner and westerner, Gentile and Jew, Catholic and Protestant, Muslim and Hindu—a family unduly separated in ideas, culture and interest, who, because we can never again live apart, must learn somehow to live with each other in peace." Dr. King called for true compassion, a revolution of values, nonviolent coexistence rather than violent co-annihilation, and interrelatedness as a moral imperative. "Whatever affects one directly affects all indirectly."[12]

Dr. King never attempted to systemize the content of the beloved community or world house images. Nonetheless, these phrases expressed his vision for church and society reformed in non-racist, inclusive ways. In a speech given in Los Angeles on February 25, 1967, Dr. King said,

> The past is prophetic in that it asserts loudly that wars are poor chisels for carving out peaceful tomorrows. One must come to see that peace is not merely a distant goal that we seek, but a means by which we arrive at that goal. We must pursue peaceful ends through peaceful means.

Continuing, Dr. King denounced the "triple evils of racism, extreme materialism and war." Evoking the story of the prodigal son (Luke 15:11–32), Dr. King called on those who love peace to organize as effectively as the war hawks,

> As they spread the propaganda of war we must spread the propaganda of peace. We must combine the fervor of the civil rights movement with the peace movement. We must demonstrate, teach and preach, until the very foundations of our nation are shaken. We must work unceasingly to lift this nation that we love to a

12. King, "The Quest for Peace and Justice." *Where Do We Go from Here?*, 167–91.

higher destiny, to a new plateau of compassion, to a more noble expression of humane-ness.[13]

These words reverberated in the United States and worldwide. Like many others (but unlike millions who opposed Dr. King) I was inspired by Dr. King in 1963 when he spoke in support of African Americans as they marched on Washington DC to demand civil rights, in 1967 when Dr. King condemned the war in Vietnam, and again in 1968 when he demanded economic and social rights, not just for African Americans, but also for poor whites, Hispanics, Vietnamese, and others. Dr. King's death on the eve of a second march on Washington spurred me, along with a generation of courageous Baptist peacemakers to take up his challenge to struggle for a new world. He shaped an agenda which still includes work to eliminate every vestige of racism, to overcome poverty, to end war, and to use science and technology for good ends.

Researching, writing, and presenting the BPF-BPFNA story, I pray the prophetic witness of Dr. King and other Baptist peacemakers will resonate not only with Baptist readers. If a significant number of members of the world's faith traditions were to embrace one another as neighbors and together work to extricate our societies from culture-specific forms of racism, materialism, militarism, and technological determinism, the emerging planetary culture would experience a powerful surge toward enduring peace. Embedded in one another's lives, we share life on a crowded, fragile, and precious planet. May this book stimulate new thinking and purposeful action to build together a culture of peace rooted in justice and active peacemaking.

OUTLINE

Chapter one highlights the origins of BPFNA as the BPF. Members assisted Baptist COs during the Second World War.

Chapter two summarizes the period from 1945 until 1984, the year when Baptists from several North American bodies came together to form the BPFNA. Highlights include continued support for COs during the Korean and Vietnam conflicts; solidarity with victims of wars in Northern Ireland, Afghanistan, Central America, and elsewhere; creation of the Dahlberg Peace Prize and the naming of Dr. Martin Luther King,

---

13. King, "Casualties of the War."

Jr., as its first recipient (1964); and the journey of reconciliation to the former Soviet Union (1983).

Chapter three shifts our focus to the BPFNA. Highlights include the formation of BPFNA and the first twenty-three peace camps. At the time of writing, Weber State University in Ogden, Utah is scheduled to host the twenty-fourth, July 20–25, 2009, with the theme, "When There Is Justice, Then Peace Will Come!"

Chapter four highlights other programs including supporting local networks and partner congregations; training in conflict transformation and restorative justice; equipping youth, recognized formally as The Next Generation (now The Youth and Young Adults); friendship tours within North America; and several publications: *PeaceWork*, *Baptist Peacemaker* after 1990 when the BPFNA assumed responsibility for it, books, and the website.

Chapter five explores the emerging global Baptist peace network. We highlight international friendship tours, conferences, and training events, as well as projects in Burma (Myanmar), *México*, Central America, India, Sudan, and elsewhere supported by a bequest from the estate of Victor and Eileen Gavel.

Chapter six identifies three areas in which the BPFNA became more inclusive in its vision. Three brief case studies explore the process by which the board adopted unanimously in 1995 a statement, entitled "Justice and Sexual Orientation," initiated the Gleaners Project in 1999 to create partnerships with the poor for economic self-development, and undertook after the attacks of September 11, 2001 interfaith peace building with members of another FOR affiliated organization, the Muslim Peace Fellowship.

Chapter seven assesses Martin E. Marty's observation that the coupling of *Baptist* and *peace* is an oxymoron. Highlighting the experience of BPFNA members, this chapter points ways forward by which Baptists can "seek peace, and pursue it" (Ps 34:14).[14]

WORDS OF APPRECIATION

Books are rarely the product of one person's work, or even two. No one has helped me more than Nancy Rose Dekar. My wife for over forty years,

14. Marty, "Foreword," xi. The phrase "Seek Peace and Pursue It" was the theme of the International Baptist Peace Conference, August 3–7, 1988.

Nancy lives our praying and prays our living. This book arises from commitments shared as we have walked our journey together. BPFNA has been a spiritual home for us, for our family, and for countless others. Experiencing joy in listening to, or reading the stories of a wide stream of men and women, largely unheralded, I have appreciated Shakespeare's words,

> Whereof what's past is prologue, what to come
> In yours and my discharge.[15]

Many have responded to inquiries. Johnny Almond, Kathy Coogan, Katie Cook, Evelyn Hanneman, LeDayne McLeese Polaski, and Bob Spinks—members of the BPFNA staff—and Tom and Martha Bryson facilitated my visit to the present offices. Beverly Donald, Molly Pennington Epperson, Gary Gunderson, Grace Hammond, Sarah Hammond, Andy R. Loving, Dwight M. Lundgren, Courtney Walsh Marsh, Phil and Elaine Pennington, Ken Sehested, Tom Walsh, Paula Womack, and others have responded to questions and made suggestions about draft material. Nancy Rose Dekar, Carol Eklund, Stacy Li, Lee McKenna, Michael Webb, and George Williamson, Jr., read and commented on the entire manuscript. I have tried to incorporate as many of their suggestions as possible. I am fully responsible for the final outcome.

Friends who challenge and inspire me, George Williamson, Jr., and Ken Sehested warrant special recognition. George grew up a true-believing son of Jim Crow culture. He got caught up in the sit-in movement while a student at Wake Forest College in North Carolina. Ever since, he has sought to follow Jesus faithfully in several roles: teacher, pastor, husband, father, grandfather, and in service of the BPFNA as board president, pastor to the board, speaker, writer, and skinhead for peace.[16] In August 1984, George called me in Canada and invited me to attend a BPFNA board meeting in Granville, Ohio. I wanted to say no. I have never regretted saying yes.

---

15. Shakespeare, *The Tempest*, act 2, scene 1, lines 247–88. Antonio is speaking. The phrase "What's past is prologue" is carved on the National Archives Building, Washington DC.

16. George often wears a t-shirt, available from Northern Sun, with a picture of Gandhi and the words "Another Skinhead for Peace." For a brief biography see, Williamson, *Radicals*.

That summer, Ken Sehested had left the staff of *Seeds* magazine, then based at Oakhurst Baptist Church in Decatur, Georgia, to become Executive Director for the nascent BPFNA. Preacher, writer, and organizer, Ken was committed to work within the traditional Christian community, of which Baptists are a significant part, raising questions about what it means to name Jesus as Lord. Ken nudged me to find creative, tangible ways to live out my faith and so make a difference for a better world, especially to the benefit of those who are voiceless and powerless. BPFNA's growth over his eighteen years of stewardship attests to Ken's rare blend of insight, passion, and vision for building a culture of peace. In recognition of his peacemaking work, Ken received the American Baptist Churches' Dahlberg Peace Prize in 1995.[17]

Others have helped me to complete this book. Colleagues, staff, and students at Memphis Theological Seminary, where I served as a faculty member from January 1995 until May 2008, supported my peace activity and scholarship very concretely. I am especially grateful for the foreword by Dr. Mary Lin Hudson, Professor of Homiletics and Liturgics at Memphis Theological Seminary. Dr. Hudson led the music during the sixth peace camp at Linfield College. This proved to be a fortuitous introduction to a future colleague and friend whose gifts as liturgist, preacher, singer, and teacher have brought me and countless others joy.

I am equally grateful to Dr. Liliane Kshensky Baxter, Director of the Lillian and A. J. Weinberg Center for Holocaust Education at the Breman Jewish Heritage and Holocaust Museum in Atlanta. A former chair of the FOR National Council (2001–2003), she is married to Tom Baxter, editor of the *Southern Political Report*, who was raised a Baptist.

I have consulted two collections in addition to papers currently held at the BPFNA office in Charlotte, North Carolina. The Southern Baptist Historical Library and Archives in Nashville, Tennessee has become the main BPFNA repository. Director and Archivist Bill Sumners guided me to relevant holdings. In Pennsylvania, the curator of the Swarthmore College Peace Collection, Wendy Chmielewski, and her excellent staff, including Barbara Addison, Michelle Ciarlo-Hayes, Anne Yoder, and especially Wilma Mosholder, now deceased, helped me mine FOR's archives and invaluable BPF papers.

---

17. Cook, "Ken Sehested." For an early statement of his vision, "Plotting the Resurrection."

Introduction

For the first chapter, I have drawn on stories which Paula Womack began to record during her studies at Southwestern Baptist Theological Seminary in Fort Worth. She continued to collect materials when she served as an intern and then on BPFNA's staff.

Finally, I am grateful to Pickwick Publications, a division of Wipf and Stock Publishers, for taking on this project. In particular, Charlie Collier and Patrick Harrison have provided editorial help.

Artwork used in *Baptist Peacemaker* 21 (Summer 2001)
by Rebecca S. Ward.

1

The Baptist Pacifist Fellowship

BACKGROUND

O N APRIL 2, 1917, President Woodrow Wilson went before a joint session of Congress and called on the United States to enter what became known as the Great War. Christians generally supported his argument that the war would make the world safe for democracy. Most Christian pastors backed the war effort, as did the leaders of the recently formed Federal Council of Churches of Christ. Most denominations adopted resolutions embracing the war as a just cause. Older peace societies went into decline.

There were exceptions. These included the Historic Peace Churches (HPCs) and new pacifist organizations such as the Fellowship of Reconciliation (FOR). FOR began in Britain in 1914. The next year, on November 11, 1915, the North American FOR emerged during a conference in Garden City, New York. Sixty-eight participants included thirty-five women. The founders agreed to a statement of purpose according to which members rejected war unconditionally, proclaimed reliance on God, and expressed a determination to live according to God's revolutionary principle of love.

For the duration of the Great War, FOR offered counseling and other assistance to conscientious objectors. Among their numbers, some Baptists did alternative service or went to jail. FOR also sought to strengthen the resolve of scattered members to resist patriotic war fever and to protest the militaristic attitude of churches.

Several prominent Baptists joined FOR including Walter Rauschenbusch (1861–1918), Dores Sharpe (1885–1981), Edwin Theodore Dahlberg (1893–1986), and Harry Emerson Fosdick (1878–1969). Rauschenbusch

Edwin Dahlberg delivering "The Churches and the National Conscience" address at Hartford CT in 1959. Photo from NCC, George Conklin.

was a pastor and leading theologian of social Christianity. At the end of his career, he taught at Rochester Theological Seminary. During the first world war, he formed a "peace group" because he believed the conflict was fueled primarily by the profit motive rather than by fundamental issues of justice. Discovering the newly-formed pacifist movement, he wrote Dores Sharpe that it was "an electric shock to get together with people more radical than I am, that take the Sermon on the Mount seriously."[1]

Sharpe grew up on a farm near the St. John River in New Brunswick, Canada. During the war, Sharpe studied at Rochester Theological Seminary where he served as an assistant to Rauschenbusch. After graduation, Sharpe ministered with distinction in Canada and the United States and later wrote the first biography of Rauschenbusch. Theologian Bernie Loomer observed,

> The range and depth of his passion for justice in the economic, political, and social dimensions of our common life, and the degree of his contributions to the advance of the concerns of the kingdom constitute surely one of the finest exemplifications of the social Gospel in American Protestantism during the present century. Walter Rauschenbusch sired a worthy disciple indeed.[2]

1. Minus, *Walter Rauschenbusch*, 182; Handy, *Social Gospel in America*, for the influence of the movement.

2. Loomer, "Dores R. Sharpe," 104.

Dahlberg, onetime secretary to Walter Rauschenbusch and a Northern Baptist minister ordained in 1918, became a conscientious objector during the First World War. Though his pacifism during both world wars was controversial, Northern Baptists elected Dahlberg to head the denomination (1946–1947), and he later served as President of the National Council of Churches (1957–1960).

Many regarded Harry Emerson Fosdick as the greatest preacher of his generation. Some, including Dr. Martin Luther King, Jr., considered him a prophet. Fosdick supported involvement by the United States in the Great War. However, at the end of the war he toured the trenches and turned to pacifism. Fosdick resolved, "I must never again put my Christian ministry at the nation's disposal for the sanction and backing of war."[3] As a result, he became a member of FOR, explaining,

> Having seen at first hand what war means in the first world con-
> flict, my conscience could no longer dodge the issue: that war, in
> its cases, processes and results, is the complete denial of everything
> that Jesus Christ stands for. I welcomed then, as I do still, a fellow-
> ship which takes Christ's ways of life seriously—not simply as an
> ideal dream for tomorrow but as a practical program today.[4]

An outcome of the Great War was a strengthened resolve by Baptist peacemakers and others to work for a world without war. Many recognized that the Great War and the terms of settlement by which the conflict formally ended set the stage for a second global war. In part, this was because the United States, a new superpower, refused to ratify the Treaty of Versailles. Despite the failure of the United States to join the League of Nations, FOR and other international organizations sought to eliminate war as a means of resolving disputes.

Animated by a vision of a world without war, peace advocates worked for disarmament and to eliminate the causes of war. Pacifism flourished. Speaking on December 14, 1930 at the Ritz-Carlton Hotel in New York City, Albert Einstein argued that there were two ways of resisting war. In countries where there was a draft, the pacifist could refuse military duty. "If only 2 percent of the men liable for war service were to refuse," Einstein said, "there would not be enough jails in the world to take care of them." The other option was for pacifists in countries such as the United States

3. Fosdick, *Living of These Days*, 293.

4. FOR USA pamphlet, 1958.

and England where no draft existed at the time to declare publicly that he would not, under any circumstances, bear arms. He and Mrs. Einstein got an ovation.[5]

On February 9, 1933, students at Oxford University in England debated the resolution, "That this House will in no circumstances fight for its King and Country." It passed 275 to 153. In 1934 in the United States, the Northern Baptist Convention imbibed the spirit of the times and called on Baptists to agree to a non-aggression pledge, saying "I will cross no national boundary line to kill and to destroy, nor will I support my government in sending its army or navy to do so."[6] In Canada during the 1930s, pacifist sentiment was even greater than in the United States. FOR chapters sprang up in several regions of Canada.

Baptist pacifists understood that sin operates individually *and* collectively and that the reign of God would not come easily. Applying pacifist sentiments to concrete issues, such as war in Ethiopia or Spain, was left to individual believers. Yet Baptists, especially those influenced by Rauschenbusch, Fosdick, and other leading proponents of social Christianity, did not simply give voice to conscience. They actively undertook local initiatives for positive peace.

Dr. Martin Luther King, Jr., formulated this concept during the 382-day Montgomery bus boycott (December 1, 1955–December 21, 1956). In a sermon preached at Dexter Avenue Baptist Church on March 18, 1956, early during the Montgomery campaign, Dr. King contrasted "true" or positive peace with negative peace:

> [Jesus says] I come to declare war over injustice. I come to declare war on evil. Peace is not merely the absence of some negative force—war, tension, confusion, but it is the presence of some positive force—justice, goodwill and the power of the kingdom of God. . . . Peace is not merely the absence of this tension [race relations], but the presence of justice. . . . If the Negro accepts his place, accepts exploitation and injustice, there will be peace. But it would be a peace boiled down to stagnant complacency, deadening passivity, and if peace means this, I don't want peace. If peace means accepting second-class citizenship, I don't want it. If peace means keeping my mouth shut in the midst of injustice and evil, I don't want it. If peace means being complacently adjusted to a deadening status quo, I don't want peace. If peace means a willingness to

5. Cited by Baker, *Human Smoke*, 23.

6. Trulson, "Baptist Pacifism," 211.

be exploited economically, dominated politically, humiliated and segregated, I don't want peace. So in a passive, nonviolent manner, we must revolt against this peace.[7]

Dr. King returned to the theme when he went to Birmingham to participate in the civil rights movement there. In January 1963 a group of white clergy pleaded in an open letter to call off the demonstrations and to allow for the courts to achieve integration. Finding himself in jail, Dr. King responded on April 16 in the form of an open letter. He cited biblical examples of civil disobedience and turned to more recent examples of resistance to unjust laws. He recalled that everything Hitler did in Germany was legal and everything the Hungarian freedom fighters did in Hungary in 1956 was illegal. Dr. King suggested that, had he lived in Germany or Hungary at the time, he would have advocated disobedience of the unjust laws. Dr. King continued,

> I must confess that over the past few years I have been gravely disappointed with the white moderate. I have almost reached the regrettable conclusion that the Negro's great stumbling block in his stride toward freedom is not the White Citizen's Councilor or the Ku Klux Klanner, but the white moderate, who is more devoted to "order" than to justice; who prefers a negative peace which is the absence of tension to a positive peace which is the presence of justice; who constantly says: "I agree with you in the goal you seek, but I cannot agree with your methods of direct action"; who paternalistically believes he can set the timetable for another man's freedom; who lives by a mythical concept of time and who constantly advises the Negro to wait for a "more convenient season." Shallow understanding from people of good will is more frustrating than absolute misunderstanding from people of ill will. Lukewarm acceptance is much more bewildering than outright rejection.
>
> I had hoped that the white moderate would understand that law and order exist for the purpose of establishing justice and that when they fail in this purpose they become the dangerously structured dams that block the flow of social progress. I had hoped that the white moderate would understand that the present tension in the South is a necessary phase of the transition from an obnoxious negative peace, in which the Negro passively accepted his unjust plight, to a substantive and positive peace, in which all men will respect the dignity and worth of human personality. Actually, we who engage in nonviolent direct action are not the creators of

7. "When Peace Becomes Obnoxious," *King Papers* 3, 207–8.

tension. We merely bring to the surface the hidden tension that is already alive. We bring it out in the open, where it can be seen and dealt with. Like a boil that can never be cured so long as it is covered up but must be opened with all its ugliness to the natural medicines of air and light, injustice must be exposed, with all the tension its exposure creates, to the light of human conscience and the air of national opinion before it can be cured.[8]

In distinguishing between negative and positive peace Dr. King acknowledged the influence of Baptists, notably Rauschenbusch, Fosdick, and other leading proponents of social Christianity. Those involved in FOR were especially crucial in creating a Baptist tradition of nonviolent direct action. George Collins (1892–1991) illustrates pre-WWII positive peacemaking efforts by Baptists. Though he was 6′5″ tall, people called him "Shorty." Graduating in 1915 from the University of California, Berkeley, Collins was commissioned in the army. He was preparing to go to the front in France just as the Great War ended on November 11, 1918. As a result, he escaped combat duty. Later, after hearing then FOR co-executive secretary Norman Thomas give a talk on area of race relations, Collins became a committed pacifist. He joined the staff of FOR and became its first organizer in the south where he influenced Howard Thurman and other African Americans by confirming that meaningful shared experiences among people are more binding than creed, ideology, or race.

Kenneth L. Cober was pastor of the Baptist church in Canandaigua, New York. Influenced by Howard Thurman he joined FOR and, in November 1932, organized a "peace week" as an experiment in educating the entire community in world peace and friendship. Drawing together pastors from several churches, educationalists, librarians, and other civic leaders, Cober organized public forums, a poster contest, school programs, and other activities.[9]

Between 1919–1939 examples of positive peacemaking attempts abound. A review of the historiography of the period indicates that historians have studied efforts to eliminate war as an institution and create a culture of peace. Little real progress was made in either arena. To what extent were people aware the world was not at peace, especially when Internet or television did not exist and even radio and cinema newsreels may have been luxuries? Notably through the Great Depression North

8. King, "Letter from Birmingham City Jail," in Washington, 295.
9. Cober, personal communication.

Americans had their own struggles and generally did not experience war first hand, at least not until Pearl Harbor Day.

Yet during these years, United States forces intervened on at least a dozen occasions in Latin America: Nicaragua, Mexico, Haiti, Dominican Republic, Cuba, Panama, Honduras, Guatemala, Costa Rica, and El Salvador. Violence boiled up around the world. On April 13, 1919, a British slaughter of peaceful protesters in the sacred Sikh city of Amritsar was a bleak day in the annals of British India. Japan seized Manchuria in 1931 and attacked China in 1937. Civil strife in Brazil in 1932 led to the deaths of hundreds. In 1935, Italy invaded Ethiopia. In 1937 hundreds of Haitians were massacred in the Dominican Republic. Germany moved into Austria in 1938 and Czechoslovakia and Poland in 1939.

On September 1, 1939, United States President Franklin D. Roosevelt sent out a two-paragraph letter to the governments of Germany, Poland, Italy, France, and Britain. His appeal read in part,

> The ruthless bombing from the air of civilians . . . during the course of the hostilities which have raged in various quarters of the earth during the past few years . . . has sickened the hearts of every civilized man and woman, and has profoundly shocked the conscience of humanity. . . . I am therefore addressing this urgent appeal to every government which may be engaged in hostilities publicly to affirm its determination that its armed forces shall in no event, and under no circumstances, undertake the bombardment from the air of civilian populations or of unfortified cities, upon the understanding that these same rules of warfare will be scrupulously observed by all their opponents.[10]

President Roosevelt's intervention did not break the march to war. He probably could not have done so despite the conviction of many Baptist pacifists that the only way to prevent war was to abstain from any participation in it. The public generally recognized that entry was inevitable by the United States, and a just cause.

THE BAPTIST PACIFIST FELLOWSHIP

However much Baptists differ by ethnicity, nationality, or theology, many in the 1930s agreed that the Bible portrays God as condemning violence as inherently sinful, that Jesus rejects war, and that the appropriate response

10. Cited by Baker, *Human Smoke*, 134.

to the extraordinary circumstances of war is to live peacefully. Many regarded such precepts of social Christianity as compassion, forgiveness, humility, nonresistance, and truth-telling as marks of a Christian peacemaker in daily life.

By the later part of the 1930s, war clouds menaced on the horizon despite efforts by some Baptists to apply precepts of social Christianity by challenging the war system, seeking to create a just economic system, and promoting inter-faith harmony. Resolutions were introduced at several assemblies of Northern Baptist Convention condemning war as evil. In 1939, the denomination decided:

> Whereas war is utterly contradictory to the spirit and ideals of Christianity, carries with it destruction of spiritual and moral values and is always accompanied by propaganda, unbridled lust and other forms of evil; therefore, be it resolved, that we declare our emphatic opposition to the whole war system and all things related to it; furthermore be it resolved that we give our support to pacific means for settling international disputes, and that, as fundamental to this, we work for the establishment of the Kingdom of God on earth.[11]

Individual Baptist peacemakers indicated their unconditioned refusal to engage in armed conflict. On Monday evening May 6, 1940, over radio station WSYR in a broadcast entitled "The Minister and War," Edwin Dahlberg reminisced briefly about his own decision not to bear arms or kill in World War I. He continued:

> Now it is 1940; once more the ministers of church must seriously consider their responsibility to Christ. Nothing could be more important than that we study what the Master of men had to say about war and peace. Peace convictions must be founded in something deeper than party platforms. Unless they are rooted in the will of God and some basic religious philosophy, they will not stand up against the pressure of public opinion in wartime.[12]

Such resolutions and addresses expressed grave concern about preparation for war on the part of the United States. Some estimated three and a half million would declare themselves conscientious objectors (COs) to

11. From the first BPF brochure.
12. Dahlberg, *Edwin T. Dahlberg.*

war. This did not happen. Confronting stark choices, only 100,000 took this stance.[13]

Abraham Johannes Muste (1885–1967) and John Neven Sayre (1884–1977), co-executive secretaries of FOR USA, recalled the harsh treatment of COs during the Great War. They foresaw that members of denominations or religions who did not share a tradition of pacifism, like the HPCs, would need support if they exercised their right of conscientious objection.

The Rauschenbusch Fellowship, later called the Roger Williams Fellowship, was formed in 1935 with several goals including raising awareness of Baptist principles and engaging controversies within the Baptist family with integrity and open dialogue. Members discussed the idea of forming a Baptist Pacifist Fellowship (BPF) at some of their early gatherings. This led to a meeting of Baptist pacifists at the home of FOR staff member and Baptist pastor Laurence T. Hosie on November 18, 1939. This date marked the beginning of the Baptist Pacifist Fellowship (BPF), one of the parent organizations of the Baptist Peace Fellowship of North America.

Those in attendance included Dahlberg, Shorty Collins who was serving as campus pastor in Madison, Wisconsin, and Edwin McNeill Poteat, Jr., who at that time was pastor of a congregation in Cleveland, Ohio. They saw the need for creation of a mechanism to bring together like-minded Baptists in fellowship and to support COs in the event the government instituted conscription.

After the meeting, the group sent every Northern Baptist Convention congregation a letter signed by Collins, Dahlberg, Fosdick, Hosie, and others. Stressing the principle of supremacy of conscience, these prominent Baptists recognized that, in the event of war, there would be conscription. They called for treatment of Baptist COs similar to the exemption from combat duty which would be accorded Brethren, Friends, or Mennonites.

On April 9, 1940, the New York Chapter of the Rauschenbusch Fellowship authorized the Reverend Gordon R. Lahrson, chair of a Committee on Arrangements, to plan a peace breakfast. The committee invited every delegate to the denomination's upcoming convention at Atlantic City, New Jersey, to attend a breakfast meeting. The objective

---

13. *Baptist C.O.* 3 (November 1945) has a partial list of Baptist COs. See also *Directory of Civilian Public Service, May 1941 to March, 1947.*

was to consider organizing a Baptist pacifist group which, the invitation stressed, would be an unofficial body.

Over one hundred fifty persons gathered on May 24, 1940. Participants approved a motion giving the Committee on Arrangements to determine the organizational structure and to select officers for a BPF. At a follow-up meeting, Edward C. Kunkle of Mount Vernon, New York, and president of the denomination was named BPF President. Edwin T. Dahlberg of First Baptist Church in Syracuse, New York was First Vice President. Ruth E. Murphy, a religious educator, was named BPF Secretary Treasurer. The group established seven regional groups and a statement of commitment which read: "As I view my loyalty to the Person, Spirit and Teachings of Jesus Christ, my conscience commits me to His way of redemptive love and compels me to refuse to participate in or give moral support to any war." Of the $2 dues, $1 would go with permission to FOR. The officers arranged reciprocity for Baptists joining FOR.[14]

In a letter to "Peace Makers," President Kunkle proposed an array of activity. He encouraged Baptists to conduct Schools of Conscience or to form local discussion groups for study and fellowship. He encouraged cooperation with work carried on by FOR, the American Friends Service Committee (AFSC), and other peace groups. He corresponded with other pacifists, offering encouragement and a willingness to participate in cooperative service projects. He urged Baptists to undertake any one of a number of spiritual practices: fasting; giving the money saved to war-relief; intercessory prayer individually and with group members; and reading devotional literature such as Muriel Lester's pamphlet *Training*.[15]

The BPF was downright radical. Members resolved to eradicate the many social ills out of which war springs. They endeavored to work out nonviolent alternatives for solving conflicts. They developed healing processes. They offered spiritual guidance to all who wanted such help. They made available to Baptist pacifists strength and comfort to be derived from knowing that there were others prepared to support each other in the time of testing and crisis that lay ahead.

To refuse participation in the institutions of war, or to give moral support to COs were not popular options in wartime. Through the war years, travel restrictions prevented the holding of regular meetings.

14. A.J. Muste memo to Edward C. Kunkle, December 18, 1940, SCPC FOR DG13, section II, Series E, box 22, BPF General correspondence folder, 1935–1953.

15. Circular letter by Edward C. Kunkle, September 30, 1940.

Nonetheless, the steering committee found ways to increase the effectiveness of the BPF, for example, encouraging local action in opposition to a peace-time draft, publishing a newsletter, and maintaining a spirit of reconciliation with those who did not share their Christian pacifism. Speaking at the BPF's breakfast on May 23, 1941, Edwin Poteat emphasized, "Bluster is the most odious sin of the Pacifist. A creative spiritual act is rarely spectacular. A bursting bomb is spectacular, a bursting bud is undramatic; but slow, patient growing is constructive."[16]

Agreeing to work with other pacifist bodies, the BPF participated in a conference convened on April 16, 1941 by the National Service Board for Religious Objectors. It was the sense of the meeting that the National Service Board would keep all groups working with COs informed, through the issuance of frequent bulletins and cooperation in financing COs assigned to Civilian Public Service (CPS).

According to legislation of the day, COs had three choices: noncombatant military service, alternative service in church-run camps, or prison. Neither the government, nor any other agency provided financial help. This placed an incredible burden on COs, their families, and those committed to ensure their livelihood. After vigorous debate, the 1940 assembly of the Northern Baptist Convention adopted a resolution which expressed approval of maintaining a registry of Baptist COs. The resolution explicitly stated that this action was not to be construed as approval of any effort either to recruit COs, or to persuade military conscripts to seek assignment to noncombatant work. Consenting to have the convention keep his name in permanent records, COs signed "My Purpose Concerning War," a statement in which they agreed to an understanding of pacifism as a positive stand for peace and as a daily duty.

The BPF sent a letter to everyone who signed the declaration of purpose or inquired as about provisions of the Selective Training and Service Act of 1940 pertaining to conscientious objection.[17] The Northern Baptist Convention agreed to maintain a registry. Implementation of this obligation fell to the Home Mission Society (HMS), which seconded Professor John W. Thomas of Crozer Divinity School to the AFSC to provide counseling and a mechanism permitting those who so desired to designate gifts through the World Emergency Forward Fund. In 1942

16. Minutes, Annual Meeting, May 23, 1941.

17. Mitchell, "To Christian Conscientious Objectors to Military Service of the Northern Baptist Convention."

individuals and local groups sent $35 per CO per month for 80 Baptists in CPS camps, a total of nearly $34,000. In solidarity, the executive urged members to spend a day a week in fasting and prayer. Based on a review of the published financial reports, Northern Baptist Convention paid the HPCs approximately $46,500 towards support for Baptist COs in CPS camps and ended with an unpaid debt of around $52,000. The 1947/48 HMS report lists the unpaid balance at $59,244.81, and a bit over $7000 was listed as paid after that.[18]

Towards the end of the war, Baptist pacifists debated the merits of withdrawing from the system. One issue concerned the treatment of COs. Obliged to do menial or meaningless work without pay, CPSers found themselves enmeshed in what Harry Emerson Fosdick described as "a system of internment camps at which forced labor without pay is exacted . . . as the price for being allowed to hold a religious belief."[19]

Another concern related to the fact that, by agreeing to manage part of the Selective Service System (SSS), the churches appeared to nullify the witness of COs and to cross the boundary separating church and state. M. Palmer Bryant expressed the view, "No religious or pacifist group should continue to administer this evil business for our present government." Having recently walked out of CPS Camp #76 in Glendora, California, Palmer faced a prison sentence. Another former CPSer criticized the BPF role in administering the camp at Skillman, New Jersey and one or more additional CPS units. Identifying himself as JHS, he wrote,

> With this development we compromise our position completely. We align ourselves with Selective Service; we agree to carry out their orders and their program (with the implications of permanent conscription which lie behind it); we pay for their program, not ours. By doing so we lose our chance of being an effective and 'free' group. We forfeit our chance of being of real aid to the pacifists in prison and in the camps.[20]

The BPF accepted the will of these and other CPSers and the lead of FOR USA, the Quakers, and other religious pacifist bodies. Advising the Home Mission Society to withdraw from the system, the steering committee emphasized,

18. James R. Lynch to Paula Womack, September 27, 1990.

19. *Baptist C.O.,* 1 (1945) 3.

20. *Baptist C.O.,* 2 (1945) 5.

... if the churches continue in CPS they will be administering peace-time conscription. Instead ... we believe churches should put their energy into opposing it. We believe Baptists, with their heritage of separation of church and state, should be especially wary of an arrangement with the government to put men to forced labor.[21]

By resolving the debate in this manner, the BPF accentuated positive and negative aspects of peacemaking. On the one hand, Baptist pacifists sought a way of service and sacrifice. They drew strength and encouragement from the example of Jesus. They believed Jesus lived and taught love for all, returned good for evil and overcame evil with good. On the other hand, they offered a critique of war and all that contributes to war. Through this dual witness, Baptist pacifists believed they were able to continue influencing denominational positions on the war, as they had earlier.

For example, in 1942, a debate developed over a resolution commending the Young Men's Christian Association (YMCA), Young Women's Christian Association (YWCA), and AFSC for their work in feeding the starving peoples of the world as a means of creating the mutual trust and fellowship necessary for a just and durable peace. Justin Wroe Nixon, chair of the resolutions committee, Dr. Daniel A. Poling, and other denominational leaders attempted to emasculate the resolution, first by a trick of parliamentary procedure and then by an emotional appeal to the "mothers and fathers of 20,000 Baptist young men in the nation's armed forces." The effort to turn the resolution into a blessing of war failed. BPF leaders Gene Bartlett, Shorty Collins, Lilburn B. Moseley, and others mobilized on the floor of the convention to defeat the proposed changes. A delegate wrote, "This morning there was a heated debate over one of the resolutions ... advocating feeding the starving and oppressed peoples of the world as a means of creating the mutual trust and fellowship for a just and durable peace."[22]

A similar debate at the 1944 convention resulted in adoption of a resolution recognizing COs as sincere fellow Christians and urging congregations to render them the same kind of service in respect to securing jobs and finding a place in the community, as given those who have borne

21. *Baptist C.O.*, 3 (1945) 1.

22. LeRoy Day, letter October 25, 1990, quoting a letter written in June 1942 to Bette Mae Keith, at the time his fiancée.

arms. Subsequently, an article appeared in *The Watchman Examiner*. The author complained about the pacifist lobby. Carl W. Tiller, onetime official of the United States Office of Management and Budget and BWA associate secretary, recalled the concern on the part of many delegates that a resolution supporting Baptists in the war effort would probably have undergone "a process of emasculation at the hands of a strong group of pacifists who, somehow, always manage to get themselves elected to get themselves elected to the Committee on Resolutions or else attend its critical sessions."[23]

Even while considering withdrawing from direct engagement with the SSS, the BPF supported a Northern Baptist Convention decision to set aside Sunday December 3, 1944 as a day of sacrifice. In a letter to a thousand friends and members of the BPF, Secretary Treasurer Ronald W. Wells called for an enthusiastic response to a need for $20,000 to continue support for Baptist COs.[24]

Having explored formation within the Northern Baptist denomination of a pacifist body, and BPF support for COs, we may consider what was happening in other Baptist groups. By action at its 1940 annual meeting, the Southern Baptist Convention instructed the steering committee to provide facilities for COs to register with the denomination, thus enabling the steering committee to make accurate certification to the government concerning them at any time it should be called for.[25]

By December 1940, 106 potential Southern Baptist draftees had already submitted their names to the steering committee for registration as conscientious objectors. This figure was not comprehensive, as one could gain conscientious objector status without this procedure. When they declared themselves conscientious objectors, Southern Baptist pacifists received certification of their religious affiliation from the denomination.

The issue of conscientious objection again came before Southern Baptists at their 1944 annual meeting. The Social Service Commission reported that twenty-three members of Southern Baptist congregations were assigned to CPS work and that the cost of their maintenance, which was being born by the HPCs, was over $10,000. The denomination took no action in providing financial support to Southern Baptist COs.

23. *PeaceWork* (May–June 1989) 3. 1944 *Northern Baptist Convention Annual,* 280; the article: June 8, 1944, 568.

24. Circular letter, November 18, 1944.

25. Registration card, citing p. 96 of the 1940 *Southern Baptist Convention Annual.*

The issue again surfaced in 1946 when the Social Service Commission reported that more than fifty men were still working in non-combatant jobs in camps, hospitals, and various auxiliary roles. The report urged that these men not be overlooked. They received no pay and could claim no aid from the government after their time of service. The report called them "our Christian brothers who have followed their conscience at great cost. We urge the churches to honor their sincerity and courage and their religious convictions by helping them to get jobs and giving them a friendly welcome back to their churches, homes and communities."[26]

While the denomination was under no legal obligation to those who so served, the report also recommended that the steering committee reimburse the peace churches $17,708.17 to cover the cost of supporting these Southern Baptists conscientious objectors. The steering committee did not act on this recommendation.

A Southern Baptist minister William Wallace Finlator (1913–2006) picked up the story and wrote critically, "Though our indignation is far from spent, proportion and propriety enforce a restraint which permits us but to say that it is an honest debt dishonestly disavowed." Finlator added, "It is small wonder when the official family of the dominant church of the South so acts that we are still called 'the fire-eating south.'"[27]

In his role as head of the steering committee, John H. Buchanan responded to Finlator and reiterated that the Southern Baptist Convention never officially accepted responsibility to provide food and shelter for COs. "Whether the failure of the Convention to recognize this is wrong is another question."[28] The steering committee did not act. The issue never came to a full assembly for a vote.

By contrast, the Northern Baptists administered CPS unit number 74, the Eastern Shore State Hospital in Cambridge, Maryland, and CPS unit number 136, a village for Epileptics in Skillman, New Jersey. The BPF held a breakfast meeting at the annual denominational assembly giving those who said "no" to war a chance to discover like-minded believers and to receive pastoral care. After the war, the BPF continued to meet. In 1946 the Convention again adopted a resolution urging Baptists to accord

26. Sandra Hack Polaski, 23.

27. Finlator, "Christianity in Spite of the Churches," 43–44.

28. Buchanan to Finlator, March 3, 1947.

returning conscientious objectors the same welcome into the churches as given returning servicemen and women.

What was the wartime experience of the COs? And what were the consequences for their principled stand? Several hundred Baptist COs refused to bear arms. They served in a variety of roles. Some conscientious objectors worked in the Medical Corps or accepted other assignments that did not involve combat. Some fought forest fires or did land or farm reclamation work. Some administered relief to interred Japanese-Americans or Japanese-Canadians. Others helped resettle refugees in Europe after the war. Some were attendants for the mentally ill.

Some served as human guinea pigs in starvation projects, drifting in life rafts, or experimenting with new drugs for malaria or pneumonia. One Baptist, Warren Dugan, volunteered for a medical experiment, contracted polio and died August 26, 1945 of the disease he sought to wipe out. Another Baptist, William O. Atkinson, died at CPS Camp #21, Cascade Locks, Oregon, on March 26, 1942 of complications from a carbuncle, abscesses caused by bacterial infection, most commonly *Staphyloccus aureus*. The infection was contagious and could, as in this instance, prove fatal.[29]

John Y. Elliott was assigned to Byberry Mental Hospital in Northeast Philadelphia. He was required to follow such guidelines for controlling patients as this: "Hit them on the top of the head with the base of your close fist. It will leave no visible marks, but it will bring them to their knees." Conditions were horrible. Inmates rioted frequently. The facility is now closed.[30]

William R. Schorman worked in CPS before he became a human guinea pig in medical experiments on hepatitis. Twice a week he was injected with drugs to see if he would get jaundice. After a year of these tests, doctors discovered he had tuberculosis. After three and half years of CPS, he was released.[31]

When he grew up, Paul Alexander Wilhelm attended Bellevue Baptist, a Southern Baptist congregation in Memphis, Tennessee. When he studied at Washington University in St. Louis, he attended Delmar Baptist Church during the pastorate of Dr. Roland Dutton. As his pacifist

29. *Baptist C.O.*, 2 (1945) 1; on Dugan, see also "Faith of a Conscientious Objector," 5.

30. Letter to Paula Womack, October 22, 1990.

31. Letter to Paula Womack, August 6, 1989.

convictions developed, Jesus's teaching that God is love was his principle of faith; human politics contravened that love and caused war. He claimed CO status. An architectural draftsman, he was assigned to build privies, grade parking lots, and do plantings for the improvement of a nearby state park and nursery.

Wilhelm was housed at an interracial camp near Plainfield, New Jersey. As there were local protests, the camp moved to Powellsville in southern Maryland. Under supervision of the Soil Conservation Service, Wilhelm and other COs cleared swamps. Again, the CPSers encountered hostility. People argued that COs were making it easier for Hitler's submarines to land. As it was in an urban area close to Washington DC, "Anyone wandering off from camp was likely to get beaten up."[32]

At least thirty-three Baptists refused to cooperate with the system altogether and went to jail, including Alfred Hassler (1910–1991), first treasurer of the Baptist Pacifist Fellowship and future FOR Executive Director. In his *Diary of a Self-Made Convict*, Hassler observed, "I had no reason to go to war. . . . I'm not mad at anybody, so why should I shoot them?" Jailed at Lewisburg Penitentiary from 1944–1945, Hassler joined others to protest segregation. This pressure helped lead to integration of the military. Hassler wrote, "it is only a Christianity whose adherents are willing to face that kind of suffering [dying for faith] . . . that can hope to make a dent in this very bad world."[33]

Another Baptist CO who exercised his conscience and ended up serving a prison sentence was Theodore Dettweiler, a member of the Kensington Avenue Baptist Church in Kansas City, Missouri. In early 1945, he was sent to the minimum-security Federal Prison Camp in Springfield Missouri to serve a second term.[34]

Exempt from the draft, pastors had other decisions to make than whether or not to serve in the military. Some chose to declare their conscientious objection in the pulpit. In 1941 Kenneth L. Cober was serving a congregation in Buffalo. After the Japanese attack on Pearl Harbor he preached on war as a violation of the principles of Jesus. This is what he said:

---

32. Letter to Paula Womack, November 26, 1990; the SCPC houses Wilhelm's papers.

33. Hassler, *Diary*, 108, 135.

34. *Baptist C.O.*, 2 (1945) 1; the next issue carried a list of COs then in prison, or on parole from prison.

Jesus rejected the philosophy used to defend war, namely, that the end justifies the means. Beginning with the Beatitudes, he extolled all the anti-war virtues: meekness, mercifulness, and peace making. He demanded love of one's racial foes and enemies. He advocated universal brotherhood. He forbade killing, attempts to kill, and even the inner attitude of hate that leads to killing. He demanded that evil be overcome with good. He ordered nonresistance of evil. He advocated forgiveness of one's enemies. He condemned reprisals. He did not resist his enemies, physically. He forgave his enemies. He rebuked Peter for using the sword. He proclaimed and lived the great commandment of love. He required a life of self-sacrifice as a test of discipleship. He asserted that the individual had infinite worth. He required supreme loyalty to God. I must choose, either to make war, or to follow Christ. I cannot have both. . . . I renounce war . . . [but] I am not trying to convince you or win you over. I am trying to save my self-respect by speaking the truth without fear. Time will come when I will leave this position but I cannot do so without walking among you as a liar and a coward. To whatever extent my thinking is in accord with the divine purpose, may God give me the strength to remain true to my vow.[35]

His congregation did not dismiss Cober for his views. Nor did the Kentucky congregation of Pete Gillespie. On several occasions he offered pastoral prayers for the enemy as well as for "our boys." While congregants doubted his theology and patriotism, they allowed him to give voice to his conscience. In this way they recognized the tradition by which Baptists exercise spiritual freedom.

Other Baptist congregations, less tolerant towards their pastors, fired those who dissented from the prevailing consensus. For example, Gaylord Pierce Albaugh (1910–2003), was serving on the staff of University Baptist Church in Chapel Hill, North Carolina after he graduated from Colgate Rochester Divinity School. When the United States formally entered the war effort, Albaugh faithfully ministered to the needs of those in active military service despite holding pacifist views. The wartime atmosphere of aggressive patriotism led him to preach on *The Spirit of Christ or the Spirit of the Bayonet,* and he was dismissed from his pastorate. Nathaniel Parker, a former Southern Baptist then serving as principal of McMaster Divinity College in Hamilton, Ontario, invited Albaugh to teach church history. He retired from that position in 1976.

35. Letter of October 23, 1990.

Carroll S. Feagans lost his position at Sullins College, now King's College in Bristol, Virginia. He was sent to CPS camp #108 in Gatlinburg, Tennessee, where he cleared trails for the National Park Service.

As World War II moved towards an anticipated victory, many Baptists turned their attention to relieving suffering caused by the war worldwide. In cooperation with other denominations, the BPF appealed to its constituency to contribute generously in support not only of COs, but also of relief agencies such as the interdenominational Church Committee on Overseas Relief and Reconstruction, the AFSC, the China Committee for China Relief, the International Missionary Council, and the International YMCA and YWCA.[36]

AFTER WAR-TIME SERVICE

How did the decision to claim conscientious objector status influence Baptist peacemakers after the war? Whatever forms their conscientious objection took—CPS, alternate service, or jail—the men resumed civilian life and became moral leaders of the first generation to face the threat of nuclear annihilation. Yet they faced the challenge of being regarded, at least in some circles, as slackers or traitors who should "surrender all moral rights to the benefits of citizenship."[37]

After the war, those who served in the mental hospitals protested conditions and recommended changes that were acted upon. Others brought pressure to bear upon political leaders and popular opinion to integrate the armed forces and end segregation in the prisons. Others, including Gene Bartlett, campaigned against legislation that sanctioned post-war conscription and compulsory peacetime military training.[38] Others joined social movements against nuclear weapons, for the environment, and for civil rights in the United States. For example, Kenneth L. Cober journeyed south in 1964 to stand with demonstrators demanding integration of public facilities in St. Augustine, Florida. In 2000, *The "Good War" and Those who Refused to Fight It: The Story of Conscientious Objectors in World War II*, a Bullfrog Films documentary, highlighted these post-war activities.

---

36. *Baptist C.O.*, 1 (1945) 4.

37. Kelsey, *Social Ethics among Southern Baptist*, 115.

38. David Bartlett, email, January 3, 2006; Ernst, "Twentieth-Century Issues," 313.

Richard Cummings served in various denominational positions, concentrating on civil rights and the rights of workers. He remained committed to pacifism and nonviolence. LeRoy Day became a college teacher and endowed an annual lecture and program on peace and justice at Sioux Falls College. Two conscientious objectors did graduate work at the University of Wisconsin where Shorty Collins encouraged them.

One was Rodney Hood who received a PhD in mathematics. During both the Korean and Vietnam wars, he advised students opposed to the wars, joined demonstrations against the wars, and marched for disarmament as recently as 1982 in New York City. In his congregation, he spoke out against the display of the flag and singing militaristic songs in church. He became a tax resister.

Another was Ben Willeford who went on to teach chemistry at Bucknell College in Lewisburg, Pennsylvania. There, he also visited prisoners at the near-by federal penitentiary. He helped form a campus FOR chapter and urged scientists to refuse research funding from sources linked to the military industrial complex, so-called by President Dwight D. Eisenhower in his January 17, 1961 farewell address. Willeford marched against the war in Vietnam and opposed United States intervention in Central America. In 1996, he participated in a delegation hosted by the *Centro Christiano de Reflexion y Dialogo* in Cardenas, Cuba. On return he called for "more dialogue, not less" and an end to the embargo against Cuba.[39] He now marches with an interfaith group against the war in Iraq.

After working in Civilian Public Service, Ercell V. Lynn was assigned to the national office of the Church of the Brethren Service Committee in Elgin, Illinois. There he worked with William M. Hammond, Jr., another one of fifty Southern Baptist COs whose story was told in a pamphlet published in 1945, *The Story of 50 Southern Baptist Civilian Public Servicemen.*

From 1943–1946, Hammond was Director of Placement for the Public Service Program of the Brethren Service Committee with responsibility for liaison with dozens of hospitals, public health and agricultural experiment stations, schools and government agencies. In an article published

---

39. *Baptist Peacemaker* 16:1 (1996) 8.

in *Christian Frontiers*, he championed the cause of fifty Southern Baptists who received no financial support in CPS from their denomination.[40]

In 1949 Hammond founded Horizons Unlimited, through which he arranged and led overseas tours to study the application of Christian principles to international relations. IFOR leaders Muriel Lester, A. J. Muste, Martin Niemoeller, and Kirby Page were among the resource people who led seminars for the tours.[41] From 1953–1961, Hammond served as Secretary and Treasurer of the BPF and edited the organization's newsletter.

Paul Wilhelm provided draft counseling through several organizations. In retirement, Wilhelm worked with the National Interreligious Service Board for Conscientious Objectors, now the Center on Conscience and War.

During the war, at least two medical students lost scholarships when they refused to participate in mandatory military drills. While exempt from military service, one of them, Marion Marshall Young, set up a clinic in Chattanooga that provided free medical service to poor African Americans. Later, he traveled to South America on health delegations. Inspired by King's August 28, 1963 "I have a dream" speech at the Lincoln Memorial, Young advocated diverting money from the military to the health sector.[42]

In March 1965, Carl Tiller joined Dr. King in the first day of the march from Selma to Montgomery while his wife Olive Tiller tried to cross the Edmund Pettus Bridge in Selma. In 1985, she was arrested protesting apartheid at the South African embassy in Washington DC.[43]

Victor Gavel and his wife Eileen became tax resisters. They wrote on their returns "not to be used for war." Together in 1964 they endowed a prize in honor of their former pastor, Edwin T. Dahlberg. Over the years, the Dahlberg Peace Prize has recognized several recipients for championing life-long peace with justice and freedom, including BPF founders Shorty Collins, Carl Tiller, and Olive Tiller. The Gavels also left a bequest to the Baptist Peace Fellowship of North America. The BPFNA board used part of these funds to establish the Gavel Memorial Peace Fund to sup-

40. Hammond, "They Serve Without Weapons."
41. Helen Hammond to Paula Womack, November 24, 1990.
42. Young, *Journey of Discovery*.
43. Olive Tiller, "Crossing the Edmund Pettus Bridge," 25.

port Baptist peace workers in international conflict zones such as Burma (Myanmar), Nagaland, Indonesia, the Philippines, and various African nations.

During the Vietnam War, Dahlberg also became a tax resister. In 1983, at the age of 93, Dahlberg accompanied a delegation of American and Southern Baptists to the Soviet Union, where he preached in Moscow. This friendship visit led to formation of the BPFNA.

WOMEN AND CONSCIENTIOUS OBJECTION

What about Baptist women? As women remained exempt from the draft, they faced different choices. Most stayed on the home front but were deeply affected by the absence and loss of sons, brothers, fiancés or husbands. Lois Tupper, who taught High School in Saskatchewan in the early war years, recalled the pain of being unable to prevent the deaths of her fiancé, relatives, former students, and friends.[44] Many responded to government campaigns that mobilized workers for the war effort and entered the labor force. Others volunteered for the Red Cross or other service organizations. Still others ran households efficiently in spite of wartime shortages. They assumed responsibilities on farms and in family businesses.

A minority were pacifists. Because of their gender, they had little opportunity to register their dissent. Elise Boulding, the noted peace scholar, told a biographer, "I remember feeling, like many women did, that I wished I were a man so that my conscientious objection could be recorded."[45] Though they were not in any legal sense conscientious objectors, many women distanced themselves from the culture of war. Some put their careers on hold to follow their conscientious objector husbands or fiancés to the CPS camps where they worked as dietitians, nurses, or educators.

Approximately two thousand women, and perhaps half as many children, lived in or near CPS camps. The majority of these families came from the HPCs or groups like the BPF which supported the make-shift facilities for COs at Skillman, New Jersey. The village could only house

---

44. Interview, April 22, 2005. Born in 1911, Dr. Tupper taught at McMaster University from 1948–1971. She was the first woman to hold a tenured faculty position in a theological college in Canada.

45. Goossen, *Women against the Good War*, 3.

childless couples or singles who served the community in such roles as medical doctors, cooks, and supervisors.[46]

Baptist women who held pacifist convictions responded in other ways as well. Some participated in BPF chapter meetings. Some believed their primary role was to find ways to confront "war hysteria with its blindness to truth and its fanning of hatreds."[47] In a letter to Carl W. Tiller, Mary Martin Kinney, Chicago-based secretary for the Woman's Home Mission Society, wrote of sharing her testimony "in understandable terms, quietly and intelligently."[48]

REFLECTIONS

The experience of the World War II Baptist COs enables us to consider, first, that the historical record has been largely silent about them. This silence skews history and fosters the dangerous illusion that no one resisted the culture of violence then prevalent. Historian Herbert Butterfield wrote, "If history could be told in all its complexity and detail it would provide us with something as chaotic and baffling as life itself; but because it can be condensed there is nothing that cannot be made to seem simple, and the chaos acquires form by virtue of what we choose to omit."[49]

World War II Baptist COs have received little recognition in part because they were not members of the HPCs, whose traditions are better documented. As well, for most Baptists, as for most citizens, the years during and immediately after World War II were marked by a strong belief that the United States had participated in a just war. The majority culture tended to denigrate World War II COs as deviants, draft dodgers, wrong, or even criminals.

The government of the United States did everything possible to marginalize them. While their treatment was more severe during WWI, the WWII COs and CO couples suffered inequities. In the United States after the war, many lost their jobs because they refused on principle to take loyalty oaths during the Communist scare. Not wanting pacifists to infect the body politic, the government sought to ensure that their legacy is rarely if ever taught in public schools. This may explain why, in interviews and

46. *Baptist C.O.*, 1 (1945) 2.
47. Elizabeth B. McKinney to Carl W. Tiller, February 2, 1942.
48. Kinney to Tiller, February 4, 1942.
49. Butterfield, *Whig Understanding of History*, 97.

letters, they stated, "I don't think this reply is apt to be of any value to your research" or "I doubt my experience can be of much help."

Second, we may honor the often lonely witness by which these modern prophets denounced the immorality of killing. They saw conscientious objection as a matter of conscience and insisted that any infringement on their liberty was a threat to the rights of others. In the face of powerful war rhetoric, they peered into the abyss of war and refused to bear arms. They articulated a strong biblical basis for their war resistance. In the face of the fusion of religion and politics during the Second World War, they became mentors to others wrestling with questions about the morality of war.

Finally, many associate religion with war and violence. The story of Baptist pacifists gives a more nuanced perspective. During and after WWII, Baptist COs acted on the basis of a vision of the common good. Choosing to resist evil and to fight without guns, they played a positive role in nonviolent efforts to forge a more just and peaceful world.

There are many throughout the world crying out to reclaim religion from the terrorists, fundamentalists, and politicians who do not speak for them. There is a world waiting for acts of compassion, healing, and reconciliation, qualities by which I characterize the historic engagement of WWII-era Baptist pacifists.

By the end of the Second World War, several thousand Baptists worldwide had a pacifist affiliation, including those who joined a sister Baptist pacifist group in Britain. In Canada, where only a few Baptists did alternate service or went to jail as COs, Tommy Douglas, then a Co-operative Commonwealth Federation (CCF) member from Saskatchewan in Parliament, took unpopular stands in defense of civil liberties. Archie McLachlan of Vancouver was one of two Canadian Baptist pastors who stood publicly against the internment of Japanese Canadians.

During WWII there were Baptists in Canada, Britain, the United States, and possibly *México* who joined FOR but did not identify with the BPF or its counterparts in the southern United States and Britain. Though the numbers were small, what was remarkable was that there were any Baptist pacifists at all. Given war propaganda of the time, hostility which COs confronted, and overwhelming support by Christians for the war effort, I am awed by their courage and steadfastness.

After 1945, as a result of the fateful circumstances which ended the Second World War, Baptist peacemakers lived under the shadow of global nuclear annihilation. Moreover, they found themselves an increasingly tiny minority within their denominational family. Members of the Southern Baptist Convention—the largest Baptist denomination—tended toward pre-millennial, apocalyptic, and fundamentalist views. The overwhelming majority of Baptists in the United States supported the military build-up and interventions of a succession of United States administrations. In chapter two we shall consider the forty-year period between 1945 and 1984, during which BPF members supported COs during two regional conflicts and—together with new Baptist peace groups—joined the worldwide campaign for nuclear disarmament.

Artwork by Norma Young used with Ann Sims, "My War (3/25/03),"
Baptist Peacemaker (Summer 2005) 14.

2

Living in the Shadow of Nuclear Annihilation

AFTER THE WAR

WORLD WAR II ENDED after the detonation of nuclear weapons at Hiroshima on August 6, 1945 and at Nagasaki on August 9, 1945. Living in the shadow of nuclear annihilation became a new Baptist Pacifist Fellowship (BPF) focus. However, the Home Mission Society (HMS) still needed to staff an office on Christian Ministry to Service Men and Conscientious Objectors. This provided a channel for those wishing to facilitate the transition of COs back to civilian life and to support them financially.

On November 30, 1945, Northern Baptist Convention President Anna C. Swain and C. O. Johnson, chair of the World Mission Crusade, appealed for funds to assist both several hundred COs still in Civilian Public Service (CPS), and to meet the education and rehabilitation needs of COs. These men were not included under The Servicemen's Readjustment Act of 1944, commonly known as the GI Bill of Rights.[1]

In the southern United States, articles in a Southern Baptist periodical *Christian Frontiers* urged that the denomination accept its responsibility to help with the CPS service of those who had claimed CO status.[2] When the denomination did not act on reimbursing the historic peace churches (HPCs) for support of Baptist COs, an editorial in *Christian Frontiers* recommended that the Brethren Service Commission be reimbursed in full for expenditures made by them on behalf of bona fide Southern Baptists. In the event the denomination did not reopen the matter.[3]

---

1. Online: http://www.gibill.va.gov/GI_Bill_Info/history.htm.
2. Buckhart, "The Church and Returning Service Men and Women."
3. "Conscientious Objectors Again," 173.

Until 1947, when the last service personnel were released from their duties or their jails, including COs in noncombatant roles and those in CPS, a key issue concerned those imprisoned for exercising their conscience. The Northern Baptist Convention called upon the President of the United States to declare a general amnesty for all COs, restoring to them full civil rights.[4] The Southern Baptist Convention did not. This prompted *Christian Frontiers*, a Southern Baptist journal, to editorialize that "a presidential amnesty in their behalf would be in keeping with our American ideals of democracy and individual freedom."[5]

Summarizing the experience of COs completing five-year jail sentences, a "letter" in *Christian Frontiers* by a "voice of a Southern Baptist Prisoner" addressed readers as follows,

> I am a P.O.W.—prisoner of war. No foreign camp is it in which I languish for these five long years. It is a U.S. Federal prison—I am a prisoner in my own land. My loyalty has never been denied by the government, and I am innocent of crime; yet they made me a criminal and put me away in prison.

Grateful that the independent and unofficial Southern Baptist peace community ministered to many WWII COs, the author observed that fifteen or more men faced the reality that, upon their release from prison, they would not have full rights. The letter continued,

> The fact that nearly all sentences will have been completely served within a year from now does not justify optimism over the status quo, for the loss of rights to vote, hold office, secure civil service employment or enter licensed professions, etc., is a lifetime punishment, unless presidential amnesty is granted. The appointment of an amnesty review board by the President has meant only a speeding up in the parole of men remaining in prison—parole under special conditions far less liberal than those for criminals. It has indicated no interest in the restoration of civil rights.

Accusations that a pardon would excuse those who sympathized with the Nazi cause and had moral scruples about fighting them enflamed the issue. Newspaper editorials around the country and a flood of public opinion supported some form of clemency. President Truman refused to authorize a general pardon. He did order several limited amnesties.

4. *Northern Baptist Convention Minutes*, 1947, 187.
5. Finlator, "Free the Conscientious Objectors," 181; "They Made Me a Criminal."

On December 24, 1945, the President pardoned civilian prisoners who had volunteered for military service and who received an honorable discharge upon completion of a year's duty or more. The effect of the pardon was to restore their full civil and political rights.

Truman then established a three-man review panel to examine some fifteen thousand cases of draft evasion. On December 24, 1947 Truman granted yet another Christmas Eve pardon to 1,523 draft evaders who had served or were serving prison terms. Aware that this covered only one out of every ten cases it reviewed, the board defended its choices in these words:

> We found that some founded their objections on intellectual, political or sociological convictions resulting from the individual's reasoning and personal economic or political philosophy. We have not felt justified in recommending those who thus have set themselves up as wiser and more competent than society to determine their duty to come to the defense of the nation.[6]

On December 24, 1952, Truman granted full pardon and restoration of civil and political rights to former convicts who had served in the peacetime army between August 14, 1945, the end of active hostilities in WWII, and June 25, 1950, the start of active hostilities in Korea, and who had not been covered by his earlier pardon. In addition, he pardoned all convicted peacetime deserters from the military up to June 25, 1950.

AFTER THE WAR, WAR AGAIN

If only for a while, some COs continued in the work they had been doing during the war. Many of those who had done social work went on to make it their career. Some went back to their pre-war occupations, where they experienced nothing like the hostility that WWI COs had faced. The WWII draft operated from 1940 until 1947 when its legislative authorization expired without further extension by Congress. During this time, more than ten million men had been inducted into military service. With expiration of the Selective Training and Service Act (STSA), no inductions occurred in 1947. However, the Selective Service System (SSS) remained intact.

After the STSA expired, a second peacetime draft began with passage of the Selective Service Act in 1948. The new law required all men, ages

6. Damon, "Amnesty."

eighteen to twenty six, to register. It lowered the induction age to eighteen and a half and extended active-duty service commitments to twenty-four months. It also created the system for the "Doctor Draft" aimed at inducting health professionals into military service. Unless otherwise exempted or deferred, these men could be called for up to twenty one months of active duty and five years of reserve duty service. Congress further modified this act in 1950 although the post-WWII surplus of military personnel left little need for draft calls until Truman's declaration of national emergency in December 1950. Only 20,348 men were inducted in 1948 and only 9,781 in 1949. Between June of 1950 and 1953, Selective Service inducted 1,529,539 men to meet the demands of the Korean War. Another 1.3 million volunteered. Most joined the Navy and Air Force.

In 1951, Congress enacted the Universal Military Training and Service Act. To increase equity in the system, President Eisenhower signed an executive order on July 11, 1953 that ended the paternity deferment for married men. In large measure, these changes in the draft arose because of the Cold War, with a focus on the Soviet threat.[7]

During the Korean conflict, the American Baptist Convention repeatedly voiced its full support of the principle of the right of conscience above the law. While the Convention did not endorse the pacifist position, it recognized the right of any of its members to take such a position.

After July 27, 1953, with the signing of the Korean Armistice, there was no general amnesty for military deserters or draft evaders. Though BPF members began to breathe easier, technology brought new promises and threats. United States air and nuclear power fueled the Eisenhower doctrine of "massive retaliation" articulated in a message to the United States Congress on January 5, 1957. This policy demanded more machines and fewer foot soldiers, so the draft slipped to the back burner. But the head of the SSS, Lewis B. Hershey (1893–1977), urged caution. In May 1953, he told his state directors to do everything possible to keep SSS alive in order to meet upcoming needs.

Dissenting voices continued to appeal to the history of voluntary military service in the United States as preferable to universal military training or conscription. Fearing that the massive French defeat at the Battle of Dien Bien Phu at the hands of Communist revolutionary forces in May 1954 portended a future conflict in Vietnam or elsewhere, the BPF

7. Online: http://en.wikipedia.org/wiki/Conscription_in_the_United_States.

executive urged "all persons who do not want to see the Congress permanently fasten upon America the Hitler, Stalin type of militarism known as Universal Military Training and Conscription" to join a caravan going to Washington DC to lobby Congress, or to write their members of Congress and the Senate.[8]

WAR AFTER WAR AFTER WAR

Though many Baptists followed the lead of the surrounding culture, supporting the nation in its new obligations as leader of the so-called "free world," something else was stirring as well. As early as 1943 the Southern Baptist Convention appointed a World Peace Committee with the purpose "to develop, clarify and mobilize the sentiment of Southern Baptists for a righteous and lasting peace . . ." The following year, its first report listed six principles:

1. Condemning isolationism;
2. Affirming the obligation of the strong to protect the weak;
3. Affirmation of the need for an effective international organization which could restrain aggression;
4. An acknowledgment of the reality of racial prejudice and listing it as among the roots of war;
5. Analyzing economic injustice and poverty as roots of war; and
6. Reasserting the need for religious liberty.

The World Peace Committee was authorized a budget to promote these principles "through every channel of denominational information." One response was to encourage the formation of congregational study groups to focus attention at the local level.[9]

Through the 1950s, the BPF membership generally numbered a few hundred. The executive published a newsletter on an irregular basis and occasionally sent mailing informing members and other interested persons about major developments. These were all important initiatives. However, with a small membership and no staff, the BPF could not sus-

8. Action Memo, April 1955. FOR DG 13, Series E, Section II, Series E, boxes 22–28, denominational groups: BPF.

9. Southern Baptist Convention, *Annual*, 149–50, cited by Sehested, "Conformity and Dissent," 6.

tain this level of activity every year. As a result, the BPF profile increased slowly, so much so that several times pundits prematurely pronounced the BPF dead!

John M. Swomley, Jr. (1915–), at the time FOR Executive Secretary, inquired on April 22, 1954 about establishing mechanisms to improve correspondence about BPF-FOR membership. One of the BPF officers John Thomas responded, "I am not sure as to what I ought to say . . . I am afraid BPF is dead beyond resurrection. I do not know what Forest [Ashbrook] would suggest. My own feeling is that BPF must be marked down as one of those good efforts that came into being, lasted awhile, and now is gone."[10] Yet BPF members carried on with a crucial focus on the spiritual basis of peacemaking. Resisting the temptation to spiritualize or privatize the Biblical concept of peace, BPF members formed groups for Bible study, prayer, and action. This emphasis led to a theological perspective which understood peace more broadly than the absence of war. BPF members also were widening the scope of their vision.

This was evident at a convocation held between February 12–14, 1946 of denominational and other pacifist bodies. Representing the Northern Baptist Convention and BPF, S. B. Cloward offered $1,000 towards the goal of forming a structure for a continuing functional co-operation both in the joint campaign against peacetime conscription, but also in working towards such goals as "world government, world responsibility, world disarmament, world relief, and world reconciliation."[11]

With an understanding of the scope of Christian peacemaking that embraced work for positive peace, BPF members undertook a wide range of peace initiatives. Among these was an educational ministry. Believing that every generation must be taught and inspired to love peace, the BPF executive compiled a list of speakers available to visit campus around the country and circulated the information to members, colleges, and seminaries.[12]

In 1956 and 1957, BPF members participated in several tours to Europe. They met with representatives of eastern European peace committees, the NATO Supreme Commander, and prominent figures in

10. Swomley to Thomas, April 22, 1954; Thomas to Swomley, April 26, 1954, FOR DG13, Section II, Series E, boxes 22–28: denominational groups, general correspondence, 1935–1954.

11. "Proceedings at Atlantic City Conference," BPFNA papers.

12. *BPF Newsletter* May 1955.

the international peace movement. These included Martin Niemoeller (1892–1984) a German pastor who had resisted the Nazis and Kaspar Mayr (1891–1963), one of the first Catholics in leadership of the International Fellowship of Reconciliation, the largest religious pacifist organization in the world at the time. They also met with André Trocmé (1901–1971) and his wife Magda (née Grilli, 1901–1996). This French couple had resisted the German occupation and protected Jews during the pastorate of André in Le Chambon-sur-Lignon.[13]

American and Southern Baptists formed "Initiatives for Peace". This was an organization chaired by pacifist author Culbert G. Rutenber (1909–2003). On November 14, 1958, the steering committee met for the first time in Chicago. The gathering identified a number of initiatives. These included encouraging more exchange visits with people from abroad. They wanted to foster a program of prayer for peace. They supported a joint American and Southern Baptists effort on behalf of Trick or Treat for the United Nations Children's Fund (UNICEF). They offered literature to help Baptists discern biblical and theological sanctions for Christian peacemaking. Members agreed that the basic causes of war include hunger, population pressure, national rivalries, and racial tensions. They further agreed that, if humanity were not to fall over the brink of a suicidal race conflict, Christians must emphasize a kinship not only with one another, but also with all creation. "Concern for the survival of the human family must drive the Christian people to confront the issues which lead to war."[14]

Edwin T. Dahlberg was perhaps the most influential member of this early Baptist peacemaking group. As a BPF member, he served on its advisory board. On December 6, 1957, he became President of the National Council of Churches. On taking office, he declared as utter folly and futility spending forty billions of dollars on a system of defense that could not possibly defend us. He challenged the churches of the United States to lead in a plan of massive reconciliation based on the Christian Gospel of love rather than adhering to the policy of massive retaliation: bomb for bomb, rocket for rocket, Sputnik for Sputnik. He reminded Christians that we are not prevented from taking God into account simply because

13. Tom Cornell, "How Catholics Began to Speak Their Peace," originally appeared in *Salt of the Earth*. Online: http://64.191.235.137/issues/peace/tcorn.html.

14. "Minutes of the Meeting of American Baptist and Southern Baptist Commissions on Peace." BPFNA files.

we are faced with governments and secular agencies of society which do not take God into account (the United States included). He called not only for new ways of thinking about international relations, but also for a nationwide effort in race relations.[15]

Acknowledgment of the reality of racial prejudice as a root cause of war and impediment to creating positive peace led Baptist peacemakers to promote interracial harmony, to condemn lynchings,[16] and to focus broadly on inter-faith relations.[17] One initiative illustrated the broadening scope of Baptist peacemaking.

In the 1930s, Clarence Jordan, an agriculture student at the University of Georgia, participated in reserve officer training. Unable to reconcile the Sermon on the Mount with the war machine, he abandoned thoughts of a military career and became a popular Southern Baptist preacher and Bible teacher at Southern Baptist Theological Seminary in Louisville, Kentucky.

World War II challenged Jordan's pacifism. During meetings of the Louisville chapter of the FOR, Jordan, his wife Florence, and Martin and Mable England, American Baptist missionaries on prolonged furlough due to the war in Asia, talked of trying to do something concrete about conditions among poor southerners: inadequate housing, welfare, unemployment and despair. In the fall of 1941, Jordan gave up the security of the seminary to work first with inner-city poor. In 1942, the two families left for Georgia to undertake a venture in discipleship. They bought a 440-acre rundown farm near Americus, Georgia. They renamed it Koinonia Farm. While the Englands later returned to Asia, the Jordans worked to create an interracial community which held property in common (Acts 2:44–45; Eph 2:14–16).

From the start, Koinonia Farm engendered hostility. For example, members of the Jordans' congregation, Rehobeth Baptist Church, unhappy with the views of its Koinonia Farm members on issues of peace and race, suggested in 1948 that they resign voluntarily. The Jordans declined to do so and were told that they were no longer welcome.

One strategy used against Koinonia Farm was a boycott, which sought to prevent Koinonia from marketing its farm produce. There were

15. Dahlberg, "The Task before Us"; *Baptist Peace Fellowship Newsletter* #7 (December 31, 1957).

16. *Christian Frontiers* 1:9 (1946) 275–76.

17. Cutten, "The Intolerant Baptists."

also sporadic acts of hostility such as machine-gunning of buildings, cancellation of insurance policies, beating of Koinonia workers, and the visit of a 70-car Ku Klux Klan deputation. On one occasion, Jordan approached his brother, a successful banker, for assistance. His brother refused. Jordan confronted him with the memory of having been baptized together and promised to follow Jesus, not just to admire Him.

BPF members were among those who responded to appeals for help. Many traveled for varying periods of time to Georgia to work on the farm. Others assisted with gifts of encouragement, energy, and ideas. Jordan imbued Baptist peacemakers with the conviction that it is not the case that God is in heaven and all is well on earth. Rather God is here and all hell is breaking loose! After years of controversy and nonviolent struggle, Clarence Jordan died in 1969 followed, in 1987, by Florence. Their prophetic voices have continued to challenge Baptists and others through the ongoing ministry of the Koinonia community.

There were additional examples of BPF activism during the 1950s. Members petitioned President Eisenhower to call off nuclear weapons tests. On another occasion, the executive requested members to pray in support of the crew of the "Golden Rule," a trawler that in 1958 sailed to a Pacific Ocean nuclear weapons test site. Members of the crew were arrested five nautical miles from Honolulu and sentenced to sixty days in jail. Their act of nonviolent protest against the testing of nuclear arms and the nuclear arms race attracted worldwide media coverage and inspired similar actions by members of the Vancouver-based "Don't Make a Wave Committee." In 1971, the group formed Greenpeace, an independently funded organization which works to protect the environment.

In the early 1960s, BPF members continued to get together at the time of the annual meetings of the denomination. On the eve of each convention, the executive mailed a letter to some six thousand pastors inviting them to attend the annual gathering. These were usually breakfast meetings, occasionally luncheon meetings, and once an evening meeting. A featured speaker addressed a peace subject.

Long time BPF member and president for 1964–1966, Victor H. Gavel said in an address at the fifth annual BPFNA summer peace camp in Ottawa, Ontario, July 6, 1990, "We were not an integral part of the convention, but we were tolerated. We managed to obtain a booth at our conventions in the exhibit halls—not always on the 'mid-way,' sometimes back in a corner—but we were there."

Former BPF and American Baptist President Carl W. Tiller also reflected on the ability of the organization to carry on.

> At the beginning we were composed of conventional pacifists. From the time that nuclear weaponry came to be understood we had a great many people who, in effect, became "just war pacifists," that is, they felt that any future war would be a nuclear war and a nuclear war could not be a just war. And therefore, many people who were aghast at the thought of nuclear warfare came to be interested in what the Baptist Pacifist Fellowship was doing.[18]

In 1963 BPF formally adopted a new name: Baptist Peace Fellowship. In 1970, it became the Baptist Fellowship for Peace. The name changed again in 1974, when the group took on the name American Baptist Peace Fellowship.

In the early 1960s, the BPF focus remained the spiritual basis of peace at a time of threatened nuclear war. Members organized a annual convention exhibits distributing information about peace organizations, campaigns, and gatherings such as the All Christian Peace Assembly held in Prague, Czechoslovakia, June 13–18, 1964 or deliberations of the Church Peace Mission, a FOR project, in San Francisco May 19–23, 1965 under the theme "One Lord, One World, One Mission." Secretary/ Treasurer Lillian M. Robertson represented BPF.

During the Vietnam War period, issues related to conscription and selective conscientious objection again became concerns for many men. In 1965, Edwin T. Dahlberg shared in a FOR-sponsored clergy visit to Vietnam and renewed his call for massive reconciliation. In one talk given January 2, 1967, Dahlberg acknowledged that more was involved than ending the war in Vietnam. He called for development of a theology of peace to take the place of the theology of war. He appealed to the churches to come to grips with the power structures which keep the war system going: industry, government and education, and to undertake a radical transformation, a move which, as he understood it, would entail a movement away from private religion and into places where the struggles for freedom must be won. Ultimately, he stressed, "we must go deep down into the soul of man if we are going to have a massive reconciliation." In another talk, he concluded, "Massive reconciliation may seem like an

---

18. Yurke, "Reaping," 3.

impossible task. But man has been given the intelligence, the imagination, and the power to effect it. Will he have the faith?"[19]

Echoing Dahlberg's call for massive reconciliation, the Reverend John C. Zuber of Anderson, Indiana, challenged BPF members to present challenging new visions for the day after his election in 1968 as BPF President. As a possible basis for action in the future, he suggested formation of "guerilla groups for peace."

> Our state department and military services command thousands and millions of men. Guerillas for peace will have to speak and act out of study in depth. At this time in history many gaps (poverty, race, religion, culture) desperately divide our world. Men of peace will have to step into the gaps to gain knowledge in the midst of action. Then the polarized peoples of the world may begin to build the bridges of understanding in an unsurveyed terrain. We need bridges of mutual concern and care.[20]

In 1970, BPF, in concert with the Division of Christian Social Concern of the American Baptist Convention, sought to develop a Peace Education Action Community Enterprise, with the goal of focusing more directly on war and peace issues and developing strategies relating to these issues at the local level. One example was the formation, in 1971, of a Baptist Peace Action Task Force with theologian Norman Gottwald and others charged to reach out to college campuses and seminaries around the San Francisco Bay Area. They noted two phenomena: first, there seemed to be too few new peace supporters; and second, pastors and seminarians, who they expected to have Jesus' peace ethic as central to their ministry, generally did not see peace or nonviolence as central to the Gospel or were too timid about being prophetic voices for peace.[21]

In 1970 the BPF experimented by hiring an intern, James R. Lynch, a theological student at Bethany Theological Seminary in Chicago. He set up regional training seminars, encouraged the formation of local peace groups, improved the newsletter, and corresponded with Baptists inquiring about conscription and conscientious objection. A benefit of paid staff

19. Dahlberg, "Consideration of Massive Reconciliation."
20. *Baptist Peace News* (July 1968) 2.
21. *BPF Newsletter* (December 1970).

was greater BPF activity. Lack of a secure funding base made it impossible to continue beyond a year.[22]

In the early 1970s, BPF membership did grow. The draft continued until 1973 when United States ground participation in the Vietnam War ended. According to the Veteran's Administration, 9.2 million men served in the military between 1964 and 1975. Nearly 3.5 men million served in the Vietnam theater of operations. From a pool of approximately 27 million, the draft raised 2,215,000 men for military service during the Vietnam era. It has also been credited with "encouraging" many of the 8.7 million "volunteers" to join rather than risk being drafted. Of the nearly 16 million men not engaged in active military service, 96 percent were exempted because of jobs including other military service, deferred (usually for educational reasons), or disqualified (usually for physical and mental deficiencies but also for criminal records to include draft violations). Draft offenders in the last category numbered nearly 500,000 but less than 10,000 were convicted or imprisoned for draft violations. Finally, as many as 100,000 draft eligible males fled the country.[23]

During the 1970s, local Baptist congregations and groups around the country like the San Francisco Bay Area American Baptist Peace Action Task Force undertook some peace activity. In keeping with traditional Baptist polity, this approach did little to influence public policy.

After United States involvement in Vietnam ended, BPF and other groups called for forgiveness of Vietnam War resisters and deserters. Also, a great many issues had gotten worse while the peace movement was preoccupied with Vietnam, and these issues desperately needed attention. These included several crises around the world, including the Israel-Palestine conflict, fighting elsewhere in the Middle East and in Northern Ireland, the struggle against South Africa's apartheid regime, the war for independence of Rhodesia (Zimbabwe), and the continuing arms race.

With limited resources, BPF networked with other organizations. For example, the steering committee asked one of its members, Martha S. Miller, to represent BPF on a journey of reconciliation to Ireland from November 28–December 6, 1977. There were two purposes for the trip. The first was to stand with the peace people in their nonviolent efforts to end the troubles and terrorism so that the root causes of the violence

22. Interview with James R. Lynch, February 22, 1989.
23. Online: http://en.wikipedia.org/wiki/Conscription_in_the_United_States.

could be dealt with. The second was to participate with them in a peace rally on Sunday, December 5. Subsequently, Miller reported she went not to judge, but to learn; not to pass lightly through, but to experience the daily life of the people of both the Republic of Ireland and Northern Ireland; and to experience the fears and a few of curtailments of the freedom of the people. Among other recommendations, Miller encouraged BPF members to sign a "Declaration of the Peace People," to write letters of solidarity, and to find ways to cut off the flow of guns and bullets to perpetuators of violence.[24]

The Irish peace initiative was one of many signs of vision and hope manifest during the 1970s. Olive Tiller, BPF president for 1977–1981, challenged BPF members as follows,

> Remember during all those long years of the Vietnam War, how we fondly hoped that, once that war was over, the U. S. military budget would be reduced drastically, and most of that money could be channeled into constructive efforts to build a better society at home and abroad? One wonders what it will take to bring down the expenditures for weapons, armaments, and war preparations! The ending of the war, the SALT talks, the United Nations special session on disarmament [May 23–July 1, 1978], the closing of many of our military installations—none of these has seemed to have any slowing effect on the constant upward spiral. It's time for Christian people who take seriously the peace ethic, to speak up and speak out, to let the President and the Congress know that enough is enough.[25]

On July 27, 1980, during a meeting of denominational peace fellowships affiliated with FOR at Berea College in Kentucky, Martin England reported that the BPF was trying to get the American Baptists Churches-USA to declare itself a peace church on the basis of previous resolutions passed at assemblies.

As evidence of a heightened commitment to peacemaking, the American Baptist Churches USA formed an office on international affairs based in Washington DC. The Reverend Robert W. Tiller was its first director.

24. Memo, June 25, 1977, FOR BPFNA file 4.

25. *BPF Newsletter* September 1978. UN Special Sessions on Disarmament also took place in 1982, 1988, and 1997.

NEW STIRRINGS

In 1980, the ABCUSA Board of National Ministries established a Peace Concerns Program. A brochure entitled *Breaking Down the Walls* provided a list of biblical, theological, and practical resources for peacemaking and summarized key themes shaping the program goals of the new office, as follows,

> People are important to God ... Since God created and values each person we are of great worth to each other. We are expressions of God's love. During war, we destroy people created in God's image and in so doing inhibit the sharing of God's love.
>
> The life, death and resurrection of Jesus Christ brought us back into right relationship with God; and through the power of God's grace we can be reconciled to other people. As Christ broke down the dividing walls of hostility between Jew and Gentile (Eph 2:11–19), we must break down the walls of hostility among nations. The message of the peacemaking power of God's love is a message that needs to be learned and lived by all people regardless of nationality. Nationalism must not be allowed to divide people and prevent them from sharing God's reconciling love. ... When persons are just in their relationships with one another violence is minimized. And when we as nations and as a world community establish institutions which define and express our ideas of justice, war can be eliminated.[26]

Program goals included the following,

1. stimulate discussion in the American Baptist Churches USA on issues related to Christian ethics and war and how Christians can contribute to making a more peaceful world;

2. publicize and provide resources to American Baptists for study and action for peace;

3. empower individuals and churches by identifying speakers and providing workshops and seminars on peacemaking;

4. witness to the political structure to seek peace through non-military means;

5. identify persons and churches within the denomination providing leadership on peacemaking;

26. *Breaking Down the Walls.* Pamphlet.

6. hold conferences, consultations, workshops, and seminars; and

7. define and articulate a theology of peacemaking with and for American Baptists.

Larry Pullen was the first to staff this program followed, from 1987–1996, by Daniel L. Buttry. Since 1996, Dwight M. Lundgren has continued in the position of Coordinator of Intercultural Ministries and Reconciliation.

Anticipating growth, BPF undertook new projects. In 1980, it sponsored an essay context. On April 14, 1981, Olive Tiller wrote a "special URGENT" plea that members act to stop military aid from going to El Salvador's governing regime. After its 1981 annual meeting in San Juan, Puerto Rico, the executive circulated a questionnaire, a petition for a nuclear weapons freeze, and a newsletter announcing several transitions: a new look and name for the publication, new officers, new emphases, "and (we hope) new resolve and enthusiasm for our task!"[27]

The Ohio Baptist Peace Fellowship (OBPF) was founded in September, 1981, at the headquarters of the Ohio Baptist Convention (OBC) in Granville, Ohio. John Sundquist, then OBC Executive, called together a group of Ohio Baptist peace and justice activists to give them opportunity to form some sort of common cause within the denomination. This included Steve Hammond, Tom Gentry, several members of First Baptist Church of Granville, two of whom were members of the OBC staff, and the congregation's new pastor, George Williamson, Jr. Williamson had come to the church three months earlier as a new member of ABC, having been a lifelong Southern Baptist with a history of activism in peace and justice movements.

The meeting resulted in the formation of OBPF with Williamson as president. Most of the founding members were not members of or at all knowledgeable about the American Baptist Peace Concerns Program or the older BPF, with which the OBPF was not affiliated. From the beginning, and for the next decade, the OBPF met monthly, and mobilized Ohio Baptists in several ways. First was to activate peace groups in local churches, and raise peace and justice issues—particularly the nuclear freeze movement which was the peace issue then most prevalent—before congregations. Second was to publicize these issues in various forums of

---

27. *PeaceWork* September 1981.

the OBC, especially its annual convention, to have a peace breakfast there, displays at its display area and to sponsor statements of concern before the convention. Third was to join with other groups in local and statewide peace and justice activities.

The conservative mainstream of OBC was angered and activated by the presence of this new group. Opposition gathered against the purported influence of the OBPF, which had about fifty members with no local groups. At the 1982 OBC convention, Williamson and a leading OBC fundamentalist debated the topic peacemaking, which was widely held to be unbiblical in OBC, if not a sign of the anti-Christ, before a plenary session between.

These fresh BPF and OBPF initiatives paralleled a notable stirring among Southern Baptists. There was a long and rich history of discussion among progressives who were linked through their time at Southern Baptist Theological Seminary in Louisville. Many shared church historian E. Glenn Hinson as mentor, guide, and model. In 1972, before fundamentalists took control of the seminary and Hinson left to became Professor of Spirituality and John Loftis Professor of Church History at Baptist Theological Seminary in Richmond, Virginia, Hinson offered a course on Christian devotional literature. In the last class session, Hinson observed that becoming a peacemaker flows from the quality of our personal and corporate spiritual lives. According to Robert C. Broome, this principle chased him for years and was the seed for his role in helping start both the *Baptist Peacemaker*, and a series of pamphlets on Baptist spirituality.[28]

A few years later, a group of students and faculty at Southern Baptist Theological Seminary in Louisville began discussing the need to address the challenge of living with the threat of nuclear war. The group organized a meeting in February 1979 at Deer Park Baptist Church in Louisville. Billed as a "Southern Baptist Convocation on Peacemaking and the Nuclear Arms Race," the gathering brought together four hundred people. The high level of enthusiasm resulted in several responses. One was the formation of congregational peace groups. Another was the publication of quarterly paper, *Baptist Peacemaker*, launched on December 1980. A two-day retreat of *Seeds Magazine* and *Baptist Peacemaker* staff held at Glendale Baptist Church in Nashville, Tennessee brought together lead-

28. Broome, "Birth of *Baptist Peacemaker*." In three volumes, Hinson published the *Classics*. Until Broome's death on July 11, 2009, he lived in Louisville where I interviewed him at an early stage of this project.

ers working in several southern communities. Southern Baptist women in ministry began to organize. And thirteen Southern Baptists participated in a journey of reconciliation to the Soviet Union in May 1983 with thirty-six American Baptists.

The stage was set for Baptists to break new ground. The biennial convention of the ABC took place that summer in Cleveland, Ohio. The OBC and the Cleveland Baptist Association, a city society independent of and more liberal than OBC, were co-hosts. Through the offices of the Cleveland Baptist Association, OBC, OBPF offered an afternoon peace seminar. The annual ABC BPF breakfast took place the next morning. Members of the group who had just returned from the Soviet Union did a presentation.

A large group from OBPF, most of whom had not been involved with BPF before, attended the breakfast meeting. There was considerable excitement, both about the Soviet Union trip—the first thing the BPF as an organization had ever done beside their biennial breakfast—and about OBPF's size, activism, and enthusiasm. Ed Crabtree, a Cleveland Baptist pastor and the ABC BPF member instrumental in arranging the breakfast. His leadership at the time of the biennial convention was so crucial that he was the obvious person to be elected president of ABC BPF. He was, however, involved in a crisis in his church which ultimately resulted in his leaving Cleveland, so he declined the nomination for president.

Meanwhile, "acting secretary, and BPF newcomer" George Williamson, Jr., described a new openness to seeking to increase membership of the BPF. Two things followed. First, the BPF membership elected Williamson as president (he first had to join), Crabtree as vice president, and a board of directors with the goal of raising funds and initiating some form of collective peace and justice activism within the ABC. Williamson was authorized to lead an extensive effort to raise funds and engage issues. Expectation was that *Peacework,* the mimeographed newsletter edited by Olive Tiller, would be expanded and would appear more frequently.

Second, it was agreed no longer to consider the BPF a pacifist organization. Members agreed to be open to issues of peacemaking however they presented themselves. In this connection, the board officially endorsed the statement of concern on Nicaragua and El Salvador and instructed George to communicate this endorsement to the Convention during the debate (he didn't get the microphone).[29]

Energized by the success of the journey of reconciliation to the USSR and of the biennial breakfast, Williamson, other BPF board members, and Southern Baptists who had been part of the May friendship tour in Washington DC, where from August 27–28 they marked the twentieth anniversary of the March on Washington. They discussed the possibility of forming an umbrella organization for American and Southern Baptist peacemakers.

A follow-up conversation during the newly-elected BPF board meeting, held in Chicago, was more negative than positive. Most board members knew little about Southern Baptists, except their negative role in the Civil Rights Movement and their expansionist policies. Williamson, who until 1981 had been a lifelong Southern Baptist, introduced them to the *Baptist Peacemaker*, and described the many liberal and activist Southern Baptists he knew who lived on the fringe of the convention and who longed for fellowship with people of like mind. Given that ABCUSA members of the BPF lived by and large on the fringe of their denomination as well, the possibility of some sort of cooperation began to seem a possibility worth pursuing.

Williamson traveled to Louisville and met with Hinson, Carman Sharp—pastor of the Deer Park congregation—and Glen H. Stassen, at the time professor of ethics at the Southern Baptist Theological Seminary in Louisville. Over a period of months agreement was reached to hold an exploratory meeting at Deer Park church.

With formation of the Baptist Peace Fellowship of North America in May 1984, the BPF came to an end as an organization binding together members of American Baptist congregations. In continuity with earlier BBF peace work, American Baptists have continued to staff a peace portfolio within the Board of National Ministries of the American Baptist Churches USA. Dwight Lundgren, the incumbent member of staff responsible for the Peace Concerns Program, has continued to represent American Baptists on the BPFNA board of directors and to oversee selection of Dahlberg Peace Prize recipients.

29. Email, Williamson to Dekar, January 3, 2009.

DAHLBERG PEACE PRIZE

In 1964 longtime BPF members Victor and Eileen Gavel endowed an award in honor of their former pastor and BPF founder Edwin T. Dahlberg. They wanted to give recognition to American Baptists who have worked constructively for peace with justice and freedom. Initially, the denomination lodged responsibility for the award with the General Board. More recently, the office of Board of National Ministries has administered the award.

Drawing primarily on the Dahlberg Peace Prize files, we may review achievements of the thirty individuals honored to date. Readers interested in a full description of the recipients' biographies will find considerable information about each person in denominational literature and other sources.

- **1964** Martin Luther King, Jr. (1929–1968) was cited for his nonviolent leadership for racial justice and for his constructive efforts for peace with justice and freedom. In 1964, he received the Nobel Peace Prize.

- **1965** L. Kijungluba Ao (1907–?) was cited for efforts to end violence in India stemming from a war against India for its having reneged on a commitment in 1947, when Britain granted India independence, to grant autonomy to Nagaland, a hill state located in the far north-eastern part of India.

- **1966** William Alvin Pitcher (1913–1996) was cited for work in civil rights and economic development among African Americans. He taught at the University of Chicago and became deeply involved in civic life on the South Side of Chicago. He served several Hyde Park churches in both ministerial and lay capacities, worked with Operation Breadbasket, an arm of the Southern Christian Leadership Conference, and participated in several development projects in the Woodlawn neighborhood.

- **1967** Kyle Haselden (1913–1968) was cited as an "opinion maker" in the arenas of race relations and international peace. A former managing editor, he began his four-year editorship of *Christian Century* in 1964 with an editorial endorsing President Lyndon B. Johnson for re-election. He was in the forefront of growing opposition to the Vietnam War by several major religious journals.

61

- **1968** Leon Howard Sullivan (1922–2001) was cited for work in the development of economic opportunity for low income African Americans and for working to end apartheid in South Africa. Pastor of Zion Baptist Church in Philadelphia from 1950–1988, he created Global Sullivan Principles of Social Responsibility for investment or divestment in South Africa in 1997.

- **1969** Zelma Watson George (1903–1994) was cited as a distinguished sociologist, educator, diplomat, humanitarian, singer, actress, and authority on Negro music. In 1960, President Eisenhower named her as a member of the United States delegation to the fifteenth General Assembly of the United Nations, where she represented the United States on the Economic and Finance Committee. From 1966 until 1974 she was the director of the Cleveland Job Corps.[30]

- **1970** Frank Morey Coffin (1919–) was cited for building solid foundations for peace through his leadership in international development assistance. Elected to represent Maine in the Eighty-fifth and Eighty-sixth Congresses (1957–1961), he became managing director of Development Loan Fund until October 1961 when he became deputy administrator of the Agency for International Development and served until 1964. Appointed to serve as United States Representative to Development Assistance Committee of the Organization for Economic Cooperation and Development, Paris, France, 1964–1965, he completed his professional career as a judge.[31]

- **1971** George (Shorty) Collins (1892–1991) was cited for a lifetime of campaigning against war and for peace. After the Great War, he committed his life to pacifism and served on FOR's staff in the area of race relations. Ordained in 1927 by the Northern Baptist Convention, he was campus pastor at the University of Wisconsin in Madison for thirty years and influenced many men to become COs during WWII. He later served as pastor of Grace Baptist

30. Online: http://en.wikipedia.org/wiki/Zelma_Watson_George.
31. Online: http://en.wikipedia.org/wiki/Frank_M._Coffin.

Church in San Jose, California. He once said, "There are no reasons for war—not ever. There is always a better way."[32]

- **1972** Harold Edward Stassen (1907–2001) was honored for his role in creating the United Nations, and for his work for social justice as a private citizen, public leader from the time he served as Governor of Minnesota from 1939 to 1943, and American Baptist leader. In its tribute to Stassen, the Dahlberg committee cited his address on "peace with justice" at the twelfth congress of the BWA meetings during 1970 in Japan. Dr. Stassen stated, "It is not enough that we cry out for peace; we must relate the great moral principles and concepts of our religion to the constructive steps necessary for peace."[33]

- **1973** William Sloane Coffin, Jr. (1924–2006) was not at the time related to an American Baptist Church. Nonetheless, the Dahlberg committee cited his leadership in opposing the Vietnam War during his tenure as chaplain at Yale University. He went on to serve as Senior Minister at The Riverside Church in New York and as President of Sane-Freeze (now Peace Action), one of the nation's largest peace and justice groups.[34]

- **1975** Mabel Benjamin Martin was cited for her service as an American Baptist "professional volunteer," notably twenty-five years as American Baptist accredited non-governmental representative to the United Nations. When she received the Dahlberg Peace Prize, she stressed that the issues of the day demanded global approaches and that, ". . . .only global solutions will suffice . . . *we* must delay no longer in seeking these solutions. I believe the Church must be in the lead in its concern for Humankind—it must not follow from afar."[35]

- **1977** Robert Andrew Hingson (1913–1996) was cited for his role in eradicating epidemics through invention of the "peace gun," a tool which has enabled efficient mass needle-less inoculation

32. *Fellowship* 57 (June 1991) 22.

33. Obituary, *Baptist Peacemaker* 21 (Spring 2001) 13; additional information online: http://en.wikipedia.org/wiki/Harold_Stassen.

34. *Once to Every Man: A Memoir* (1977); additional information online: http://en.wikipedia.org/wiki/William_Sloane_Coffin.

35. Remarks, June 26, 1975, BPFNA files.

worldwide against such diseases as smallpox, measles, tuberculosis, tetanus, leprosy, and polio. In 1958, Dr. Hingson, in association with the Baptist World Alliance, conducted a medical
mission survey. This led to creation of My Brother's Keeper, a
non-government agency linking the medical resources of the
United States to global health care needs. He once stated,

> We leave the luxury of our living room with its color televi-
> sion and stuffed furniture and hurry across our manicured
> grass lawn. But then, alas, as if through magic, our neighbor's
> eight-room house and his garden of flowers have vanished.
> In their place is a grass hut. A toothless, tuberculous, blind-
> from-trachoma grandmother, old at forty-six, stands in the
> doorway. Your neighbor's wife has just died in childbirth, ly-
> ing on a straw mat over a mud floor covered with flies. Two
> of the children are sick with malaria; all have worms; two are
> coughing following recovery from measles. The year-old baby
> died last week from malnutrition. None of the children have
> shoes. Only one has ever been to school. All are physically
> and physiologically hungry. The father makes $900 a year. . . .
> Your tendency is to doubt your eyes and your ears and your
> brain. Yet this is a true picture. A billion people in the world
> live under the conditions just described.[36]

- **1979** Jimmy Carter (1924–) was cited for his role in negotiating
  the Camp David accords between Israel and Egypt. He served as
  the thirty-ninth President of the United States from 1977 to 1981
  and in 2002 received the Nobel Peace Prize.

- **1981** Gustavo Parajón (1938–) was cited for his work in Nicaragua
  where he served from 1964–2003 as a medical missionary with his
  wife Joan. He founded two organizations: PROVADENIC which
  provides primary health care in twenty-five rural communities
  by training local health promoters to treat and prevent common
  illnesses; and *CEPAD*, Spanish acronym for *Comité Evangélico
  Pro-Ayuda al Desarrollo,* the Evangelical Committee for Aid
  and Development, which has worked in over a hundred communities, bringing the good news of empowerment and holistic
  development to hurting and hungry people regardless of race,

36. Online: at http://www.brothersbrother.org/founder.htm. For an obituary, see
http://www.asahq.org/Newsletters/1999/09_99/hingson0999.html.

religion, or political affiliation. Founded in 1972 to aid victims after an earthquake took more than 10,000 lives in Managua and around the country, *CEPAD* has broadened its ministry.[37]

- **1983** Anna Dorothy Wylie (1906–) was cited for her role in putting the nuclear weapons freeze on the ballot in Michigan and in the field of race relations. Earlier, during WWII, she helped form the Women's Action Committee for Lasting Peace, believing that peace could come about only through understanding and helping "the enemy." After this group terminated, she became active in local chapters of the United Nations Association, Amnesty International, and Sane-Freeze. In 1980 Kalamazoo College conferred upon her the honorary degree, Doctor of Humane Letters.[38]

- **1985** George W. Hill (1918–2003) was cited for a ministry which held up issues of peace and justice as central. He chaired the National Peace Academy Campaign, which in 1984 led Congress to establish and fund the United States Institute of Peace, an independent, nonpartisan, national institution. Hill held several pastorates during a half century of ministry.

- **1987** George H. (Nick) Carter, Jr. was honored for his ministry of peace-seeking and peacemaking. As national co-chair of the Coalition for a Nuclear Weapons Freeze, he was part of a high-level delegation which met face to face with Soviet leader Mikhail Gorbachev (1930–) and high-ranking United States officials during the 1985 Geneva Summit talks. Carter's group presented Gorbachev with one million petition signatures calling for a halt to nuclear weapons testing and he personally presented Gorbachev with a packet of letters and drawings from school children in the United States. Subsequently in 1988, he became the Executive Director of the newly formed Sane-Freeze campaign, a position he held into the early 1990s. Following his work at Sane-Freeze, Carter provided leadership for the Comprehensive Nuclear Test Ban Treaty Coalition, authored *Who's Who and What's What in Nuclear Non-Proliferation*, and served as the national co-chair of

37. Online at http://www.internationalministries.org/read/3776.

38. Nomination, Jean M. Batts to the Dahlberg Committee, June 7, 1982, National Ministries.

the Alliance for Our Common Future. He is now the President of Andover Newton Theological School.[39]

- **1989** Lucius Walker, Jr. was cited for his work as executive director of the Interreligious Foundation for Community Organization (IFCO). He also served as Associate General Secretary of the National Council of Churches of Christ from 1973 through 1978. In January 1979, he returned to IFCO, which has the distinction of being the only national ecumenical foundation committed exclusively to the support of community organizing. Subsequently, he founded Pastors for Peace, which organizes humanitarian aid caravans as a way to assist the victims of US foreign policy. IFCO/Pastors for Peace has delivered caravans of aid to Nicaragua, El Salvador, Guatemala, Chiapas, *México*, and Cuba.[40]

- **1991** Carl and Olive Tiller were cited for their lifetime commitment to peacemaking. Together, they were involved in the founding meeting of the BPF. Later, both served as president of the body. As well, Carl was president of the American Baptist Convention. He helped found the Institute for Life and Peace in Uppsala, Sweden. Olive has served on FOR's National Council.

- **1993** Margaret (Peg) Sherman was cited for her work as American Baptist representative to the United Nations.

- **1995** Ken Sehested (1955–) was cited for passionate leadership first as co-founder and director of education for *Seeds* and subsequently as BPFNA Executive Director. During the first ten years of his BPFNA service, the organization grew to over 1500 members and 12,000 readers. In addition to traveling around the world as an ambassador for peace, he published articles in journals and books. He edited *Dreaming God's Dream*, books which celebrated the life and legacy of Dr. Martin Luther King, Jr. Sehested currently serves as co-pastor of the Circle of Mercy Congregation in Asheville, North Carolina.

39. Nomination, Dahlberg Committee, December 1986; *PeaceWork* (May–August 1987) 19.

40. *PeaceWork* (July–October 1989) 21; Biographical sketch online: http://www.speakoutnow.org/userdata_display.php?modin=50&uid=153.

- **1997** Marian Wright Edelman (1939–) was cited as president and founder of the Children's Defense Fund (CDF), a children's rights organization. In 1968, she moved to Washington DC, as legal counsel for the Poor People's Campaign which Dr. Martin Luther King, Jr., began organizing before his death. She founded the Washington Research Project, a public interest law firm and CDF parent body.

- **1999** Mary Ruth Crook and Roger H. Crook were cited for over fifty years of peace and justice ministries. They have focused on positive relationships with the citizens of Cuba and the former Soviet Union and community-wide action to affect national legislation on disarmament. The Crooks have provided leadership in a Peace and Justice group at Pullen Memorial Church in Raleigh, North Carolina. Roger Crook served as chair of the Department of Religion and Philosophy of Meredith College. Mary Ruth Crook has created banners for several BPFNA peace camps.[41]

- **2001** Gordon C. Bennett and Mark Odom Hatfield shared the award. Bennett taught Communication Arts at Eastern College (Eastern University since 2001). Nurturing a new generation of peacemakers, he regularly led students to Washington DC to present their views to members of Congress on nuclear disarmament and other issues. He was an organizer of the Delaware Valley chapter of Pastors for Peace. Since his retirement from teaching at Eastern University in 1998 he has developed the Global Wellness Fund Treaty, and with several colleagues from Eastern and Central Baptist Church in Wayne, Pennsylvania CBC, made a five-year effort to secure backing for it within the United Nations.[42]

- Mark Hatfield (1922–) represented Oregon in the United States Senate for thirty years. He focused on hunger and sponsored legislation advancing peace. Retiring in 1996, he has remained active in Oregon, where he co-authored a statewide initiative to repeal the death penalty.

41. *Baptist Peacemaker* 19 (Spring 1999) 11.
42. Online: http://levellers.wordpress.com/dahlberg-award-winners/.

- **2003** John Robert Lewis (1940–) was cited for peace and justice work. As chair of the Student Nonviolent Coordinating Committee, he spoke at the August 28, 1963 March on Washington. Since 1987 he has represented Georgia's Fifth Congressional District in the United States House of Representatives.[43]

- **2005** Charles Z. Smith (1927–) was cited for his work on the Stockholm Accords on Ethnic Cleansing and other justice and peace work. He was dean of the law school of the University of Washington and served on the State of Washington Supreme Court. President of the ABCUSA during the 1975–1977 biennium, he handled tensions in a fair and even-handed way as lesbian, gay, bisexual, and transgender people sought to be included at the American Baptist table.[44]

- **2007** DeeDee Coleman was cited for her work with ex-offenders, substance abusers, and high risk youth. A native New Orleanian, she has served as pastor of the Russell Street Missionary Baptist Church in Detroit since 1999.[45]

As a collective portrait, these thirty honorees are lawyers and politicians, pastors and teachers, housewives and househusbands, doctors and writers, business people and movement people. Cumulatively, the Dahlberg Peace Prize recipients attest to the capacity of committed people and small groups to stimulate the transformation of neighborhoods, nations, and even global institutions. They encapsulate the dreams and achievements of the communities, non-government organizations, and social movements of which they are members. The denomination has highlighted their achievements during the denomination's biennial meeting while acknowledging the importance of the context where the activists have contributed.

REFLECTIONS

Before we look at the experience of BPFNA members over the past twenty-five years, we pause to recall that the creation of a strong Baptist peace

43. Lewis and D'Orso, *Walking with the Wind*.

44. Mixon, "Charles Z. Smith Receives Dahlberg Peace Prize."

45. Coleman, "A Dangerous Mission." Online: http://www.russellstreetmbc.org/pastorbio.htm.

movement has been built on the shoulders of BPF's founding generation. To paraphrase syndicated columnist Ellen Goodman from the Summer 2001 issue of *Baptist Peacemaker*, I have never been especially impressed by people who hold great titles or make great claims about changing the world. Rather, I have been inspired more by people who have been willing to respond to their calling and struggled to make one small difference after another. They have challenged me, and inspired countless people to work for the common good.

For a century, Baptist peacemakers gave given voice to their objections to war and to their conviction that the God of love wills peace. Courageous and prophetic, they were like a lightening rod, attracting the disdain of the majority of their national compatriots, even other Baptists.

The BPF did achieve acceptance of a place within the Northern Baptist Convention and a succession of denominational re-organizations. Several times, American Baptists elected pacifists as denomination presidents, including Edward Kunkle (1939–1940), Edwin Dahlberg (1946–1947), Carl Tiller (1965–1966), and Culbert G. Rutenber (1968–1969).

The consistent witness of BPF members to the Gospel of peace led them into ministries of transformation and reconciliation. By their strategies, faith, and life work, they have contributed in truly extraordinary ways to the creation of a culture of peace.

Coming into being in 1984, the new BPFNA confronted fresh challenges amidst heightened Cold War superpower tensions and regional conflicts in Central America and elsewhere around the world. In the next four chapters, we review ways by which the BPFNA members have responded to the trials of a world which appeared to be on the brink of catastrophe. At varying times they have joined millions and millions to communicate a clear and consistent message that what people around the world need and want is peace, not war; disarmament, not nuclear weapons; and inclusion, not intolerance. In working to these ends through nonviolent strategies, ordinary people have helped shape the largest coordinated global social movement in the history of the world.

Artwork by Sharon Rollins, *Baptist Peacemaker* 19
(Winter 1999) cover.

3

Creating a Network of Resistance, Affirmation, and Celebration

BREAKING NEW GROUND

AMERICAN AND SOUTHERN BAPTISTS who visited Soviet Baptists in 1983 came home determined to start something new. In spring 1984, a meeting in Louisville, Kentucky gave birth, kicking and screaming, to the Baptist Peace Fellowship of North America (BPFNA).

The meeting took place on March 30–31 1984 at Deer Park Baptist Church. Wanting to bring these two groups of Baptists together and to reach out to Baptists from other traditions around North America, organizers invited some of the participants in the 1983 friendship tour and others to attend a meeting of American and Southern Baptists to join together in common peacemaking efforts. The idea was to work for peace not only in the nation and in the world, but also between two parts of a divided family. There was also the desire to extricate "peacemaking" from its association with passivity. Finally, some peacemakers were searching for a way of grounding their peacemaking firmly in Baptist life rather than siphoning Baptists off into organizations alienated from local congregations.[1]

Participants had to overcome doubts and fears on the part of both parties. On one side, American Baptists had a solid peace organization dating back to the early 1940s. What could be gained by talking with a group of Southern Baptists with a history marred by complicity in racism and efforts to evangelize in areas where American Baptist congregations

---

1. George Williamson letter of invitation; Rachel Gill's presentation to the fifth BPFNA summer conference in Ottawa, Ontario, July 6, 1990 and Sehested, "The Road to Rome."

ministered? On the other side, Southern Baptists were committed to their own independent initiatives. There seemed little to gain in a merger.

There were hours of honest dialogue around doubts and fears, desires and dreams. Just when the group seemed to reach consensus on a statement of purpose for a joint peace venture, the *Baptist Peacemaker* staff decided not to support the proposal that the newsletter become the official voice of a new organization.

Chaos ensued. American Baptists felt betrayed. Southern Baptists were frustrated. Finally, calmer voices prevailed. George Williamson, Jr., newly elected President of the BPF steering committee and pastor of the First Baptist Church in Granville, Ohio, was determined to bring these two groups together. Steve Shoemaker, pastor of Crescent Hill Baptist Church in Louisville, insisted there was no breach of faith. The proposed organization could do without the paper.

The crisis passed. Those who took part in this meeting committed themselves to join Baptists and others working for peace in a warring world. They gave birth to a new organization and called it the Baptist Peace Fellowship of North America (BPFNA). Participants identified an executive and several goals: establishing peace groups at the regional, state, associational, and local church levels; facilitating communication between these groups and bringing them together for common purposes; and encouraging all the Baptist groups and conventions in North America to engage in active peacemaking. With a chorus of emotions, participants committed themselves to seek peace and to pursue it, beginning with self-examination and working together with others in pursuit of these goals.

At the first board meeting, held in Granville, Ohio on May 3, 1984, it quickly became clear that the excitement, sense of limitless possibility, and very real potential for a peace and justice organization among 30 million North American Baptists was much more significant than could be accomplished by this small group of volunteer leaders. An executive director, with a formal, expanding program was the only means by which anything significant could be achieved. However, none of the predecessor groups had ever raised more than a few hundred, collectively, a few thousand dollars, and none of the leadership knew the first thing about fundraising. As a compromise, the decision was to authorize Williamson to hire a secretary for BPFNA in his Granville office, and to devote significant time toward expanding and funding the organization.[2]

2. Minutes.

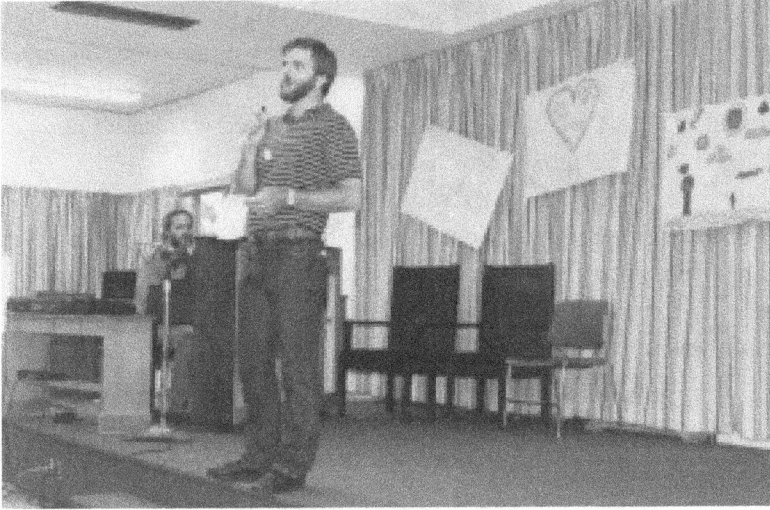

Ken Sehested and Ken Medema at Peace Camp 1986.

By September 22–23, 1984, when the executive committee next met, again in Granville, it had recruited BWA and Canadian, General Conference, National, and Progressive National Baptist members. Mexican, Puerto Rican, Seventh Day, and other Baptist peace groups would soon find a place within the new umbrella organization and expand its vision.

Ken Sehested, one of the Vice Presidents, stayed in the home of George Williamson, Jr. After the session on the first evening, over a glass of wine, Sehested proposed to Williamson that he resign his position at *Seeds,* and become executive director for the new organization. He suggested that in his work at *Seeds* he had developed enough contacts to be confident that he could raise sufficient money, both to pay himself a living salary, and to fund the sort of program which would justify an executive. The dreaming conversation consumed the rest of the night and several bottles of wine. The following day, Sehested made the formal proposal to the board that he be named executive director with a modest salary and an organization budget of $50,000. This plan had the effect of increasing the previous collective fundraising efforts of the predecessor organizations by fifteen-fold. Sehested further proposed several fail-safe milestones, according to which, if not reached by given dates, the agreement could be rescinded.

The response of the board was of the "this guy must be crazy, but, why the hell not" variety. The Sehested budget was adopted, the fail-safe mechanisms set in place, and Ken was hired. A year later the fail-safes were out of date, the budget met, and Ken Sehested was leader of a growing and dynamic Baptist peace movement.

Over the next ten years came a series of board meetings characterized by then president George Williamson, Jr., as apocalyptic events. The home congregations of board members provided hospitality for these meetings, including First Baptist Church in Granville, Ohio, where George was pastor from 1981–2004. After the meetings board members often participated in the host congregation's Sunday morning worship. Appendix five provides an example of prayers by then-board member Lee McKenna and staff member Katie Cook.

Sometimes the board met on holy ground such as Koinonia Farm near Americus, Georgia (February 1987), Jubilee Partners in Comer, Georgia (October 1995), and the King Center in Atlanta, Georgia, on the occasion of the first Martin Luther King, Jr., holiday in the United States. Board members joined others in signing a pledge card that reads, "On January 20, 1986, I commit myself to living the dream by loving, not hating; showing understanding, not anger; making peace, not war."

Sometimes, the board met outside the continental United States, beginning with one that included a friendship tour to Nicaragua in May 1986. Meetings followed in Toronto, Ontario (October 1986), Puerto Rico (May 1989 and October 1994), during which board members joined protests against ongoing United States military presence on Puerto Rico, and Mexico City (May 1996). The effect of these meetings was not simply that board members gained a first-hand experience of the issues with which first peoples and other nationals around the continent were dealing; it also enabled the movement to address two imperative needs.

The first was the need to transcend the race divide. In the United States, especially, people of European-American background have dominated the peace movement. African Americans, Asian Americans, Hispanic Americans, and Native Americans have stressed organizing for justice. Sometimes these constituencies have found each other and formed alliances, but intentional efforts to work together in a multi-racial organization have been rare.

A second, equally compelling need was to overcome parochialism. Whether one works on a particular issue such as reducing the threat of nuclear war, or more generally for healing among the peoples and nations of the world, peacemakers must not only recognize, individually and collectively, their particular national identities, but also transcend them.

The rich diversity of North American Baptist life offered the nascent BPFNA a chance to form an institution which addressed both needs. At the time, most Baptist peacemakers were probably not preoccupied with the need for a new organization, certainly not a multi-racial, international one. Doing what they could in their daily lives and through church and community affiliations, most were already working for peace and justice in ways which rarely made the news. Some were pastors, educators, or denominational employees. Others were lay people with diverse ministry emphases. A few had undertaken highly visible and sometimes controversial acts of discipleship. Busy people, they did *not* need one more cause to join, one more meeting to attend, or one more check to write. Conscious and hurting about what was happening at home and around the world, they were already living into God's dream of "healing among the nations" (Rev 22:2).

With a primary purpose of nourishing, empowering, and training people to act with courage and imagination in their local contexts, BPFNA leadership sought to create a unique collaboration for peace. It remained to be seen whether this was, in the words of Ken Sehested after only a few months as Executive Director, "the naïve fantasy of a handful of sheltered idealists or a genuine movement of the Spirit, bringing life and light from unexpected places."[3]

In this balance of this chapter, we look at one of the first ways chosen to involve and encourage Baptists to develop an interracial and international perspective, an annual conference affectionately known as peace camp. Inviting the involvement and sharing of peacemakers from different ethnicities, denominations, and nationalities, in the relaxed setting and pacing of six days, BPFNA sought to inspire participants to leave at the end of each week with renewed energy and ideas for the work of ensuring the wholeness, security, prosperity, righteousness, justice, and political, economic, and spiritual well-being of all persons.

3. Director's Report, January 17, 1985.

PEACE CAMPS

Departing from the Baptist Pacifist (Peace) Fellowship's practice of organizing a breakfast during the annual or biennial American Baptist meetings, BPFNA's leaders planned a gathering to take place from June 30 to July 5, 1986. Over two hundred persons convened at the Green Lake Conference Center in Wisconsin. The Reverend James A. Forbes, Jr., from 1976–1989 professor of homiletics at Union Theological Seminary in New York City, preached on the conference theme, *Announcing the Reign of God* (Matt 4:23; Luke 4:16–22, and other texts). Ken Medema rocked the walls and awakened hearts with his music. Jane Smith Medema generated fresh insights with her Bible studies. Two Canadians, Nancy Dekar and Jan Swaren, organized and led a creative program for over fifty children. Roger Velásquez challenged the North American church to respond to the cries of neighbors to the south. The gathered community encircled and commissioned him to ministry in Nicaragua. From the watchtower of her father's shoulders, baby Sarah Burkett gave cues for clapping, smiling, dancing, and shouting "Koolebah," an African word meaning freedom.[4]

Peg Wallace recalls how the Green Lake conference inspired and prepared her for a life of peace rooted in Jesus.

> God called me to pulpit ministry through the inspiring preaching of Nancy Sehested (who also preached at my ordination a few years later). I didn't know Nancy then; or anyone else to tell the truth. I came to the conference to find out what peace and justice was. . . . Twenty-five years later I look back on my ministry as challenging and spirit-filled. I continue to be awed at the ways that God calls.[5]

For many conferees it had been a long time since it felt so good to wear the Baptist label. My stories of mostly unknown Baptist "saints" allowed contemporary peacemakers to see themselves as part of a larger narrative rather than as aberrations in Baptist history. In a recent email, Alan Selig has recalled,

> [in] Green Lake, Wisconsin, there were many children and youth present as I recall. I remember Paul Dekar told stories of some of the heroes of Baptist peacemaking.

4. Sehested, "Revive Us Again"; Nancy Hastings Sehested's presentation to the fifth BPFNA summer conference in Ottawa, Ontario, July 6, 1990; and my personal journal.

5. Email forwarded by LeDayne Polaski, January 29, 2009.

Our children at the conference decided to engage in an act of quasi-civil disobedience. Concerned that the electric fence surrounding the Rose Garden on the grounds would provide a painful shock to the deer in the area (for whom the rose bushes provided a delicious snack) unknown persons crept out one evening and cut the wires.

The perpetrators were never identified, and since they would now be around 30 years of age, the statute of limitations has undoubtedly run out on the crime. The ensuing conversations considered whether or not the act fit into the category of "peacemaking." No conclusions were agreed upon. However, the practice in subverting the authorities (administrative and parental) was undoubtedly good preparation for future activity.[6]

Many have seen revivals as high in emotion and imparting a self-centered piety leading away from a confrontation with the world rather than toward it. However, this has not always been the case. At times in the history of North American Christianity, revivalism has motivated some attendees to reach out to the marginalized. In eastern Canada, revivals have sometimes deepened appreciation of the social significance of personal religion.[7] In the United States, revivals have sometimes led to ministry in the gaps.[8] In Puerto Rico, evangelical leaders have been imprisoned for protesting the presence of United States occupation forces.[9]

Billed as part conference, part revival, peace camp enabled participants to reclaim and rejoice in what had been an embarrassing part of their heritage. Rejecting lop-sided Christianity, conferees could share in this significant aspect of their religious culture.

For the second BPFNA peace camp (July 6–11, 1987), peacemakers met at Mars Hill College in Asheville, North Carolina. Words of Jesus to his closest friends on the eve of his execution provided a focus: "In the world, you will have tribulation, but be of good cheer, for I have overcome the world" (John 16:33, *RSV*). The theme, *Be of Good Cheer*, made known the possibility of hope amidst suffering.

6. Email forwarded by LeDayne Polaski, February 2, 2009.

7. Goodwin, *Revivals, Baptists, and George Rawlyk.*

8. Jordan, "II Atlanta (II Corinthians) 5" in *Cotton Patch*, 81, for the gap image, ". . . through Christ, [God] bridged the gap between himself and us and has given us the job of also bridging the gap."

9. Dussel, 208.

Hope sprang from an unanticipated and unwanted circumstance. On Thursday, July 9 George Williamson, Jr., BPFNA board president and pastor of First Baptist Church of Granville, Ohio, fell off a precipice while climbing in the mountains near the conference grounds. What followed can only be described as Spirit-filled. Faith healing has rarely been common in Baptist worship yet during the worship that evening, two hundred Baptists as well as a few non-Baptists reached out for one another's hands and forged a strong prayer chain. On bended knees, they prayed for George's survival. The group was not concerned about announcing God's reign, making peace, or anything else. At that precise moment they were Gospel. They were peace. They were *shalom* in the widest biblical sense of the word.

The next day, word came that George was on a path towards healing. Spontaneous dance broke out.

There were other highlights. Baptists and non-Baptists of different ethnicities and nationalities discovered the close connections between the many justice and peace issues. Joseph Roberts and Yamina Apolinaris preached passionately. Jane Medema led revealing Bible studies. Ken Medema, Darrell Adams, Kim Christman, Stan Dotson and Currie Burris provided a wealth of music and introduced some folk to unfamiliar instruments like the dulcimer. Longtime peacemaker and civil rights leader C. T. Vivian gave a soul-stirring address. Motlalepula Chabaku told her story. She cut her teeth in the struggle against oppression in 1949 organizing farm workers to protest against pass laws in the northern region of South Africa known as the *Transvaal* (Afrikaans for *beyond the Vaal River*). Canadian Douglas John Hall offered theological input on the theme. Paul Dekar shared stories of Baptist saints. Over fifty children, skillfully directed by Karen Peters and Olivia Kay Clyde, led creative worship during several sessions.[10]

The third peace camp met July 4–9, 1988 near Atlanta, Georgia at the Simpsonwood Conference and Retreat Center of the North Georgia Conference of the United Methodist Church. The theme was *Love Your Enemies* (Matt 5:44). My vignettes of Baptist saints emphasized the theme.

For many, women in leadership and preaching, including the subtle difference which this entailed was a highlight. The Reverend Nancy

10. "Be of Good Cheer," 5–6.

Hastings Sehested, then pastor of Prescott Memorial Church in Memphis, Tennessee, was the preacher for the week. The Reverend Carman Pagan from Bayamon, Puerto Rico, gave her testimony on how God called her to peacemaking. Women artists of all kinds led through dance, drama, and music.

Building on the growing reputation of peace camp as a family camp, Judy Webb and Mary Meadows involved children and youth in every aspect of the worship, including Jenny Selig of Dubuque, Iowa. Then aged 11, she wrote and read this poem:

> Deep inside
> a little child's head
> fairy elves creep
> and nobody's dead.
>
> Love is powerful
> overall
> pixies watch you run
> and never let you fall.
>
> Wars are gone
> in the innocent fantasies
> no need for band-aids
> on the un-cut knees.
>
> Grass is green
> on all sides of fences
> parks are equipped
> with colorful benches.
>
> The child is creating
> Unknown to us all
> A little piece of heaven
> With love enough for all.[11]

Evaluating the Atlanta conference, one participant said, "This is the only conference our children have ever looked forward to. Driving away they asked what the dates for next year would be!"[12]

Several hundred Baptist peacemakers gathered during July 10–15, 1989 at Keuka College in the Finger Lakes region of upstate New York,

11. "A Child's Mind," 8.
12. "News Story," 9.

with the theme *Prisoners of Hope* (Zech 9:12). For yet a fourth peace camp, I provided a window into Baptist history through stories of Baptists who served time in prison in various contexts.

In the spirit of the Hebrew prophet, conference preacher Roger Velásquez stressed that Nicaraguans could not understand why the United States supported military operations against their country. Yet they prayed for North American Christians and looked expectantly to the future.

At the time, Velásquez was working with Evangelical Committee for Aid to the Victims, known by its acronym in Spanish, *CEPAD* (*Comité Evangélico Pro-Ayuda al Desarrollo*). A Protestant relief and development organization in Nicaragua, *CEPAD* works in more than a hundred communities, bringing the good news of empowerment and holistic development to hurting and hungry people regardless of race, religion, or political affiliation.

Sarah Hammond, then aged 13, encapsulated similar fears and dreams in a poem she composed and delivered, as follows:

Hope.   This simple word
        Throughout the centuries past
        And those to come
        So essential to the survival of humanity
Hope.   A crystal, bubbling spring of life
        Buried deep within our souls
        Joyously rushing up
        Renewing our strength
        When our most precious dreams
        Are swept away
Hope.   The strand of threat we cling to
        When life threatens
        To drag us down and drown ourselves
        In the overwhelming, bitter depths
        Of sorrow and suffering.
Hope.   In many ways
        The cruelest of emotions
        For it indeed imprisons us
        Enslaves our souls
        Drawing its iron chains
        Tightly around our hearts
        Sometimes our only wish
        Is to be able to stop hoping
        To spare ourselves the torture

> Of holding on to faith
> To take an easier road
> Than this steep, narrow footpath
> With its sudden twists
> And seemingly impenetrable barriers
> Of frustration and fear
> We plead to be set free
> From this anguishing bondage
> Because we are afraid
> Afraid. Of being let down or broken
> If we hope to no avail.
> Afraid. Of baring our hearts
> Only for them to be trampled upon.
> Afraid. To trust for an outcome
> We cannot be sure of
> Hope. Leaves us vulnerable
> Offering no protection
> Against deep and wrenching pain
> But if we choose the narrow path
> Working and struggling together
> To carry them out
> It is on the hopes
> Of we who dare to dream
> About a new and better world
> That the firm foundation
> For a bright and shining future
> Of global unity and understanding
> And of true, secure peace
> Will be laid.[13]

A surprised Larry Crockett listened to speakers like Roger and Sarah. On his way to his home in Vermont, he had decided spontaneously to visit the Keuka College campus for the first time since 1969 when he had to resign from the faculty as a consequence of his peace activism and ended up attending peace camp. At the end of a session, he was given the microphone and said, "If you feel discouraged in your peace work, keep working and be patient and come back in twenty years and see the harvest of your work. We never know how the seeds we're planting are going to grow."[14]

13. *PeaceWork* (July–October 1989) 8.
14. Ibid., 7.

Between July 2 and 7, 1990 Carlton University in Ottawa, Ontario, was host campus for the fifth peace camp. Those who came early enjoyed the July 1 Canada Day festivities, one of a number of ways the vision of the Americas broadened, particularly for United States citizens who spent their Fourth of July holiday in another nation.

The theme was *Justice and Peace Will Embrace* (Ps 85:10). Leading the daily Bible study, Miguel Tomás Castro of Emmanuel Baptist Church in San Salvador, El Salvador, stressed the implications of solidarity with the poor and suffering. Drawing from his personal experience of having been arrested, tortured, and released into exile in Canada, Castro stated, "We can't work for justice without paying the cost." Conference attendees raised funds for an ad in the Salvadoran press expressing hopes for negotiations then under way under the auspices of the United Nations between the government of El Salvador and the rebel *Frente Farabundo Martí para la Liberación Nacional* (FMLN), or Farabundo Martí National Liberation Front. The ad read in part as follows:

> Lord of love and mercy, we pray that all violence and human rights violations should stop, a cease-fire prevail and negotiations lead to restoration of peace. May leaders be granted commitment to justice and wisdom to bring peace and justice. May prosperity return to the land, families be reunited, the resources of war be diverted to the healing of the nation and children one day dance and sing throughout the land, for *todos niños son Cristo con nosotros* [all children are Christ with us].[15]

Participants also raised $1,000 towards the efforts of the Innu (human being) to preserve their homeland, Nitassinan (Our Land) in the Quebec-Labrador peninsula. From the early 1980s NATO conducted low level flight training over land claimed by the Innu. In 2000, the Canadian Department of National Defence agreed to call off the high speed flights and to negotiate with the Innu. Talks led to a permanent reduction of military training and clean-up of Goose Bay.

Conferees also raised $16,268 in cash and pledges to purchase a bus for the *Universidad Politécnica de Nicaragua* (UPOLI), a university of the *Convención Bautista de Nicaragua* in Managua.[16] Free Williams, then a ten-year old fifth grader, donated $80. He said that he had heard Roger

15. *Baptist Peacemaker* 10 (Summer–Fall 1990) 7. The Chapultepec Peace Accords were signed on January 16, 1992.

16. Online: http://www.upoli.edu.ni.

Velásquez the previous year. "It looked like they felt real bad, and I wanted to do something." For George Williamson, Jr., "Our summer get-togethers are often the occasion for miracles. This is a small gesture—though it's plenty big for our little flock of members—to remind our Nicaraguan friends, especially our Baptist brothers and sisters, that we've not forgotten them since their country's future is now fading from newspaper headlines."[17]

During the successful two-year campaign, people contributed $40,000. The bus was purchased, loaded with medical and other humanitarian supplies, and driven to Managua. On June 18, 1991, the bus arrived at the campus of UPOLI. Describing the scene, Tom Burkett, one of the drivers and a Granville, Ohio middle school teacher, commented,

> The perception was not that the *bus* was a gift, but that *we* (the BPFNA members who drove it) were a gift sent by the BPFNA to be a gift (to Nicaraguan Baptists). They (the Nicaraguan Baptists) knew this bus came from the richest country in the world, but not from the richest people. It came from people just like them who knew the need and wanted to express love.[18]

In keeping with a new program focus timed to coincide with the 1992 quincentenary of Columbus' historic voyage to the "new world," the campaign would explore the legacy of colonialism in the Americas. Entitled "The Longest War: 500 Years Since Columbus," the program sought to educate the dominant European American culture of North America about the history of colonization for which Columbus and his 1492 voyage are primary symbols. In keeping with this goal, the 1991 and 1992 peace camps featured Native American speakers and a curriculum on first peoples' cultures for the children's program.

Linfield College in McMinnville, Oregon, was host campus for the sixth peace camp July 1–6, 1991. The theme was *Be Not Afraid* (Exod 14: 13; Luke 12:4). Dr. William Baldridge, associate professor of Native American ministries at Central Baptist Theological Seminary and a member of the Cherokee nation, did a series of Bible studies in which he shared stories from "The Old Testament of Native America." With these, along with stories of Jesus recorded in the Second Testament, a Native American theology might emerge.

17. *Baptist Peacemaker* 10 (Summer–Fall 1990) 9.

18. *Baptist Peacemaker* 11 (Fall 1991) 1.

... if the Gospel of Christ is translated into the Native American sense of reality, rather than being offered as a transliteration of the Euro-American culture, Indians will respond and Indians will take up their own bed and walk.

I hope for the day when Native Americans walk out from under the oppression of the dominant community; walk away from the racism and paternalism that still can be found in some of our missionary attitudes; walk over and set the drum beside the pipe organ, walk over and put some sage in the censer, walk over and set the communion pipe beside the communion cup.[19]

Mary Lin Hudson of Memphis Theological Seminary organized musical reflections. In her program notes, "In Praise of Darkness (When Enlightenment Means Oppression)," Mary Lin observed that perhaps nothing has compromised the work of the Gospel more than when it has been used to justify the so-called enlightenment of Native Americans. This has entailed forms of evangelism that have justified violence, devastation, and destruction aimed at an entire people.

Psalm 27:1, Luke 2:9, John 6:20, and other passages in Scripture counsel people not to be afraid. George Williamson, Jr., preached on this theme from Revelation and said that John wrote the book to encourage "patient endurance" among Christians who had to choose between their life and their way of life. John wanted to create the faithful witness. Williamson drew parallels with what was going on in the contemporary world,

Because of the [Persian] Gulf War and its aftermath, the contemporary church is thrust into the apocalyptic situation. We read the Book of Revelation in church as we cry out, "Who is God?" "Why?" "What must we do?" What we get is not an answer but a story, a dark, obscure drama. We are left with no certainties in this radical questioning to which we have been driven, only a hope.[20]

For the seventh peace camp, held June 29 through July 4, 1992, over 325 persons convened at Hollins College in Roanoke, Virginia. Psalm 24:1, which reads *The Earth Is the Lord's*, highlighted the interconnectedness of humans and the land and provided the theme for input by two Native American speakers, theologian Bill Baldridge (Cherokee) and writer Kim Mammedaty (Kiowa). Baldridge drew attention to the fact that five hundred years had passed since the wake of the little wooden ships carrying

19. Baldridge, *Be Not Afraid*, 8.
20. Williamson, *Who Is God*, 34; *Be Not Afraid*, 14.

the Christ-bearing colonizer Christopher Columbus inundated the contours of this hemisphere.[21]

Offering the experience of her ancestors, Mammedaty described living on the edge of the circle, on the fringe.

> To know the experience of exile is to know the experience of Jesus. We must enlarge our community and brace ourselves to endure. There is a greater community out there waiting to experience us. And after we know the greater community, we will no longer fear following Jesus, looking at the tracks we've left. As the Christian story says, we will not die but we will be changed.[22]

Many participants signed a statement which offered encouragement to two congregations in North Carolina disfellowshipped from the Southern Baptist Convention for supporting gay men, lesbians, bisexuals, and transgender people. The statement read in part,

> We appreciate the courage you showed in dealing openly with a controversial issue; your sincerity in seeking the will of God, in searching the Scripture and seeking the leadership of the Spirit; and your willingness to follow that Spirit as you see it. We suffer with you the pain of rejection and offer you our consolation. We also experience the pain caused to all Baptists who cherish the autonomy of the local church and the tradition of speaking for the disenfranchised.[23]

Homosexuality remains a lightening-rod issue for many Christians around the world. We will return to the BPFNA stance on this issue in the sixth chapter.

From July 26 to 31, 1993, Miles College, a historic African American institution, hosted the eighth peace camp in Birmingham, Alabama. The Reverend Fred Shuttlesworth told personal stories of the civil rights movement in Birmingham during the 1960s. He shared how he narrowly survived bombings, faced down Eugene ("Bull") Connor, infamous director of public safety, and negotiated with white leaders. He told of the children's marches and of the bombing of Sixteenth Street Baptist Church on September, 15, 1963, when four teenage Sunday school children died.

---

21 Baldridge, "The Quincentenary," 1.

22. *Baptist Peacemaker* 12 (Fall–Winter 1992) 11.

23. Ibid., 10.

Christopher Hamlin, then pastor of Sixteenth Street Baptist Church, developed the theme, *Walk Together Children, Don't You Get Weary*. Pastor Hamlin warned that darkness still enveloped the United States. Racism, sexism, classism, and other isms were tearing at the nation's fabric. But, he said, God through Christ has affirmed light in us. "We will not revert into darkness while the world is in need of hearing the Gospel in clear, illuminating words that influence the lives of all people."[24]

During the Friday evening worship service at Sixteenth Street Baptist Church, I joined other conferees in presenting the congregation a check for $4,625 and "The Birmingham Confession" with over 1,100 endorsements. The statement read, in part,

> . . . Our preaching has not been faithful. Our most ambitious missionary endeavors are undermined by the continuing reality of racial injustice within our own ranks.
> Therefore, we ask for your forgiveness. In doing so, we acknowledge that our own healing is at stake, that racism impedes our own development as a people and discredits our own preaching . . .
> Finally, we acknowledge that the dream of the beloved community is painfully slow in coming. The roots of racial discrimination are deeper than we thought. The larger work of confession, repentance and restoration is yet to be completed.

Signatories further committed themselves "to diligent patience, to sustaining the struggle against racism for all the days of our lives, to the small steps of reconciling action which will someday blossom forth in the healing of communities, of cities, of the very nations themselves."[25]

As a token of solidarity, conferees raised $1000 for installation of handicap access ramps at Miles College. Several helped prepare a shelter for HIV-positive women. Mary's House, part of the Catholic Worker network, opened a few weeks later. Thirty-three teenagers took part in a variety of activities related to challenging and overcoming racism.

First Baptist Church in Granville, Ohio, hosted the ninth peace camp, July 4–9, 1994. More than 300 persons, including a hundred children and youth, came from around North America. The theme, *We've Come This Far by Faith*, enabled conferees to look back at BPFNA's first ten years. Several participants described key moments in BPFNA history.

24. "BPFNA Summer Conference Report," 4.
25. *Baptist Peacemaker* 13 (Summer 1993) 1.

Walk Together Children (#8 Birmingham 1993)

Others challenged participants to push to the frontiers for justice. George Williamson, Jr., Bible study leader and pastor of the host congregation, proclaimed that one of the frontiers was where the breakthrough of God overwhelmed religious evil. Williamson defined religious evil as "religion alienated from the breakthrough of God, done at other peoples' expense, obsessed with death and without repentance.... Breakthrough is simply what God does. It occurs wherever history is soft, wherever masses of people, beat down by religion done at their expense find voice and community."[26]

Kyle Childress, 1985 BPFNA intern, pastor of the Austin Heights Baptist Church in Nacogdoches, Texas, and one of three preachers, described the movement's growth as a journey,

> ... Starting off with little money but a lot of faith and grit, here we are stronger and healthier but still living on faith and grit.
>
> Along the way we have become one model, one embodiment, that the broader church looks to for guidance, challenge, and even inspiration, building bridges across racial lines and geographic and national boundaries, speaking out with a load voice against [the first Iraq War] when there was little more than a whimper from the rest of the U.S. Willing to walk along on faith with Native Americans and trying to be faithful with gays and lesbians as they struggle. For 10 years we have kept finding ourselves wrestling with one thing after another and as soon as we tried to catch our breath, something or someone else came along and we moved further down the road.

26. Williamson, *This Far By Faith,* 24.

87

That someone is Jesus. The one thing that has been constant for 10 years is that we have sought to follow Jesus. . . . Each summer, we gather and stop at our Peace Camp, find a safe place and get some perspective and nourishment, but by the end of the week someone yells, "Hey, Jesus is on the move again! Come on!"[27]

Canadian human rights activist Lee McKenna used Luke 10, Jesus' commissioning of seventy disciples, to draw parallels with BPFNA's witness. She summarized,

> . . . 70 (more or less) have gone to every town from San Juan to Halifax, from Vancouver to Decatur. Their travels took them to Sjövik and Pretoria, to Moscow and Managua, from Havana to Myanmar [Burma]. They stood, hands on hips, before the principalities and powers of San Salvador and Washington, Mexico City and Ottawa; they stood, without shoes, before the courts and cathedrals of the collaborators and opened their embrace to the homeless, the disabled; they preached Good News to the victims of human rights violations and spoke alternatives to and liberation from the shackles of a consumptive culture. . .[28]

Luis Collazo, literature professor at *La Universidad Interamericana de Puerto Rico* (Inter-American University of Puerto Rico) and the third conference preacher recalled the theme of peace camp 1993, *Walk Together Children, Don't You Get Weary*. Collazo exhorted conferees not to get discouraged. "A vital component of the Old Testament is that faith orients us toward the future, toward faith, toward the journey."[29]

Participants sent a telegram to a United States District Court judge in North Carolina handing down sentences for the "Plowshares Four." On December 7, 1993, John Dear, Lynn Fredriksson, Bruce Friedrich, and Philip Berrigan were arrested and charged for actions of civil disobedience at Seymour Johnson Air Force Base in Goldsboro, North Carolina. The four were denied bail because they were determined to be a "danger to the community" and had already served seven months in prison. The Conference telegram asked the judge to make the activists' sentences equal to time already served. "We believe that justice has already been served in this case. These four are not criminals in the narrow sense, but

27. Childress, "Always Between Places."

28. McKenna, "Seventy (More or Less)."

29. Collazo, "By Faith We Will Walk into the Future." The Spanish text is also available.

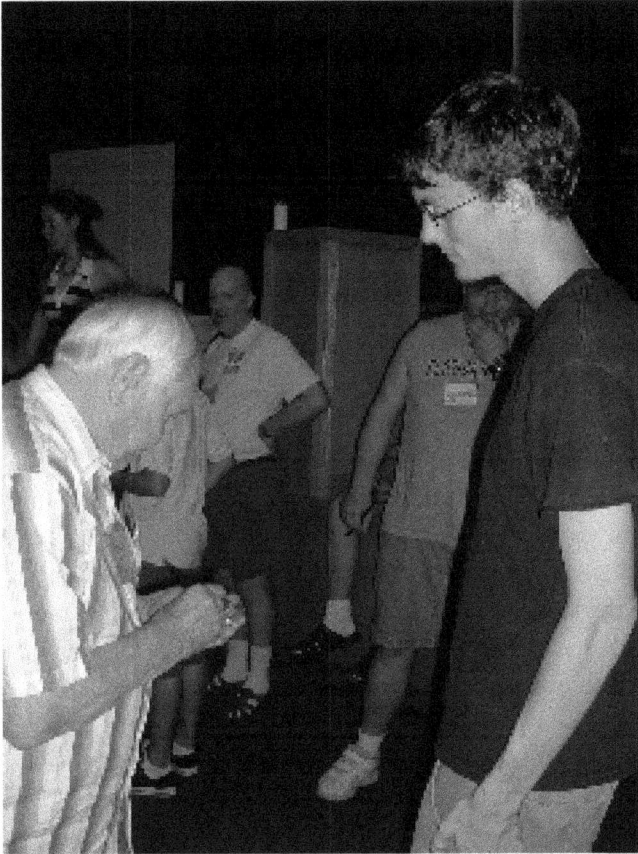

Two COs from the 2005 McMinnville conference.
Tracy Gipson and James Reiswig.

are people of conscience appealing to the conscience of the nation. We appeal to you, as a man of conscience, to act out of a sense of justice and not retribution."[30]

The tenth peace camp (July 10–15, 1995) was housed at the Mount Alverno Conference Center, a former convent located in Redwood City, California. With peace camp based near San Francisco, named for Saint Francis of Assisi, the conference theme, *Fools in the Eyes of the World*, drew on Saint Francis as exemplifying Paul's admonition to Christians at

---

30. *Baptist Peacemaker* 14 (Fall–Winter 1994) 5. For an account of the action, Dear, *Persistent Peace.*

Corinth to "become fools so that you may become wise. For the wisdom of this world is foolishness with God" (1 Cor 3:18–19).

Anne Symens-Bucher, Co-Director for Justice, Peace, and Integrity of Creation Office of St. Barbara Province of Franciscan Friars in Oakland, highlighted two aspects of Franciscan spirituality. The first has been the nurture of nonviolence as a way of being, exemplified in her role vigiling against nuclear weapons with the Nevada Desert Experience and Pace e Bene, an Italian expression of greeting used by Saint Francis for "peace and all good".[31] The second has been active service towards others, exemplified through her serving marginalized people who come for assistance to the St. Anthony Foundation.[32]

James Chuck, conference preacher and retired pastor of First Chinese Baptist Church of San Francisco, focused on two words in the name of the organization, peace and fellowship. Chuck explained that Chinese orthography renders peace as grain now and fellowship as covenant. He concluded that peace is present when everyone has food enough to live. Recalling the struggles of Chinese immigrants to North America, Chuck called for a declaration of interdependence which has as its goal alleviating the vulnerability of children, the elderly, and other marginalized people.

Jerene Broadway, an artist and minister living at the time in San Francisco, helped conferees create a panel for the NAMES Project AIDS Memorial Quilt.[33] Those who wished to do so wrote the names of friends who have died of AIDS on rainbow-colored peace cranes. These were attached to a banner with the words: "We remember and celebrate the lives of . . . our rainbow of friends. Baptist Peace Fellowship Summer Conference 1995."[34]

Peace camp eleven gathered at the University of Waterloo in Waterloo, Ontario July 8–13, 1996. The theme, *And a Child Shall Lead* (Isa 11:6), lifted up the significant role children and youth had come to play in conference activity. As in previous peace camps, children and youth provided crucial leadership through play, song, and worship. Adults followed as children danced, searched for black squirrels around the conference

31. Online: www.paceebene.org. See also my review of *Engage: Exploring Nonviolent Living*, by Laura Slattery, Ken Butigan, Veronica Pelicaric, and Ken Preston-Pile.

32. Online: http://www.stanthonysf.org/home.html.

33. Online: http://www.aidsquilt.org/.

34. *Baptist Peacemaker* 15 (Fall–Winter 1995) 4.

grounds, and offered poignant, often painful reflection on what it is like to grow up in a violent, frightening world.

Eleven-year old Amy Temple began a poem, as follows, "A young child shivers under cold wet clothes. Has she eaten? Nobody knows. Her voice is weak and her English poor. She has some friends though she needs many more..."

Sixteen-year old Free Williams, who led the morning devotions, challenged perceptions common to North American culture of ordinary children as leaders.

> C. S. Lewis used children to lead in his Narnia chronicles, and Steven Spielberg used a child as a main character in *E.T.* So the idea of a child leader is rather common.
>
> However, the idea of a child leader is not believable to us. Children are only leaders when strange things happen. C. S. Lewis paired child leaders with talking animals, and Spielberg pairs them with aliens from outer space. There's no such thing as an ordinary child leader in our culture. So how can we know what the kingdom of God is like without knowing what its leader is like.

Williams concluded the week with a litany which highlights which we are all children of God:

> Leader: Who are you?
> People: We are the children of God.
> Leader: Where do you live?
> People: We live in God's world
> Leader: How are you made?
> People: We are made in the image of God.
> Leader: Why are you here?
> People: We are here to worship and to learn.

Williams suggested that this litany is so simple that it might be close to what Jesus meant about belonging to heaven. If we can accept these simple sayings, then we, too, can belong like children.[35]

The July 21–26, 1997, peace camp drew 270 people to Eastern Mennonite University, Harrisonburg, Virginia. The focus was *Disarming the Heart, The Gospel of Nonviolence.* Female conferees from the four countries of BPFNA's core constituency, Canada, *México*, Puerto Rico, and the United States, played the key role as theme preachers.

---

35. *Baptist Peacemaker* 16 (Fall–Winter 1996) 10.

The Reverend Olivia Juárez de González, director of an extension program at Baptist Seminary in Mexico City, drew from her experience with indigenous women's organizations in Mexico. She called on conferees to become involved in the lives of those who suffer from violence, poverty, and discrimination.

> The example of the church in Antioch teaches us that giving, sharing, a common commitment, showing oneself to be brother or sister to those who suffer, bringing food to those who do not have it—this is an important part of our testimony. If our arms were like those that Paul mentions in Ephesians 6:10–20—truth, justice, peace, faith, salvation, the Sword of the Spirit—then we would not be bearers of death, but life abundant.[36]

The Reverend Tama Ward Balisky of Vancouver, British Columbia, used the story of the Good Samaritan (Luke 10:25–37) to encourage conferees to consider how much time is spent working to keep violence from happening instead of responding to those who suffer.

> Jesus doesn't spend even one verse talking about how to ensure safety on the Bloody Way ... and yet I am convinced that this passage is as much about justice as any in the Bible. It's the justice that can only come about through acts of deep, almost unexplainable compassion, through acts of nonviolence.[37]

The other theme preachers were the Reverend Nancy Hastings Sehested, then pastor of Sweet Fellowship Baptist Church in Clyde, North Carolina, and the Reverend Carmen Pagán-Cabrera, religion professor at *La Universidad Interamericana de Puerto Rico* (Inter-American University of Puerto Rico). Conference activities also included a meeting of The Next Generation (TNG), BPFNA's youth advisory committee formed in early 1997. TNG shared a video highlighting the role youth can play if given a sense of purpose. Especially through their involvement each year in peace camp, young people had assumed a clear place in leadership of the BPFNA.

Earlham College, Richmond, Indiana, housed the thirteenth peace camp, July 27–August 1, 1998 with the theme, *Proclaim Jubilee: Scripture's Vision for the Healing of Creation and All that Dwell Therein* (Lev 25). Bob Hunter, campus pastor and adjunct professor of peace and global studies

36. *Baptist Peacemaker* 17 (Fall 1997) 6.
37. Ibid.

at Earlham, used Matt 12:15 to focus on Jesus' challenge of the religious leaders of the day.

> Was it legalism or was it love? If it was a legalism, what were the exceptions to be made? If it was legalism then the rules of the Sabbath were disinterested in human well-being. If it was love then the exception would be recognizable when human well-being was at stake. Jesus' declaration is that the Sabbath was made for human beings. The human callousness coming out of legalism leads to arbitrary manipulation of people.[38]

Shortly before the conference the scheduled Bible study leader, Sharon Ringe of Wesley Theological Seminary in Washington DC, suffered an accident and could not attend. Four volunteers filled in. Jane Medema of San Francisco provided an overview of the Jubilee theme in Leviticus and Deuteronomy. Medema emphasized that the Jubilee texts did not function as a prescriptive legislative agenda for ancient Israel but as a summons to personal and public renewal. "When the jubilee vision functions properly, it is not simply a return to some romanticized past but the invitation, the enticement, to participate in God's recreation of the world."

Michelle Tooley, at the time a member of the faculty of Belmont University in Nashville, Tennessee, gave attention to the legal implications of a grassroots movement pressing the rich countries to cancel the debt of poorer countries of the world. Acknowledging that jubilee economics does not resonate easily with modern realities, Tooley said, "I hope that I pledge allegiance to the God of the jubilee vision. But I fear that I pledge allegiance to the international companies that create order in my world and make me safe."

Doug Donley, then pastor of Dolores Street Baptist Church in San Francisco, focused on the breach between worship and work. He said that to be a repairer of the breach (Isa 58:12) requires willingness to satisfy the desires and needs of the afflicted.

Steve Hammond, co-pastor of First Baptist Church (now Peace Community Church) in Oberlin, Ohio, focused on the story of the rich young ruler in Luke 18. Jesus expanded the jubilee theme by applying it

---

38. *Baptist Peacemaker* 18 (Fall 1998) 3–5 for the comments of Hunter and other speakers; Harris, *Proclaim Jubilee!*

Building a Culture of Peace (#14 Vancouver 1999).
Artwork by Christ Dupere

to the wealthy. Wishing truly to follow Jesus, they must be liberated from their bondage to security.

The fourteenth peace camp, third to be held in Canada, met July 19–24, 1999 at the University of British Columbia in Vancouver. Balancing between commitment and carnival, speakers, children, and youth explored the theme *Upon This Rock: Building a Culture of Peace.*

Drawing on words of Jesus to Matthew (Matt 16:18), young people built a church out of Lego building blocks. On each was written the name of all of conference participants. Another group made an altar-like rock garden with a prayer or wish of a child written on each rock such as "peace on earth" and "the hungry are fed." The youth dedicated one wall of the plenary room with a challenge to the larger group. Called the Wall of Peace, it was decorated with exhortations, drawings, and opportunities for adults to write their own pledges. Some of the youth created a newspaper called *Peace Soup*, which has become a regular feature of *Baptist Peacemaker.* Musicians Andrew and Wendy Donaldson of Toronto wrote the theme song,

1. The need is overwhelming
    There's so much to be done;
    So many lives in danger
    Thirst and hunger, lose their dreams—

It always seems we've just begun.
But Jesus said, Don't be afraid;
And when the mountains shake above you,
Stand firm, for I am with you.

Chorus:
Upon this rock
The saints have stood before;
Upon this rock
God is walking with the poor;
Upon this rock
The captives find release;
Upon this rock,
God works among us, building a people of peace.

2. When wages of oppression
Come rising like a flood;
When loving acts of justice
Turn against us, turn to pain,
Then we cry, Where's the reign of God?
But Jesus said, Go on in faith;
And when the cities seethe around you,
Go on, for I am with you.[39]

Wake Forest University in North Carolina was host campus from July 10–15, 2000 for the fifteenth peace camp. The theme drew from *On Earth as It Is In Heaven* (Matt 6:10). With sanctions continuing in Iraq, conference delegates raised almost enough funds to buy four chlorinators, sent to Iraq without a license from the United States Treasury Department and installed in 2001.

During a workshop, "Making the Lord's Prayer Your Own," Bob Adams wrote the following paraphrase of Jesus' themes,

You, who are so much other than we
that no name fits you
or does you justice,
yet you who are better than our best idea of parent—
Help us be careful of how we represent you to others.
May what happens among us
Be like what happens when and where you rule.
May what we most need physically
Not be such a worry for us.

39. *Baptist Peacemaker* 19 (Fall 1999) 5.

Make us a part of your putting all things right,
No matter the cost.
Help us get your reading on our doings.
Help us, even for a moment,
to catch a glimpse of how it is when what you want becomes real.[40]

The preacher for the week was Rebeca Montemayor of Mexico City. Educator and pastor, she was the first woman to be ordained among Baptists in *México*.

Oberlin College in Ohio was host campus for the sixteenth peace camp, July 9–14, 2001, with the theme, *For Such a Time as This* (Esth 4:14). A principal stop on the pre-Civil War Underground Railroad, Oberlin provided opportunities to visit historic sites and to hear local historians tell stories about Oberlin-area abolitionist activity.

Cindy Weber, pastor of Jefferson Street Baptist Community at Liberty in Louisville, Kentucky, brought to life women in the Hebrew scriptures. Board member and Toronto pastor bob paterson-watt opened each day with fresh studies of the book of Esther. The Shape-Note Singers, led for years at peace camp by the late Jack Smith, performed one evening under a new name: the Jack Smith Singers. Jerene Broadway of San Francisco helped organize creative and poignant interpretations of the conference theme such as the litany included as Appendix six.[41]

About 200 people came to the campus of Acadia University in Wolfville, Nova Scotia, for the seventeenth peace camp (July 22–27, 2002). Barry Morrison, at the time Acadia Divinity School's professor of homiletics and worship and now pastor of Wolfville Baptist Church, oldest continuing Baptist congregation in Canada, explored the theme *To Sing among the Peoples* (Ps 57:9). In powerful messages of lament and hope, Morrison insisted that "A lament is an act of faith where we raise our voices to God . . . because we dare to believe in a day when there will be no tears."[42]

Jerene Broadway guided the group through the extravagance and hyperbole of the Psalms of complaint. Using an eclectic collection of art, music, and dance, she guided participants through the dark and painful stories of Hebrew history into the light of hope.

40. *Baptist Peacemaker* 20 (Fall 2000) 5.
41. *Baptist Peacemaker* 21 (Fall 2001) 5.
42. *Baptist Peacemaker* 22 (Fall 2002) 10.

To Sing among the Peoples (#17 Wolfville, Nova Scotia).
Artwork by Chris Dupere

Various presentations and field trips focused on displaced peoples of Nova Scotia. Conferees learned of the French-speaking Acadians. Nearly three centuries ago, they were pushed out of Canada when they refused to sign an oath of loyalty to the British crown which did not allow them neutrality in conflicts between the British and the French. Further Canadian content (affectionately known as CanCon) included stories of slaves who escaped to Nova Scotia from the United States before and during the United States Civil War and of Afro-Canadian communities that have been displaced in more recent years. Native Canadians told of their displacement from traditional hunting and fishing grounds

Russell DeYoung, a scientist with the National Aeronautics and Space Administration, spoke of another form of displacement. He had recently spent six months in a federal prison for an act of civil disobedience, protesting at a combat training school for Latin American soldiers in Fort Benning, Georgia. In November 2000, the weekend before Thanksgiving in the United States, he had joined and been arrested at the annual protest during which progressive movements call for the closure of the School of the Americas, renamed in 2001 the Western Hemisphere Institute for Security Cooperation and for a new direction in United States foreign policy.[43]

43. Online: http://www.soaw.org/index.php. Most people still refer to the School of the Americas, renamed Western Hemispheric Institute for Security Cooperation in 2001.

With Such a Cloud of Witnesses (#18 Keuka 2003).
Created by Chris Dupere.

During July 14–19, 2003 more than 250 peacemakers converged on the campus of Keuka College in upstate New York around the theme *With Such a Cloud of Witnesses* (Heb 12:1). William Herzog of Colgate Rochester/Crozer Divinity School led the morning Bible studies. The keynote speaker was Mel White, founder and director of Soulforce, an organization which works for the liberation of lesbian, gay, bisexual, and transgender people from religious and political oppression through the practice of relentless nonviolent resistance.[44] Encouraging conferees to speak truth to power White challenged all to reflect on the question, "Who is the enemy that we are supposed to love? They are victims of untruth.

Since 1990, a Washington DC-based not-for-profit human rights organization School of the Americas Watch has worked to monitor graduates of the institution and to close the School of the Americas through legislative action, grassroots organizing, and nonviolent direct action. Every year, about the middle of November, more than 10,000 people gather at the gates of Fort Benning to memorialize those who have died at the hands of soldiers trained at this school and to take action opposing this training. Appendix seven has two reflections on this resistance.

44. Online: http://www.soulforce.org.

They don't want to throw out their family members [who are gay] but they think they have to. . . . The first and only weapon we have is truth."

Another speaker was Rabia Terri Harris, coordinator of the Muslim Peace Fellowship and associate editor of Fellowship of Reconciliation's magazine, *Fellowship*. She challenged conferees as follows,

> I do not believe that universalism is the answer. We all need a particular way. But we must understand our human failing, our tendency to make other people unchosen, to make us special—chosen. We do not own God, none of us.[45]

The local planning committee for peace camp 2003 asked Peter Carman, pastor of Lake Avenue Baptist Church in Rochester, New York, to write a song for the conference. He used the theme, "With Such a Cloud of Witnesses," for the song, included as Appendix eight.

The Stones Will Cry Out (Hab 2:9–11; Luke 19:40) was the theme for the nineteenth peace camp held from July 19–24, 2004 at Towson University in Towson, Maryland. Almost 300 peace campers gathered each morning to listen to creative Bible studies by Molly Marshall, Associate Professor of Theology and the first woman granted tenure at Southern Baptist Theological Seminary in Louisville, Kentucky. Shortly after the gathering, Marshall was forced to resign due to her support for ordination of women.

At a memorial service held one evening, the gathered community remembered, among others, Madeleine Paterson-Watt of Kitchener, Ontario, who died on April 28, 2004. Having just celebrated her fifteenth birthday, Madeleine was one of many whose life, spirit, and worldview have been strongly affected by attending peace camp.[46]

One afternoon, about sixty attendees went to Washington DC to protest against the war in Iraq. In front of the United States Capitol Building they distributed flyers, shot a video, and mounted a three-stone-high wall with the messages, "If we are silent, the stones will cry out!"

The protest was allowed to proceed even though the demonstrators did not have a permit to stage a march.

During August 1–6, 2005, the twentieth peace camp returned to the campus of Linfield College in McMinnville, Oregon. Among speakers, Marcus Borg, Hundere Distinguished Professor of Religion and Culture

45. *Baptist Peacemaker* 23 (Fall 2002) 4.

46. "Madeleine Grace Paterson-Watt: Remembrances," 10–11.

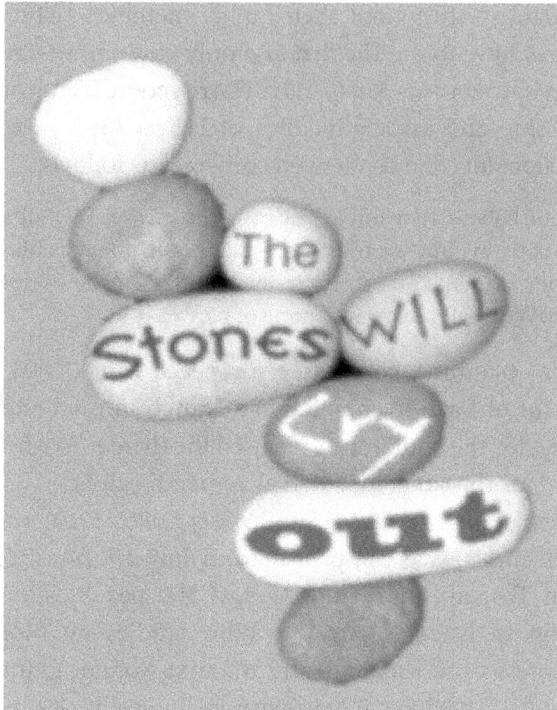

The Stones Will Cry Out (#19 Towson 2004).
Created by Claudia Esslinger.

at Oregon State University, led off introducing with the theme, *For the Healing of the Nations* (Rev 22:2). Canadian Baptist pastor Cam Watts offered creative Bible studies. I shared stories of World War II Baptist conscientious objectors. During the Thursday evening service, about a dozen COs from earlier wars joined The Next Generation. Having fashioned CO cards to carry in their wallets, young adults and youth presented a declaration of Conscientious Objection and asked for prayer. Youth and young adults also led the closing commissioning and communion service on Saturday morning.

That Friday of conference week was the sixtieth anniversary of the bombing of Hiroshima. The youth drew outlines of their shadows on the sidewalks around the church in memory of the people who had been killed by the bomb. Many conferees joined the local Yamhill Valley Peacemakers in their regular First Friday vigil protesting the continuing United States-led war in Iraq. Devon Maylie reported in the *Yamhill*

Kids at peace camp 2008 with Hector Aristizábal.

Valley News-Register that one hundred and seventy one people, from ages 5 to 90, from Canada, Cuba, and more than twenty five U.S. states lined up along downtown Adams Avenue in McMinnville in 102-degree (Fahrenheit) heat. Previously, vigils had drawn no more than twenty-five participants.[47]

Over 330 peace campers converged on Oglethorpe University in Atlanta, Georgia for the twenty-first peace camp (July 10–15, 2006). The conference theme, *Becoming the Beloved Community*, provided a focus for C. T. Vivian and others to explore how we live Dr. King's vision now. Conference activities included daily studies by Peter Paris, a native of Nova Scotia and professor of Christian Social Ethics at Princeton Theological Seminary, under the theme, "Christian Responses to Violence in All Its Varying Forms." Conferees had opportunities to visit sites associated with the Civil Rights movement and to participate in a "Katrina Roundtable" strategy session for the Churches Supporting Churches program, a network of partnerships between New Orleans churches which were devastated by Hurricane Katrina and churches in other areas of the continent. Two evenings during the week, the worship service was held at historic Ebenezer Baptist Church with Dr. J. Alfred Smith, pastor of Allen Temple Baptist Church in Oakland, California, as preacher.

47. *Baptist Peacemaker* 25 (Winter 2005) 19.

During July 23–28, 2007, three hundred people gathered at Berea College in Kentucky under the conference banner, *As the Powers Fall* (Mark 24: 25). Each morning a Mennonite minister and professor in Saskatoon, Saskatchewan, Vern Ratzlaff, offered a Bible study, with a focus on "Powers, Structures, and G-d: Creation and Power" (Genesis 1–2); "Prayer and Power" (Matt 6:9–13); "The Church and Power" (1 Corinthians 12); and "Suffering and Power" (Rev 1:4–10).

Among the speakers, Daniel Hunter, who grew up attending peace camp, was among the speakers and shared his experience doing conflict transformation around the world, "The Challenge of the Fall of Empire: Skills to Thrive on in a Fear-Based Time." Rita Nakashima Brock, a licensed minister in the Christian Church (Disciples of Christ) and Co-Director of Faith Voices for the Common Good, explored "Saving Paradise: Reclaiming Christianity's Forgotten Love for this World." Poet Wendell Berry read from his writings and led a time of open discussion.

During July 14–19, 2008, around 230 peacemakers gathered for the twenty-third peace camp at John Abbott College in Sainte Anne de Bellevue, a suburb of Montreal, Quebec, with the theme, *The Way that Leads to Peace* (Luke 1:79). Conferees focused on what each of us can do in our own personal lives to create peace—starting with peace within ourselves and circling out to our ways of being in our families, congregations, neighborhoods, and the world.[48] Jim Loney's keynote address was highlight of the week. Loney was a Christian Peacemaker Team member who, along with three others, was held hostage in Iraq for 118 days in 2005–2006. His peaceful witness before, during, and after his capture has received worldwide attention and opened many hearts to the idea of living life in a peace-filled way, even in the midst of immense violence.

Glen H. Stassen gave daily Bible studies. Stassen reinforced the idea that practical action we undertake as individuals and communities can truly move us towards peace.

In addition to workshops that covered a wide variety of issues, veterans Mary Meadows and Julie Reiswig coordinated morning sessions with young people. Hector Aristizábal—artist, human rights worker, therapist, and actor—served as a special resource leader with the youth program, using innovative theatrical techniques to teach conflict transcendence and life-affirming group processes designed to enable youth to become

48. *Baptist Peacemaker* 28 (September–October 2008) 4.

part of transformative communities. Long-time children's leader Elaine Pennington once again coordinated the morning program for children. Hector Aristizábal, David White, and various other conference leaders shared their skills of art, drama, story-telling, music, and conflict transformation to help the children develop as peacemakers.

The youth led the Friday evening worship and displayed an impressive depth of awareness to a broad array of current peacemaking issues around the globe. As had become a custom, during the closing worship the young people served communion. There were several stations where different elements were available. First-timer Daphne Hunt recalled being intrigued by the idea that, "I could have chips and salsa, or honey and rice cakes, or milk and cereal. I chose the traditional grape juice and bread cubes. I think it is rather like my experience living in Toronto. I can stay close to familiar things and the exotic is within easy reach from folk who can tell me about its goodness and make me feel welcome as I partake of it."[49]

At the time of this writing, Weber State University in Ogden, Utah is scheduled to host a twenty-fourth peace camp, July 20–25, 2009, with the theme, *When There Is Justice, Then Peace Will Come!* What began in 1986 as a modest gathering in Green Lake, Wisconsin, has become a tradition.

REFLECTIONS

Year after year, peace camp has created space for Baptists of differing hues, nationalities, gifts, and ages to come together for worship, play, networking, strategizing, field-trips, hands-on community service, and encouragement. Reflecting on the role of peace camp in relation to the BPFNA vision, Ken Sehested commented at the ninth peace camp, "Our greatest joy comes in the hearing of stories of unheralded men and women everywhere who labor quietly as agents and witnesses to the coming Reign of peace. Our greatest calling is to call forth this same vision and courage in others."[50]

Peace camps have been held in five Canadian cities: Ottawa and Waterloo, Ontario, Vancouver, British Columbia, Wolfville, Nova Scotia, and Montreal, Quebec. They have also been held in sixteen communities across the United States, returning on only three occasions to a host

49. Email forwarded by LeDayne Polaski, January 29, 2009.

50. Press release, *This Far By Faith.*

city for a second time (Atlanta, Georgia, Keuka Park, New York, and McMinnville, Oregon). This has made peace camp accessible to more people than were it held in one place year after year. Cost and logistics have precluded going to *México* or Puerto Rico.

In terms of the importance Baptists generally accord the Bible, a crucial dimension of peace camp has been the opportunity for Baptists to explore, through the leadership of many talented expositors of Scripture, the relation between Biblical faith and peace and justice issues. A Biblical text has tended to generate unity for the diverse input at each of the peace camps.

On four occasions, the conference theme has not been a biblical passage. These exceptions have highlighted BPFNA priorities, creating an international membership and a multi-racial organization. *Becoming the Beloved Community*, the theme for the twenty-first peace camp, drew from Dr. King's vision of a world house free from racism, poverty, and war. A "Negro Spiritual," provided the theme for the eighth peace camp: *Walk Together Children, Don't You Get Weary.* Conferees visited sites associated with the Civil Rights Movement in Birmingham, Alabama.

The ninth conference also drew its thematic unity from a hymn, *We've Come This Far by Faith.* This theme acknowledged that, during its first ten years, the Baptist Peace Fellowship of North America had created a community of resistance, affirmation, and celebration among some Baptist peacemakers. With the theme *Disarming the Heart: The Gospel of Nonviolence,* the twelfth peace camp highlighted the means by which this community has encouraged work to end the threat of nuclear war and to promote healing among the peoples and nations of the world.

Some people attend peace camp to learn new skills. For example, a variety of skilled trainers including Daniel L. Buttry, Lee McKenna, Daniel Hunter, and Dwight M. Lundgren have offered extended workshops in conflict transformation.

Perhaps the most incredible aspect of peace camp is the varied peacemaking experiences of people who attend. Sharing together for a week of play, prayer, study, worship and deepened friendship, folk have recovered a sense of vitality in their work for peace and justice and of confidence that they were, and are helping to create a culture of peace. As conferees communicate ideas, encouragement, and recognition to one another, many are inspired to undertake new peacemaking activities.

It was liberating to be in a setting where one could be both a Baptist and a peacemaker at the same time. Indeed, it was liberating, inspiring, and very humbling, to be surrounded by people who put their faith into peacemaking action day after day, for whom "Baptist peacemaker" is not an oxymoron but a living reality.

For our daughter, the conference was a radical experience, seeing compassion for the oppressed and the poor rooted in Christian faith, and Christianity rooted in compassion. Being involved in the youth program was a deep coming-of-age event for her.

My wife and I are also very grateful for the opportunity to take the Conflict Transformation Training given by Dwight Lundgren. Both of us expect to make use of what we learned, and I am contemplating further training.

Much of this past year was a difficult journey in the wilderness; the BPFNA Peace Conference was for me and my family an oasis in the desert, a respite, a refreshment, a God-given infusion of spiritual sustenance that made our very survival possible. Thank you for giving us this wonderful gift.[51]

To allow for this gift to unfold, organizers have recognized the importance of giving conferees the opportunity during meals, workshops, and free time to tell their stories to one another. They have encouraged and reminded each other that they are not alone and that others are also "out there" struggling for peace and justice in many ways and many places.[52]

As another way in which peace campers have expressed their creativity, each year since 1986, a BPFNA member has created a wall hanging to express visually the theme for the year's peace camp. At every peace camp, the new banner hangs, front and center, where the group gathers for worship, teaching, and fellowship. Surrounding the worship space on the walls are the previous peace camps banners, now a remarkably rich expression of artistry.

Over the years, a high percentage of BPFNA members have been able to attend at least one peace camp. Nonetheless, cost, time, interest, priority, work, and or other factors have kept some people away. Moreover, for some, not everything about peace camp is empowering. Some persons, nervous perhaps about being too publicly associated with a peace organization, have stayed away. Others may have been unimpressed by stories of what a few persons in leadership roles are doing without communicating

51. David Henry, email forwarded by LeDayne Polaski, January 29, 2009.

52. *Baptist Peace*maker 20 (Fall 2000) 4.

effectively a sense of what individuals and local communities or congregations can do.

Aware of this critique, conference organizers have encouraged local host committees to identify ways by which participants might be active in concrete peacemaking. One such opportunity was working on a shelter (Birmingham, 1993). On another occasion, virtually every conferee joined in McMinnville, Oregon a local Friday-afternoon vigil against the war in Iraq (2005). Another example was the effort to raise funds to send a bus to Nicaragua. George Williamson, Jr., observed, "We normally don't do fundraising for development projects. We're just not set up for that kind of work—we have enough trouble raising our own operating budget. But this just caught our imagination"[53]

Among regular peace camp attendees Elaine and Phil Pennington of Ooltewah, Tennessee observed,

> As we reflected on our years of experience at the summer conferences, a couple of thoughts have surfaced. Several years ago Phil told someone, it's like a church that meets once a year. It's a breath of fresh air. Living in East Tennessee makes us somewhat removed from most of the latest ideas, trips, marches, and so on to promote peace. Peacemaking is not a common topic of conversation among neighbors. The summer conference gives us a chance to catch up on what has been done and what is coming up. With these feelings toward the summer conference, we made it a family priority to attend. In just a short time I realized that I could possibly be able to use my teaching skills with our peace campers there. I volunteered in the early nineties to teach a children's class, and I've spent my conference week with the children ever since. It's such a thrill to see my former students as adults doing the work of peace.[54]

The annual gathering developed a good reputation as a family camp. Attending peace camp in 1996 at Waterloo, Wayne Soble commented,

> *And a little child shall lead* . . . Crazy, isn't it? Part threat, part promise. A vision and a voice lent to the silent agony of humankind. The voiceless, the vulnerable, the dispossessed, the desperate. Can you imagine it? . . . Judgment and grace all meanly wrapped in their prophetic little lives, condemning all that detains and defrauds and hurts and hinders. Living metaphors of a future and a hope, blessed

53. *Baptist Peacemaker* 11 (Fall 1991) 1.
54. Personal communication, October 27, 2008.

assurance of the glorious liberty of all God's children. Consult the children because those who fail to do so have no dawn! Consult the children and give their future back to them because Yahweh Sabaoth has a day![55]

In 2008, on Thursday evening after the evening program, George Williamson, Jr., former BPFNA board president who had retired from the pastorate of First Baptist in Granville, Ohio, led a large group from the plenary room down to the St. Lawrence River for an impromptu baptism. Maggie Burkett, who has literally grown up in the BPFNA and who had been preparing for baptism, expressed her desire to be baptized at peace camp. She wanted George, her pastor for most of her life, to officiate, and he did.

News of Maggie's baptism prompted one longtime BPFNA leader to remark, "Now we've had almost every kind of service at peace camp. We've had a baby dedication, an ordination, all kinds of commissioning, and now a baptism. We just need to have a wedding now." The list of participants did include one couple who, having married the Sunday before peace camp opened, celebrated their honeymoon. In 1998, Conrad Browne and Catherine Wilcox met at peace camp and married a few months later.[56] Ten years later, during the summer of 2008, Jamie Reiswig and Amy Temple, two of the young people who had grown up regularly attending peace camp, got married.

Peace camp has evolved into an annual cultural gathering of people who have been transformed in each others' presence, who love and depend on each other, whose children have grown up together in an environment of unique and inspiring values, and who have experienced God in common experience.

Responding to my request for reflections on her experience, Molly Pennington Epperson wrote,

> The best thing about Peace Camp is having the chance to grow as Christians in a way that is completely unlike what we have at home. Our whole family lives in Chattanooga [Tennessee], and my sister and I have been there most of our lives. Chattanooga, although quickly improving, is definitely a southern city with southern prejudices buried deep down. It is difficult if not impos-

55 *Baptist Peacemaker* 16 (Fall–Winter 1996) 4.

56. "Couple Finds Love at Peace Camp," 17.

Final communion at conference.

sible to find a church with views that are in line with what we truly believe about social justice as it relates to Christianity.

My husband and I attend a little tiny Presbyterian congregation at the foot of Lookout Mountain, where he is the music director. Just this past Sunday we welcomed our first African-American member. Most churches around here do not see much diversity, if any, and most churches aren't even close to being welcoming (much less affirming) when it comes to GLBT Christians. But like I said, Chattanooga is quickly improving. We will hopefully see some headway with this in the next few years. Because my family obviously has somewhat different views than most Christians around us, Peace Camp has been a bit of a refuge, especially in recent years.

My sister Amy and I have both grown up in BPFNA. I was 4 and she was 13 at the first conference and we are now 26 and 35. We have attended every conference in whole or in part except for a few in recent years due to our busy work schedules. We feel that there is a special connection with people who attend the conferences and who are called to be advocates for peace and justice in our communities. We have both made life-long friends through BPFNA, and love the feeling of "home" we get (no matter where on the continent we are!) whenever we see these friends at conferences.

George Williamson and Mary Meadows are two people who always bring a smile to my face when I think of them, no matter where I am. George's bare feet, bald head, and heart-warming smile are things that I look forward to every year. His wisdom and unending love for all he meets are true blessings! And I have to say . . . thanks to Mary Meadows who over the years has shown me what womanly strength really is. She has been a blessing in my life. Many people from summer conferences have come and gone, but there is always a special connection with them like no other I have ever experienced . . . including from a very early age hearing Darrell Adams, Ken Medema, and various other conference musicians.[57]

Year after year, with prayer, meditation, music, and worship; art and workshops; speakers, field-trips, and programming for children, youth, and young adults; impromptu happenings and many late-night discussions, peace camp has created space for people to be inspired, to experience rejuvenation, and to challenge one another with new ideas and perspectives. Through multi-racial and international participation, peace camp is a unique grassroots movement in which participants glimpse Dr. King's vision of a Beloved Community becoming reality.

57. Email, January 26, 2008.

This cartoon by Robert Darden went with "Jeremiah the War Resister" by Michael L. Westmoreland-White, *Baptist Peacemaker* 25 (Fall 2005) 6.

4

Building Blocks for a Culture of Peace

Programs and Publications

INTRODUCTION

MARTIN LUTHER KING, JR. did not announce before hundreds of thousands gathered in Washington DC on August 28, 1963, "I have a strategic plan" but rather "I have a dream."[1] Since the inception of the Baptist Peace Fellowship of North America (BPFNA), its founders wanted "Baptist" to be associated someday with concern for justice, peace, and care of creation. This dream remains today.

With this dream in mind, the BPFNA chose to influence Baptist institutions as its unique goal. Stemming from this vision and goal, the primary strategy was to develop an infrastructure of leadership on the local and regional level. Staff and group leaders sought to empower Baptist peacemakers to discover their own voices, to discern and embrace their own particular callings as peacemakers, and to get them to work cooperatively in accomplishing those tasks. Each group decided on its own tactics for accomplishing its mission.[2]

The BPFNA has explored practical ways to build a movement rooted in Dr. King's challenge to free the world of the triple axis of evil: war, racism, and economic injustice. This ongoing agenda of the freedom revolution led by Dr. King has inspired the BPFNA to empower members through several building blocks for a culture of peace: peace camps, local groups, partner congregations, relationships with other peacemaking

---

1. Adapted from an anonymous quote cited by Lowder, "Imagining Our Future."
2. Ken Sehested, "A Word about Our Network," 3.

organizations, equipping the next generation, friendship and solidarity trips, and prize-winning publications.

LOCAL GROUPS, REGIONAL NETWORKS, AND PARTNER CONGREGATIONS

Baptist peacemaking groups in Ohio and Ontario/Quebec (1981), and Iowa/Minnesota, Puerto Rico, Rhode Island, and Washington DC (1983) predated the birth of the BPFNA and gave it direction after 1984, when the new organization was created. From the start, BPFNA gave priority to nurturing these local groups and to creating others. Each related to the BPFNA through a statement of covenant relationship, an affiliation document affirming historic principles of Baptist polity. Each was autonomous but chose to relate to each other and to a larger corporate mission through the BPNFA.

The Ohio and Kentucky groups met in September 1986 to provide a forum for sharing stories, hopes, and faith with each other. A dozen regional leaders then gathered with the BPFNA steering committee the following February at Koinonia Farm in Americus, Georgia. The BPFNA convened several retreats of local group leaders over the next several years. Each issue of *PeaceWork* featured group events or action emphases.

The following is a sampling of activity during the 1980s by some of the local groups and networks. The dates reflect the priority of BPFNA members over time:

- California (1987) planned a conference aimed at sustaining Baptist work for peace and justice in the San Francisco Bay Area;

- Delaware and eastern Pennsylvania (1987) arranged a peace walk from Nazareth to Bethlehem, Pennsylvania;

- Georgia (1987) planned an annual "Feast of the Holy Innocents," an ecumenical action at King's Bay, the Trident submarine base near St. Mary's on the coast;

- Illinois (1986) studied Glen H. Stassen's *Journey into Peacemaking* and organized workshops on conflict transformation skills;

- Indiana (1987) arranged a joint retreat with the Kentucky and Ohio groups;

- Iowa, Minnesota, and Wisconsin arranged an annual tri-region retreat;
- Kentucky (1985) included the newsletter of the Sane-Freeze Coalition and membership in the BPFNA with a subscription to the *Baptist Peacemaker*;
- Michigan (1989) sponsored a touring Russian delegation;
- New Jersey (1985) arranged writing letters on behalf of prisoners of conscience;
- New York (1987) focused on increasing understanding between Muslims and Christians in the Rochester and wider Monroe County area;
- Ohio maintained a watch on the Fernald nuclear weapons facility which was closed down because of multiple safety violations;[3]
- Ontario and Quebec held an annual retreat, during which conferees drafted resolutions and proposals for workshops at the annual BCOQ convention and triennial meeting of the CBF;
- Puerto Rico organized a concert for peace;
- Rhode Island planned events during October 19–26, 1985 as part of a national peace with justice week, with a goal of half of the eighty Baptist congregations of the state convention participating. The group encouraged members to translate Christian beliefs into non-partisan political involvement by researching what was happening legislatively in Washington DC and traveling there to talk with the state's congressional delegation;
- Tarrant County, Texas (1987) focused on prisoners being given early releases from the state's overcrowded prisons;
- Tennessee (1987) planned a weekend conference on the sin of racism and on responses by Christians;
- Virginia (1990) addressed the experience of many in the group of isolation in their communities and churches; members encouraged one another in their struggle with justice and peace issues;

3. For background, Committee on an Assessment of CDC Radiation Studies, *Review of the Radiological Assessments.*

- Washington DC established a voice as Baptists among local peace coalitions; to this end, the group organized events such as "A Weekend with Walter Wink" with "On Not Becoming What We Hate" one of the theme talks;

- Baptist General Conference (1988) emphasized developing leadership and defining a role as a force for peace and justice in the denomination;

- Seventh Day Baptist (1985) drafted a statement on peace to be reviewed for endorsement by the General Conference of the Seventh Day Baptist Convention.

Many of these groups were organized during the 1980s and still exist. Others have come and gone. This is perhaps inevitable as there is a natural ebb and flow in group interests, leadership, and structures. However, another factor has been a slight change of focus in the strategy of developing an infrastructure of leadership at the local level.

BPFNA has emphasized since 1999 establishing a formal connection with the basic unit of Baptist polity, local congregations. The flexible terms of the relationship with partner congregations have included financial assistance, consultation, resources, and notification of special training opportunities. The program is designed for mutual support and continues to nurture peacemakers wanting to turn dreams into concrete deeds.

A recent issue of *Baptist Peacemaker* listed eighty-six partner congregations.[4] Articles in *Baptist Peacemaker* have profiled many of these partner congregations over the years. Readers with access to the internet can consult the websites of these congregations and others not yet profiled in the pages of the *Baptist Peacemaker* to learn more of their ministry focus at present or in the future.

Members of these BPFNA partner congregations are liberal and conservative, evangelical and ecumenical, pacifists and just war advocates. They share a peacemaking spirituality which has the potential to re-shape Christian life in postmodern society, united principally by their affiliation with the BPFNA and not by a single theological perspective.

BPFNA produced a directory of members open to providing hospitality to visitors, *Practice Hospitality: Baptist Peacemakers on the Road*

---

4. *Baptist Peacemaker* 28 (September–October 2008) 12.

(1990) to encourage members to visit these congregations. The following is a sampling of partner congregations:

- Allen Temple Baptist Church in California occupies a building once owned by the Black Panthers. The church conducts eighty-five ministries outside its walls, where the greatest needs are. According to J. Alfred Smith, Sr., senior pastor from 1970 until his retirement in March 2009, "God is not concerned with the sweet by and by. God is concerned with the nasty now in the flatlands of Oakland."[5]

- Olin T. Binkley Memorial Baptist Church in Chapel Hill, North Carolina, was named for a pastor and former president of the Southeastern Baptist Theological Seminary whose leadership inspired the congregation to become one of the vanguards of social reform among Baptists in the United States. Binkley has championed full participation of women at every level of lay and ministerial leadership, inter-faith relations, ministry among the poor, racial integration, and a welcoming and affirming stance towards gay and lesbian brothers and sisters.[6]

- Church in the Cliff of Dallas, Texas, is a liberating and authentic congregation centered in Biblical witness and prayer. The church is part of a contemporary and provocative environment tucked in a wing of an old Mental Health-Mental Retardation building, among beauty shops and other sometimes quirky businesses. With art on all of the walls, down every hall, the congregation encourages openness to all, nourishes spiritual growth, and challenges people to be active in peacemaking. Its statement to prospective visitors says, "You will experience this community as a winsome gathering of God's children."[7]

- *Comunidad Evangélica Amoxcalli*, a Nahautl word which means gathering place, was organized by Lazaro Gonzales and Olivia Juarez, Baptist leaders among indigenous peoples in *México*. The community gathers on the only day when they are free from work, to find relief from low-paying domestic work, isolation

5. *Baptist Peacemaker* 26:1 (2006) 7; http://www.allen-temple.org/ for update.
6. *Baptist Peacemaker* 24:4 (2004) 12–3; http://www.binkleychurch.org/ for update.
7. *Baptist Peacemaker* 24:2 (2004) 13; http://www.churchinthecliff.org/ for update.

from their own people, and, sometimes, mistreatment and to support one another. A congregant told members of the board of directors who attended worship in 2001 that, though their lives are difficult, "we have this community, you see. We come together on Sunday. It is a wonderful way to spend our time. It gives us strength for the week."[8]

- Community of Grace Church in Richmond, Virginia, is diverse in the economic, educational, ethnic, and national background of its members. Modeling itself in part on the Church of the Savior in Washington DC, which is characterized by carefully considered commitment to a two-fold journey inward, journey outward, the congregation tries to view as people, not as potential members, those outside the walls of the church to whom members minister; and to live out of an understanding of mission as response to spiritual callings, not as projects.[9]

- Fairview Baptist Church in Vancouver, British Columbia, encourages community formation through nurture of a common desire to explore faith in a place where all are accepted for who they are. In cooperation with neighborhood congregations and denominational agencies, members engage in the journeys inward of prayer and worship, and outward of compassion and social justice.[10]

- First Baptist of Jamaica Plain, an urban church in Boston, Massachusetts, has endured three fire-related tragedies over its 150-year history. The building was almost completely destroyed by the third of these incidents in January 2005. Before moving into a double-wide trailer, the congregation worshipped in a red and white tent under a banner, *Many Cultures. One Faith. Still Vibrant.* Since 2003, the congregation has grown fourfold. A welcoming and affirming congregation, it bridges ethnic, economic, and generational divides and lives into its mission by addressing neighborhood needs. By phone, the Reverend Ashlee Wiest-

8. Cook, "Place of Refuge."
9. *Baptist Peacemaker* 21:4 (2001) 12–3.
10. *Baptist Peacemaker* 23:1 (2003) 12. http://www.fairviewbaptist.ca/ for update.

Laird, pastor and former BPFNA board member, reported the success the previous Sunday of an alternative gift-giving fair.[11]

- First Baptist Church in Lawrence, Kansas, has a history of upholding freedom since before the Civil War in the United States. Members volunteer, serve, and reach out to impoverished people. Recent missional activity has included staffing a food pantry and providing hot meals for the city's homeless people. Such service affects not only those served, but also those who serve. As an example, around 2001, Emily Lamb (twelve years old at the time) heard a sermon about the Good Samaritan (Luke 10:25–37). Wondering how she could help the homeless, she thought, "Does anyone care enough to celebrate with them? This led to a monthly celebration for anyone who has reached a birthday but does not have friends or family with whom to celebrate. The festivities, complete with birthday cake, ice cream, balloons, and gifts bring dignity, beauty, and love to the lives of people in the margins of the economy.[12]

- Having founded First Baptist Church of McMinnville, Oregon, in 1867, members of the Linfield College community have continued to foster a climate of intellectual curiosity and progressive thought. Over the years, the congregation has consistently sought to be all-encompassing. In 1948, members stood against the rise of fundamentalism in Oregon when the majority of state's Baptist congregations joined the newly formed Conservative Baptist Association. In the 1980s, the congregation began using inclusive language in worship. In the 1990s, the congregation formed "Together Works," a support group for gays, lesbians, and transgender brothers and sisters. The decision to authorize the pastoral staff to bless same-gender unions has remained a source of "creative tension" within the congregation. Out of respect for the conscience of a conservative minority within the congregation, the pastoral staff does not use the sanctuary for its blessing ceremony. The congregation has also sought to be peace-minded,

11. Phone conversation December 15, 2008. *Baptist Peacemaker* 27:1 (Spring 2007) 8–9. www.firstbaptistjp.org.

12. *Baptist Peacemaker* 23:4 (2003) 12–3. http://www.firstbaptistlawrence.com/ for update.

seeking to broker conversations for peace within the church and with the wider community.[13]

- Grace Baptist Church in Statesville, North Carolina, is an inter-generational Christian community called and committed to the life and teachings of Jesus Christ through the experience of cel-ebrative worship, servant discipleship, the development of each member's gifts for ministry, the work of peace and justice, the activity of faith-sharing, the pursuit of responsible freedom, and the welcoming of all people to the life and work of God's realm. Its ministers are "all members of the congregation."[14]

- *Iglesia Shalom* organizes special projects among the poor of *Cuidad México* (Mexico City). Children gave the congregation its name. Members run a Bible Institute which combines biblical literacy with concrete training in conflict resolution, counseling, and cultural awareness.[15]

- Lake Avenue Baptist Church in Rochester, New York, has shifted from being a homogeneous group to one which truly reflects its location in a multiracial, multicultural neighborhood. Two signif-icant ministries have been its response to racial turmoil during the 1960s and its long heritage of involvement in refugee minis-try. A significant proportion of the congregation now consists of refugees from Burma (Myanmar).[16]

- Lakeshore Baptist Church in Oakland, California, is an inclu-sive community of believers who, empowered by the Spirit to be God's ministers, strive to embody peace and wholeness in a broken world. The congregation welcomes people regardless of sexual identity. Members have been in the fore organizing peace marches in Oakland in opposition to the war in Iraq.[17]

- MacNeill Baptist Church in Hamilton, Ontario, Canada seeks above all to serve its church family and the world with care, com-

13. *Baptist Peacemaker* 25:4 (2005) 12–3; http://fbcmac.org/ for update.

14. http://www.gracestatesville.org/.

15. *Baptist Peacemaker* 19:4 (1999) 13.

16. *Baptist Peacemaker* 21:2 (2001) 12; http://www.lakeavebaptist.org/ and Carman, "Karen Refugees" for update.

17. *Baptist Peacemaker* 25:1 (2005) 12; http://www.labcoakland.org/ for update.

passion, and love.[18] For members of the congregation, dissent and differences of opinion on important aspects of life and faith are opportunities for dialogue rather than debate, discussion rather than dispute. As part of its ministry, MacNeill seeks to honor equality and bring justice to all people. Members have supported such initiatives as refugee sponsorship, interfaith peace building, and the creation of peace studies, an interdisciplinary field at McMaster University concerned with war and peace, violence and nonviolence, conflict and conflict transformation.

- Oakhurst Baptist Church in Decatur, Georgia, housed the BPFNA during the first four years of its life. Describing itself as a diverse Christian community covenanting together to be the church of God in Christ, members have established an array of ministries for developmentally disabled people, homeless people, Cuban detainees at a federal prison, people with AIDS, and at-risk neighborhood children, to name a few.[19]

- *Primera Iglesia Bautista de Rio Piedras* (First Baptist Church) in San Juan, Puerto Rico, was organized in 1899. The original building was once a government structure and is now the home of a confident program of outreach to diverse people, especially the marginalized. Members are encouraged to understand church not as a Sunday morning place to go, but as a living with gratitude twenty-four hours daily, seven days a week.[20]

- Pullen Memorial Baptist Church in Raleigh, North Carolina, popularly called a "liberal" congregation, prefers to describe itself as "open." In the 1960s and 1970s, Pastor W. W. Finlator, along with many members, took controversial stands against the Vietnam War and for Affirmative Action programs. The congregation was one of the first among the Baptists to advocate for equal rights of women in all aspects of life and to become openly welcoming of homosexual Christians. Missional groups are active around peacemaking, earth care, poverty, and the death penalty.[21]

18. http://macneillbaptist.ca/.
19. *Baptist Peacemaker* 20:1 (2000) 15, 18. http://www.oakhurstbaptist.org/ for update.
20. http://www.pibrp.org/home/.
21. *Baptist Peacemaker* 24:1 (2004) 12–13; http://www.pullen.org/ for update.

- Shell Ridge Community Church in Walnut Creek, California, describes itself as a community living out of a commitment to local service. Projects include Habitat for Humanity, a shelter for homeless people, home-building mission trips to *México*, building interfaith relationships, and human rights work.[22]

- Underwood Baptist Church in Wauwatosa, Wisconsin, was born in the 1840s out of the struggle for justice. The ministry which began with giving shelter to fugitive slaves has continued in other forms throughout the life of the congregation. After World War II members sponsored people from Germany, Holland, and Japan for resettlement in the United States. Since then people from Cuba, Vietnam, Romania, Liberia, the Congo, and most recently a Somali refugee family, have been helped to establish a new life in the United States as they fled repression in their home nations. Members have consistently been involved in ministries which seek to bring justice to all people, offering a hand up rather than a handout through Habitat for Humanity, the Milwaukee Christian Center, Project Focal Point, and a Restorative Justice program. A body of believers, welcoming and affirming sexual minorities and families in all their forms, Underwood Church desires to grow as a multicultural and multiethnic congregation where all people feel welcome.[23]

- University Baptist Church in Austin, Texas, was organized in 1908 to minister to the University of Texas campus. Ever since, it has been known as Austin's progressive voice of faith. In the 1940s, it welcomed African-American students first to worship and then to join. In the 1970s, it became one of the first Southern Baptist Convention (SBC) congregations to ordain women as deacons. In 1995, it ordained a gay man as a deacon. On the one hand, these acts of openness have led some members to leave and, on two occasions, the Austin Baptist Association to expel the congregation. On the other hand, others have been attracted to the church. In 2001, when the congregation ordained an African

22. *Baptist Peacemaker* 22:3 (2002) 14–15; http://www.shellridge.org/ for update.
23. *Baptist Peacemaker* 22:2 (2002) 14–15; http://www.underwoodchurch.com/ for update.

American woman to the ministry, Jackie Saxon, a BPFNA board member, commented, "It *really* is a place like nowhere else."[24]

- Woodbine Heights Baptist Church in Toronto, Ontario, is defined more than by any other part of its identity by a program called "a safe place." The congregation pledges in its mission statement to be "a safe place for people to worship, to enjoy fellowship, and to grow in their faith." This emphasis has grown out of a pilot project which sought to build a healthier community by addressing the roots of violence in families and other institutions, including those in the church. It has not simply sought to ensure safety for children and support for survivors, but also to celebrate, proclaim, and reflect Christ's love by life in community and through welcoming its diversity.[25]

In the 1980s, the fledgling BPFNA sought to inspire practical action by Baptist peacemakers at the local level. Staff produced an annual Peacemakers' Calendar, "step by step" articles in *PeaceWork*, and other resources. The step-by-step series has provided practical resources on a variety of themes. These include the following:

- how to organize a public policy hearing in your congregation;
- how to lead children in corporate prayer for peacemaking;
- how to preach on peace without resorting to violence;
- how to use a shalom lectionary; how to start a human rights group in your local congregation;
- how do develop a service of commitment to the ongoing agenda of the freedom movement inspired by Dr. Martin Luther King, Jr.

Interested readers could receive off-prints at no charge by providing a self-addressed, stamped envelope.

Another strategy to stimulate initiatives by Baptist peacemakers at the local level was to encourage the establishment of peace groups and partner congregation relationships. To this end, BPFNA staff produced

24. *Baptist Peacemaker* 21:1 (2001) 9; www.ubcaustin.org.

25. *Baptist Peacemaker* 20:2 (2000) 12; for update: http://theheightsatwoodbineand-sammon.googlepages.com/index.html.

Mt. Nebo Bible Baptist Church, in the Lower Ninth Ward of New Orleans, one of the churches BPFNA is helping to rebuild through Churches Supporting Churches.

materials on how to start and sustain local groups, to facilitate communication among them, and to bring them together for common purposes.[26]

The sister church relationship between two congregations in Memphis, Tennessee offers a model. Every year since 1983, a largely white congregation located near the University of Memphis, Prescott Memorial Baptist Church, has invited an African American congregation located in Orange Mound, a few miles to the west, Beulah Baptist, to a joint dinner recognizing Thanksgiving in the United States. Reciprocally, Beulah has invited Prescott members to a Maundy Thursday service at which the pastor of Prescott preaches and its choir sings an anthem. Beulah and Prescott deacons have exchanged places during communion services and members have responded to invitations to attend special services or outreach programs, especially in the area of race relations. In various ways, the two congregations help each other. For example, when Prescott moved into a new facility which once housed a Lutheran congregation, it

26 Sehested, "How to: Start a Peacemaker Group in Your Local Church;" Sehested, *Walk Together Children.*

did not have a baptistery. Beulah offered Prescott use of its sanctuary until Prescott added a baptistery.[27]

As another example of sister church relationships, in 2005 BPFNA responded to the needs of neighborhoods devastated by Hurricane Katrina by helping to form Churches Supporting Churches (CSC). The organization is creating three-year partnerships between thirty-six African American congregations in the hardest-hit areas of New Orleans and congregations outside of New Orleans. The aim has been to pair each New Orleans church with ten partner churches which would contribute $46,000 over the three years. At this level of funding, New Orleans congregations could meet needs in such critical areas as affordable housing, health care, schools, and day care.

A crucial question after Hurricane Katrina hit the Gulf Coast was whether or not the voices and perspectives of the marginalized would be included in decision-making. This proved important in the rebuilding process as the recipients received active support by members of partner congregations through encouragement, prayer, and technical help.

One of the first cluster of partnerships linked Corinthians Missionary Baptist Church #2 with four BPFNA partner congregations: Fairview Baptist Church in Vancouver, British Columbia; Oakhurst Baptist Church in Decatur, Georgia; Shell Ridge Church in Walnut Creek, California; and Park Road Baptist Church in Charlotte, North Carolina. The commitment of these partners helped the Corinthians congregation to restore its sanctuary. As well, their experience enabled the CSC program to refine its priorities and strategies based on realities on the ground.

In another partnership, Central Baptist in Wayne, Pennsylvania and Grace Baptist Church in Statesville, North Carolina, encouraged St. John Baptist Church in New Orleans not only by providing funds for computer equipment, hymnals, and other material needs, but also by nurturing the reweaving social structures which sustain the community.[28]

Canadian Baptists have participated in efforts to rebuild homes and foster community in the Lower Ninth Ward, a predominately working-class African-American neighborhood in New Orleans. In March and November of 2007, members of Alymer Baptist Church in Alymer, Ontario, traveled south. Reaching Customs and Border Protection in

27. Womack, "Beyond the 'Aunt and Uncle' Syndrome" and Email, Tom Walsh, December 1, 2008.

28. Powell, "Environmental Racism," 12.

Port Huron, Michigan, twenty nine participants had to be processed individually before being granted "paroles" to enter the United States. Karen Hilliker, BPFNA board member and one of the organizers of the mission trip, commented, "Parole—what an interesting description for a group of people who fund-raised for four months, gave a week of their holidays, and gave up time with their families to go and help their neighbours in New Orleans." Arriving in an area particularly hard-hit by flooding during Hurricane Katrina, she asked,

> Is it God's hand or the people of God doing God's work? It doesn't matter! It's still hard to see all of the devastation and I'm still angry—a little surprising because I thought I'd dealt with all of that last time. And life and hope are here: people are returning, businesses are opening . . . If it were me, I'd curl up in a little ball in the corner and not uncurl for a very long time. Either that or I'd lash out at anyone who came near. God promises "My grace is sufficient for you." Guess it's up to all of us to take that grace and do something with it.[29]

Over the years, BPFNA has also encouraged concrete action by members and partner congregations through training in conflict transformation. A number of skilled trainers including Daniel L. Buttry, Daniel Hunter, Dwight M. Lundgren, and Lee McKenna have led workshops in North America and around the world.

Conflict is often viewed as something to be avoided, if not minimized, in human relations. Thus, the goal in many attempts at reconciliation is to reach harmony between warring parties through mediation and compromise. Although this is an understandable objective, conflict resolution may fail at times to address the underlying causes of conflicts, as well as the inherent injustices and the power dynamics which factor into a broken relationship. When this occurs, the parties do not reconcile and peacemaking has not taken place.

BPFNA is committed to building cultures of peace which take into account concerns for justice and parity in power in an effort toward reconciliation. Conflict transformation is an approach toward peacemaking which uses conflict constructively to transform the relationships between parties, enabling them to be mutually cognizant of the underlying problems, and to be individually empowered and empathetic toward others as

29. Compiled from her blog online at http://abctripping.blogspot.com; *Baptist Peacemaker* 27:4 (2007) 13.

they address their differences. The primary goal is to prepare and guide the parties for dialogue, with resolution of their conflict a common result.

During November 21–22, 2008, BPFNA sponsored a Conflict Transformation workshop held at Park Road Baptist Church in Charlotte, North Carolina. The Reverend Dwight M. Lundgren, Coordinator of Intercultural Ministries–Reconciliation for the American Baptist Churches USA trained twenty-five people who gathered to learn more about conflict and the specific techniques which can be used to address conflict in such a way as to create greater peace and justice. Those gathered included teachers, lawyers, ministers, retirees, business people, and non-profit leaders. Together they explored conflict within families, friendships, neighborhoods, churches, and communities. All left with greater skills for analyzing conflict and using the energy within it to reshape relationships in positive ways, skills which will serve them well in all the places in which they live and work.

Recent trainings have been so successful and so well-received that leading and promoting such events is becoming a major focus for the BPFNA staff. This serves the goal of encouraging as many Baptists as possible to take up the work of transforming a culture of violence into a culture of peace.

Another BPFNA initiative to nurture practical action at the local level is the restorative justice program presently led by Evelyn Hanneman. Understanding that God created *Shalom*, right relationship between and among all creation, restorative justice seeks ways to repair the harm done by crime to the victim, the community, and the offender.

Restorative justice is a growing social movement to institutionalize peaceful approaches to problem-solving and to redress violations of legal and human rights in the criminal justice system and throughout society. These have involved truth and reconciliation tribunals such as those conducted by Australia, El Salvador, and South Africa in the 1990s, in Greenville, North Carolina in the first years of the new millennium, and presently in Canada in response to abuses experienced by first peoples in church- and government-sponsored residential schools. Restorative justice programs are characterized by an effort to engage those who are harmed, wrongdoers, and their affected communities in the search for reconciliation, restoration, and the rebuilding of relationships. As a concrete illustration of this emphasis, Evelyn Hanneman, program director and BPFNA Operations Coordinator, offers a reflection prompted by the death of Amadou Bailo Diallo, killed on February 4, 1999 by four New York City plain-clothed police officers, an article reprinted from *Baptist Peacemaker* as Appendix nine.

EQUIPPING THE NEXT GENERATION

The World Summit for Children set goals in 1990 for reducing deaths, malnutrition, disease, and disability among the children of the world. In 1990 his speech accepting the Nobel Peace Prize in 1965 for the United Nations Children's Fund (UNICEF) Henry R. Labouisse, Executive Director of UNICEF from 1965–1979, observed, "The most important meaning of this Nobel award is the solemn recognition that the welfare of today's children is inseparably linked with the peace of tomorrow's world."[30] The BPFNA board of directors undertook in 1995 a year-long process of discernment of how to address the scale of violence against children and youth from the intimate environment of the home to the victimization of children in war zones around the world.

The following year, the board approved a proposal to give special priority for the remainder of the century to issues affecting children and youth. The title for the program focus—"And a Child Shall Lead"—was taken from Isaiah's vision of the "peaceable kingdom" (Isa 11:6–9) and became the theme for the eleventh peace camp. An initial project growing out of this focus was sharing in the creation and promotion of "The Family Covenant of Nonviolence," with seven goals: to communicate better, to listen, to respect others, to forgive, to respect nature, and to be courageous in challenging violence in all its forms wherever encountered, whether at home, at school, at work, or in the community, and to support others who are treated unfairly.[31]

By the time The Next Generation (TNG), BPFNA's youth advisory committee, formed in early 1997, youth had already assumed a clear place in BPFNA leadership. Youth were involved centrally in the first peace camp and have annually participated in and led worship.

Youth have created projects specific to their interests as well. One such project was an undertaking of young people associated with the

30. *State of the World's Children 1996*, 7. This has been an annual publication since 1992.

31. *Baptist Peacemaker* 16:1 (1996) 1; McGinnis and others, *Families Creating a Circle of Peace*.

Jon Buttry, BPFNA youth, at National Rifle Association vigil.

Conferencia Bautista de la Paz de Puerto Rico. In 1986 Puerto Rican youth painted graffiti on the outside of buildings in the city of Cayey. The slogan they painted read (in English) "Peace is the fruit of justice" and was accompanied by the Conference's logo. In another unique effort, Keila Collazo was instrumental in obtaining Baptist participation in putting on peace and justice festivals for children, sponsored by *Niños y Joveniles por la Paz de Puerto Rico* (Children and Teenagers of Puerto Rico for Peace).

Courtney Walsh Marsh is currently the mother of three. She grew up in the BPFNA and a partner congregation in Memphis Tennessee, Prescott Memorial Baptist Church. When she was twelve, she participated in a friendship tour of eastern Europe followed by the first International Baptist Peace Conference held in Sjövik, Sweden during August 3–7, 1988. Speaking to the gathering, Courtney announced that children and youth in the United States and Canada had an interest in the formation of Baptist Pen Pals for Peace. She invited delegates to pass the word on to Baptist children in other countries. Courtney concluded, "As our Soviet brothers and sisters say, 'Our children are our future.' Please help us build a better future and make way for the Prince of Peace by supporting Baptist Pen Pals for Peace." At the end of her talk, Ken Sehested moved acceptance of the recommendation by acclamation. Amens and further applause followed.[32]

Over the next few years, letters arrived from four hundred Baptist children, youth, and youth groups in twenty-four countries including Burma [Myanmar], Canada, Ghana, Iraq, Kuwait, Japan, Liberia, Malawi, Philippines, Sierra Leone, and the United States. As examples, Benjamin Koroma, youth President of the Ebenezer Youth Progressive Group in Liberia requested for prayer amidst civil war. Addio wrote from Ghana with a prayer at Christmas that God would bless readers and let readers have more zeal for [God's] work even as we wait His coming soon.

When interested young people wrote to Courtney, she sent them an application to fill out. When she received a completed application, she matched the applicant with an available pen pal. Project funding came from the BPFNA, the American Baptist Churches Peace Program, and individual contributions. In an interview, she observed, "It's refreshing that in a world like ours, so many kids want to join us on this journey. It helps them feel they're a part of the peace movement . . . and it deepens my faith, because I see there are people out there facing a lot worse than I have to . . ."[33]

In the summer of 1992 Courtney visited Saransk, Moldavia with the Peace Child Project, a cultural exchange program which from 1989–1994 used musical theater to promote world peace. The young people on these exchanges wrote and produced plays with kids from host countries.[34] When Courtney went on to university, the youth advisory committee of BPFNA continued Baptist Pen Pals for Peace for a while. A participant in the project Anna Odom of Bahama, North Carolina, a first-year student at Mars Hill College in Asheville, explained what motivated her to help: "I think it is important to keep contact with people from all around the world in hopes of forming friendships and to understand other ways of life."[35]

In a recent communication, Courtney reflected on how her involvement in these projects helped her to see the world on a real level,

32. Pipkin, *Seek Peace and Pursue It*, 203–4.

33. Womack, "Baptist Pen Pals for Peace." Box 1 file 35, BPFNA papers.

34. Anne Whirley interview with Courtney Walsh, *Baptist Peacemaker* 12:3 (1992) 21.

35. *Baptist Peacemaker* 17:4 (1997) 10.

Nothing could have prepared me for the positive and overwhelming interest that children from so many countries expressed! I learned about how others live and love and serve out their faith—in situations like my own and, more importantly, in very different circumstances, like a nation at war and facing widespread hunger issues. I am now a nurse-midwife, working with primarily uninsured, undocumented or under-insured women and families. From Baptist Pen Pals for Peace and BPFNA, I learned that knowing people—truly knowing them on a holistic level—gives such insight into ways to empower and guide them. This is so valuable during their pregnancy and childbirth! There is no doubt that the BPFNA taught me to value people over systems, to see a person for who she is rather than just how she appears.[36]

BPFNA has demonstrated its commitment to youth through the pages of an award-winning column *Peace Soup*, affectionately named after a youth newspaper created during the 1999 peace camp. Appendix ten offers two musings by youth of creative imagination and hope from the inaugural column in the Summer 2000 issue of *Baptist Peacemaker*.

The communications department has also assisted youth in using other media. For example, during peace camp 1997, TNG produced and shared a video highlighting the role youth can play if given a sense of purpose.

To illustrate further its commitment to young people, BPFNA has supported the Children's Defense Fund, for example, by promoting children's sabbaths and providing action ideas for kids in *Baptist Peacemaker*. Several articles drew attention to children's concerns and to the need to give them a voice in addressing their problems.[37]

As an example, the "Doll Project" began in Maryland. Citizens were encouraged to share handmade cardboard dolls with elected officials and community leaders. On each doll was the name of a real child being left behind. The dolls could be placed in public buildings for people to take and share with family or friends. Citizens helped set up service learning opportunities in which students could be involved outside the classroom. Service learning enabled students to achieve curricular objectives, to reflect throughout the service-learning experience, to develop a sense of

36. Email, December 29, 2008.
37. Edelman, "In Defense of Children." Dekar, "Children's Sabbath."

responsibility, and to gain knowledge and skills needed for the duration of the specific projects, and long-term.

FRIENDSHIP TOURS WITHIN THE UNITED STATES

BPFNA has organized friendship tours to areas of conflict not only around the world, but also within North America. In October 1989, Kim Christman and Stan Dotson, co-pastors of Providence Baptist Church in Stoneville, North Carolina, led a delegation along with a truckload of food and clothes for striking miners in the Pittston mines of southwest Virginia. In contrast with the violence which had marked the hundred-year old history of coalmine labor struggle, an outpouring of active support by religious leaders around the country and the appointment of a mediator by United States Secretary of Labor Elizabeth Dole contributed to a just outcome of the strike. In January 1990, workers accepted terms of a settlement, including provision of health care not only for active members, but also retirees. In this particular dispute, the injustice of the company and nonviolent action by striking miners served as catalysts for change in support of justice over greed.[38]

In October, 1998, nine persons participated in a tour of farm worker camps in North Carolina. Co-sponsored by the Farm Laborers Organizing Committee, the delegation visited camps, spoke with workers, and witnessed their dangerous working conditions. Participants learned of the struggles of farm laborers for better living and working conditions. Because most do not speak English, they often do not understand the terms of their employment or the rights they are guaranteed. They are also unaware of unfair charges and non-existent "taxes" taken from their paychecks. Even when they understand that they are being mistreated and taken advantage of, they lack the language and other skills to protest or defend themselves. Traveling through places close to home, participants saw a world that had never before been in their view.[39] Appendix three lists additional friendship tours.

PUBLICATIONS

Early in its history, the Baptist Pacifist Fellowship produced, between September and November, 1945, three issues of a newsletter, *The Baptist*

38. Christman and Dotson, "Beyond Jackrocks and Prayer."
39. Polaski, "Learning to See."

C.O. An Organ of the Baptist Pacifist Fellowship. After the war, one issue appeared of the *Baptist Pacifist Fellowship Newsletter* followed, sporadi-cally after 1956, by others under a variety of names including *Baptist Peace News* (May 1957–November 1969), *Baptist Peace Fellowship* (1969-May 1981), and *PeaceWork* (1981–2007).

Among members of the SBC, at least one issue appeared as the *Baptist Fellowship Newsletter*, October 15, 1945. The newsletter indicated it would be a monthly publication of news and comments about Southern Baptists' activity in regard to religious objectors in Civilian Public Service, those classified I-A-O (conscientious objectors eligible for military service in noncombatant role), or those under sentence. I am not aware, however, if any further issues appeared.

In the late 1970s, there was considerable stir among Southern Baptists around peace and justice concerns arising from the Iran hos-tage crisis, the intensification of superpower tensions, and, at the local level, the threat imposed on the community by faulty construction at the nearby Marble Hill Nuclear Power Plant. A number of Southern Baptists formed a house fellowship, which began with Tuesday evening dinners in 1977 and continues until the present. One of the group's first activities was protesting at this nuclear facility.

Glen H. Stassen, at that time a professor of ethics at the Southern Baptist Theological Seminary in Louisville, and Robert C. Broome, a former student and a member of the house fellowship became involved in a World Peacemakers mission group at Deer Park Baptist Church in Louisville. The group began talking of the need for a Southern Baptist publication with an explicit focus on peacemaking. They believed that it would be a way to find other peacemakers among the 35,000 congrega-tions of the Southern Baptist Convention.

Broome presented the idea for *Baptist Peacemaker* to the World Peacemakers on February 17, 1980. Around the same time, Glen H. Stassen and Robert Parham, then a student at the seminary, co-edited an issue of *Seeds* which dealt with the linkage of hunger and war, bread and bombs.[40] Success of the issue led people in Louisville to proceed with plans to launch *Baptist Peacemaker.*[41]

40. "Bread and Peace," *Seeds* 3:5 (1980).

41. For the following, Broome, "Birth of *Baptist Peacemaker;*" Bledsoe, "Robert C. Broome;" and "Founding of *Baptist Peacemaker,*" interview of Dr. Robert Parham by Paula Womack, BPFNA files.

The Deer Park congregation and its pastor at the time, Carman Sharp, allowed the group to avail itself of the church's bulk-mail Post Office permit and to use church facilities to gather a mailing list, receive letters and contributions, and publish the newspaper. The first issue appeared with the stated aim of engaging "Southern Baptists everywhere in a quest for peace."[42] United States Senator Mark O. Hatfield wrote the lead article entitled "Issues for Peacemakers." Other articles included a survey of precedents for perseverance on the part of Southern Baptist peacemakers by Walter B. Shurden, Dean of the School of Theology at Southern seminary, and biblical reflections on the promise of peace by Don H. Stewart, Executive Vice President of the New Orleans Baptist Theological Seminary.

After publication of the first issue of *Baptist Peacemaker* in December 1980, letters poured into the office by the hundreds. What began as a journal for Southern Baptists grew within five years into a trans-Baptist journal with a circulation of 18,000 and accountability to other church structures and interfaith peace groups. However, it remained a ministry of Deer Park church, surviving on a shoestring for nearly ten years. Four issues a year appeared in a newspaper format. Everything was done on a volunteer basis. Unpaid, staff never knew if there would be another issue until money came in. Yet enough did come in regularly.

On one occasion Robert Parham, formerly with SBC's Christian Life Commission and now with the Baptist Center for Ethics based in Nashville, Tennessee, went to a wealthy Baptist who wrote a check for $2,500 and asked his boss, who headed a corporation which dealt with computers, to make a contribution. He gave $2,500 which funded two issues.

While many of the *Baptist Peacemaker* staff found pacifism a compelling position, they initially maintained a distance from BPFNA due to its connection with the pacifist Fellowship of Reconciliation. Attempting to allay this concern, Ken Sehested explained that, "for the most part we bracket the issue of pacifism, believing it to be little more than a philosophical sinkhole, leading to endless speculations about 'what if . . . ?'"[43] Without taking sides on the debate over just war and pacifism, many BPFNA members adopted a third model, just peacemaking. Eventually

---

42. *Baptist Peacemaker* 1:1 (1980) 2.

43. Sehested, "Baptist Peacemakers in North America," 18.

BPFNA took on responsibility for publication of *Baptist Peacemaker*. The first issue after the transition appeared in the Spring of 1990, volume 10.

For nearly twenty years, BPFNA published both *Baptist Peacemaker* and *PeaceWork*. In 2007, the Communications Committee of the board of directors voted to merge the two publications. In 2008, *Baptist Peacemaker: The Journal of the Baptist Peace Fellowship of North America* appeared with a very different look. A magazine layout replaced the newspaper and newsletter formats of the previous publications. In addition to articles, "Peace Soup," poetry, news, and information about resources, the re-designed *Baptist Peacemaker* introduced new features such as a series of "peacemaking stories" and opinion/editorial pieces. In the first year five issues appeared with the new design.

In addition to its newsletter, BPFNA has published several books, beginning with *Dreaming God's Dream*, two resources for congregations wanting to celebrate the birthday of Dr. Martin Luther King, Jr. The first was a church education curriculum edited by Ken Sehested. It contained materials for six age groups, pre-school through adult, and the outline and curriculum for a day-long intergenerational workshop. The other was a family activities guide written by Kathleen McGinnis, co-author of *Parenting for Peace and Justice*. Subsequently, BPFNA worked with Kathleen McGinnis and her husband Jim McGinnis in promoting the Family Pledge of Nonviolence.

Initiated in 1993, the "Promise of Pentecost" project signaled a commitment to address the reality of racism and the hope for healing as among the top BPFNA priorities. Growing from the conviction that any broad-based movement for racial justice must be rooted in local communities, the key strategy has been to encourage local congregations in forming and sustaining cross-racial partnerships. It was for this reason that BPFNA published "Domestic Sister Churches" in 1990 and then in 1997 a greatly expanded version *Walk Together Children. An Ecumenical Resource for Congregations in Partnership across Racial Lines*, edited by Ken Sehested. That year, BPFNA also produced *Transforming Power. Bible Studies on Racial Reconciliation* by Carol Hunter and Bob Hunter.

Over the years BPFNA has published or co-published several other books including *Yo quiero paz en mi iglesia y en mi barrio*, a Spanish-language curriculum for peacemaking study groups at every age level. Other books include the following:

- *Seek Peace & Pursue It: Proceedings from the 1988 International Baptist Peace Conference* edited by H. Wayne Pipkin and co-published with the Institute for Baptist and Anabaptist Studies (1989);

- *Rightly Dividing the Word of Truth: A Resource for Congregations in Dialogue on Sexual Orientation* edited by LeDayne McLeese Polaski and Millard Eiland (1997);

- *Peace Primer*, a collection of quotes and insights from basic Christian and Islamic spiritual teachings co-edited by Ken Sehested and Rabia Terri Harris, coordinator of the Muslim Peace Fellowship (2002);

- *Radicals: Anabaptists and the Current World Crisis. A Manifesto* by George Williamson, Jr. (2005);

- *Through the Year: A Peacemaker's Journal,* a series of meditations compiled and edited by Daniel L. Buttry and Evelyn Hanneman (2005);

- *A Pilgrim in Rome: Cries of Dissent,* by Al Staggs (2008). Pastor, performer, and author, Staggs compiled reflections in response to his observations of the political, religious, and socio-economic climate in the United States at the time.

As well, articles in BPFNA periodicals have become parts of books by other publishers. For example, my talks at several peace camp and international conferences formed the basis of my book *For the Healing of the Nations,* while talks and articles by William Apel led to publication of a book on the interfaith correspondence of the Trappist monk Thomas Merton.

There have been two additional, crucial means of communication among members. One is a newsletter, *Model Ministries,* sent to BPFNA partner congregations with action ideas. Appendix eleven gives a sample issue.

The second means of keeping in touch is the website, http://www.bpfna.org/. This was created in the late 1990s and now includes links to programs, groups, publications, and information about joining or making donations to BPFNA. As well, BPFNA has released several anthologies of materials originating as talks or sermons at peace camps, as well as other resources such as bookmarks, coffee mugs, peace-and-justice calendars, and t-shirts.

Among Southern Baptists, *Christian Frontiers* appeared for three years, from 1946 to 1949. A number of the denominational offices and regional groups have published newsletters. Among these have been *To Build Peace*, a bulletin of the Department of International Affairs of the American Baptist Churches USA which appeared in the late 1960s and early 1970s, and *Baptist Peace Link, A Newsletter for Baptist Peacemakers*, read primarily by members of the Baptist Convention of Ontario and Quebec between April 1982 and February 2000.

REFLECTIONS

In this chapter we have looked at ways by which BPFNA has sought to empower members to make a difference for peace and justice. It is difficult if not impossible to assess how successful any of these initiatives have been. How does one gauge the impact of crossing a wall separating peoples or nations, participating in a workshop, signing a petition, or reading peace literature?

To address this question, I share a little of my personal journey. Over the years I have visited many of the dozens of congregations which have associated with BPFNA. One, Shell Ridge Baptist Church in Walnut Creek, was my spiritual home in the late 1950s and early 1960s. Then called Valley Baptist Church, leaders and other members of my high school youth group encouraged me, as I moved on to the University of California, Berkeley, to attend an African American congregation when I did not return home from college on weekends; to work in neighborhood projects and voter registration for the 1964 elections through that congregation; to participate in a Crossroads Africa project in Chad during the summer of 1965; and to try seminary for a year before going on to law school. I never did go on, and, over the years, I have blessed God for having found this people of God. As Shell Ridge's website puts it, these are not your ordinary Baptists!

When I took up a career in Washington DC, Shell Ridge members encouraged me to attend the Church of the Saviour in Washington DC. For a period of time, I did. I found it to be a liberating congregation from which flows unbelievable creativity. Since the 1990s, I have been involved with a sister community, the Memphis School of Servant Leadership, as well as with a movement called the New Monasticism.

Writing in the 1990s, Jonathan R. Wilson, who holds the Pioneer McDonald Chair in Theology at Carey Theological College in Vancouver, British Columbia, outlined four marks which would be needed by new movements, including the new monasticism, to sustain faithful witness: a desire to heal the fragmentation of our lives in North American culture, a way for the whole people of God, discipline, and practices and virtues by which an undisciplined, unfaithful church might recover the discipline and faithfulness necessary to realize its mission in the world.

Wilson acknowledged that theological commitment and reflection must undergird the new communities. Right theology will not of itself produce a faithful church, which he characterized as the faithful carrying out the mission given to the church by God in Jesus Christ, but that mission can be identified only by faithful theology that strives simultaneously for a recovery of right belief and right practice.[44]

Wilson was describing an insight that theological reflection informs practice; conversely, practices shape theological reflection. Jesus taught that to follow him, one must do what he taught. "Just as I have loved you, you also should love one another. By this everyone will know that you are my disciples, if you have love for one another (John 13:34–35)." For Paul, faith was lifeless without love (1 Corinthians 13–14). For James, faith without works was dead (Jas 2:26).

In the fourth century, Evagrius of Pontas wrote, "If you are a theologian, you will pray truly. And if you pray truly, you are a theologian."[45] Medieval Christians summarized in Latin, *lex orandi, lex credendi*, the law of prayer and belief.

Responding to a call to enter more deeply into the pain of the world, many BPFNA members are joining together in prayer, simplicity of life, hospitality to the stranger, lament for racial divisions within the church and our communities, service to the poor, care for the plot of God's earth given to us along with support of our local economies, and peacemaking in the midst of violence and conflict resolution within communities along the lines of the Second Testament.

---

44. Wilson, *Living Faithfully in a Fragmented World*, 76; Rutba House, *School(s) for Conversion*, xii–xiii; www.newmonasticism.org.

45. Evagrius, "On Prayer," *Philokalia*, 1, 62.

Perhaps what most characterizes engagement in peace and justice issues by Baptists is the crucial role of the local. While BPFNA nurtures involvement by Christians in peacemaking in regional, national, and international venues, its work is deeply embedded in, and committed to raising up grass-roots peacemakers and local communities of faith. The programs described in this chapter—networking at gatherings, participating in friendship tours, or reading BPFNA publications—have helped not only to sustain me in my own individual efforts as activist, disciple of Jesus, family member, and teacher, but to link me with a wider Baptist network of resistance, affirmation, celebration. Together, through our individual service in daily living, our corporate ministry in partner congregations or other organizations, and our Gospel vision, BPFNA members "provoke one another to love and good deeds, not neglecting to meet together . . . but encouraging one another" (Heb 10:24–25).[46]

The BPFNA came into being in 1984, a time of superpower tensions, of wars between and within nations, and of threatened nuclear annihilation. Prospects for building a culture of peace seemed remote. The responses of BPFNA staff, partner congregations, and members generally to these and subsequent challenges were, and continue to be of crucial importance as an incubator for peace in the world at large. In chapter five, we look at the international work of BPFNA.

---

46. Sehested, "Inciting the Saints."

Sharon Rollins created the "Flower in Gun" cartoon to go with "To Everything Turn, Turn, Turn" by Bob Barber, *Baptist Peacemaker* 22 (Winter 2002) 4, about participating in a demonstration. It was used again in *Peace Soup* with the young people's declaration of intent to become COs in McMinnville in 2005.

5

Building Blocks for a Global Network

INTRODUCTION

THE MAY 1983 FRIENDSHIP tour to the USSR took place at a time when United States President Ronald Reagan was taking an aggressive, hard-line stance towards the former Soviet Union, calling it an evil empire. By contrast, members of the delegation encountered Soviet citizens as friends, not enemies. Participants recognized they could make the world safer by learning mutually to respect differences and find solutions to common problems. Members of different Baptist communions also discovered that they had greater common ground with one another than they sometimes felt within their respective congregations and denominations.

The experience provided an impetus to create the BPFNA in March 1984. BPFNA staff, steering committee, and the general membership were worried about heightened tensions between the United States and the USSR and recognized the importance of nurturing relationships between citizens of the two countries and their closest allies. BPFNA began to organize friendship tours to the USSR and other areas of conflict in the world. Some BPFNA members celebrated Easter 1985 with Orthodox Christians in Moscow as part of a delegation to the Soviet Union organized by *Baptist Peacemaker* staff. BPFNA members cooperated with the BWA in organizing a friendship visit to the United States by Baptists from the USSR, also in 1985.

BPFNA steering committee members meeting in June 1985 experienced the list of programs undertaken during the first year as "overwhelming." Steering committee members proposed adding other opportunities for Soviet Baptists, congregation members and leaders alike, to visit the

United States. Other ideas included creating a BPFNA group in the USSR as a peace liaison between Baptists in the two countries or organizing a global peace conference that could foster cross-cultural dialogue on topics like human rights

Members of the steering committee identified the sharing of peace and justice concerns with Baptists internationally as a goal. They had a modest objective: to build a global Baptist peace network. In coming years, the BPFNA sponsored six friendship tours to the Soviet Union or to eastern Europe, co-sponsored with European Baptist Federation an international peace conference in Sjövik, Sweden (1988), and facilitated the partnering of pen pals and congregations around the world. By building a global network of resistance, affirmation, and celebration BPFNA multiplied the overall impact of Baptists engaged in peacemaking initiatives in their local contexts. The pages which follow offer a sampling of BPFNA's engagement with Baptists not only in the Soviet bloc, but around the world. Appendix three lists friendship tours. Appendix four lists international projects.

FRIENDSHIP TOURS

Building on the success of the 1983 friendship tour to the former Soviet Union, Priscilla Inkpen and E. Glenn Hinson led a delegation in 1984, followed in 1985 by one led by Paul Hayes and Chuck Mercer. Experiencing a deep level of trust, a growing number of United States and Soviet citizens experienced love flowing through encounters in churches, meetings, even on the metro, or subway.

Kaye Cooper and Howard Roberts led the fourth friendship tour to the USSR. From June 26 to July 10, 1986, thirty-one participants connected with a variety of Soviet citizens. After spending time in Moscow, participants visited several non-Soviet republics: Latvia, Estonia, Georgia, and Azerbaijan. Participants wondered if they would ever encounter these brothers and sisters in Christ again after experiencing warm fellowship wherever they went. Some thought so, especially after a young man in Tbilisi, Georgia, showed a member of the group a picture and letter he had received from a participant on the 1983 friendship tour.

Paul C. Hayes, a pastor of Greece Baptist Church in upstate New York, led a delegation to eastern Europe from December 29, 1987–January 14, 1988. BPFNA members met human rights activists in Hungary and elsewhere. In Budapest, a young Reformed Christian described the base ecclesial community of which he was a part as existing outside the formal structures of the organized church. He explained that Christians share their possessions, meet for worship three or four times per week, "do very effective work," and have a revolutionary Christian spirit "present in their daily lives." They have no official relationship to the Hungarian religious affairs bureaucracy, a "most Stalinist" government agency that sends prophetic ministers to obscure rural parishes. "The best clergy are in the country."[1]

Hayes suggested to Géza Molnár, pastor of Rákoscsaba Baptist Church, that occasional correspondence between members of the two congregations might be a way to improve relations after discovering that they were soul mates in dreaming an alternative universe. Two years later, Ferenc and Margarit Szilágyi shared Thanksgiving dinner with their friends at Greece Baptist in the United States.

The value of this visit was heightened by the remarkable revolutions sweeping at the time through Hungary and eastern Europe. Members of Greece Baptist gained a broadened appreciation of these changes, while the visitors from Hungary had the opportunity to examine the ministries of another Baptist church. Ferenc commented,

> We need to improve our knowledge of the Bible and to encourage a Christian education in our church. Young people cannot see what they can do in the church. Our church needs to see how we can respond to them and help them ... [and] we old people have to take away our old clothes and learn how to wear new ones.[2]

Immediately after the 1988 Baptist Peace Conference in Sweden, a small group undertook Friendship Tour to Estonia, Latvia, and St. Petersburg and Moscow in the former Soviet Union. Mark Trumbo and William Appel led the trip. The group used contacts made at the Sweden Conference to gain names of many of the individuals and churches met during our trip. Participants visited many churches, sharing in the fellowship, listening intently and, on occasion, preaching. Some also participated in clandestine home meetings and responded to the invitation of young Latvia Baptists to join in their celebration of their patriot's day in public defiance of waning Soviet control. The Soviet Union soon fell and the

---

1. Williamson, "Testimonies."
2. Hayes, "It Is Good in Our Hearts."

Berlin Wall came down. Who knows in what very small ways our prayers and the prayers and nonviolent actions of thousands of Baptists in this part of the world contributed to all this resurrection moment.[3]

Fifteen persons from the United States embarked on a fifteen-day BPFNA friendship tour to the Soviet Union on July 22, 1990. Co-leaders Clifford Chalmers Cain, chaplain and professor of religion at Franklin College in Indiana, and Gene Ton, executive minister of the American Baptist Churches of Indiana, billed the trip as a faith-to-faith encounter between Christians of two nations. The variety and intensity of experiences along the three-republic, four-city itinerary surpassed this modest expectation.

The policy of transparency in the activities of all government institutions introduced in the mid-1980s by Soviet Premier Mikhail Gorbachev, or *glasnost* (literally, self help), were under way. The freedoms generated by *glasnost* allowed Soviet citizens to have more contact with the Western world, particularly with the United States. Everywhere the delegation went, participants sensed the excitement generated by *glasnost*. At the same time, there were expressions of some concern and anxiety.

Soviet Christians had a new-found freedom to engage in evangelism, to receive and distribute information, and, in the case of those who could not on moral grounds participate in the Soviet armed forces, to claim conscientious objector status. But questions arose: would the Russian Orthodox Church try to reassert its supremacy? Would the economy generate funds needed by the churches? Would the Baptist churches, which tended to be conservative, attract those unchurched thinkers for whom an intellectually respectable faith and an egalitarian leadership are prerequisites? A member of the group summarized,

> Our hearts and minds [were stretched] beyond anything we ever anticipated. Our world is both larger and smaller because of this experience. Our awareness of the challenges facing both the church and society in the Soviet Union is far richer than before. Our lives, and I trust, our ministries have been greatly enriched for having had this experience.[4]

3. Email, William Apel to Evelyn Hanneman, January 28, 2009; *PW* 7–10 1988; Buttry, *Christian Peacemaking*, 63, refers to his participation in the friendship tour.

4. Cain, "Friendship Tour," 17.

The former Soviet Union ceased to be a primary focus for peace activists, including many BPFNA members, with the breakup of the USSR and the collapse of its empire. Subsequently, some Baptists have maintained some personal or institutional links with Christians in the region through sister church relationships, organizations such as the BWA or the International Baptist Theological Seminary in Prague, Czech Republic, and four international peace conferences attended by Baptist peacemakers from around the world in Sjövik, Sweden (1988), La Boquita, Nicaragua (1992), Melbourne, Australia (2000), and Rome, Italy (2009).

As Baptists confronted the evil manifest in the East-West confrontation during the 1980s, there was a corresponding growth in resistance by Baptists to the demonic spirit manifest along another axis, which runs between the countries of the rich North and the poor South. Baptists were among the tens of thousands who signed a "pledge of resistance," a commitment to oppose any United States invasion or escalation of "low intensity war" against Nicaragua. In the United States and Canada, several Baptist congregations declared themselves sanctuary churches for refugees of Salvadoran political violence. Baptists participated in acts of civil disobedience at South African embassies or at corporate headquarters of companies doing business as usual in South Africa, and were arrested. Baptists risked fines or arrest by ignoring sanctions imposed by a succession of administrations in the United States against Cuba and by taking medicines and other essentials to Cuba.

BPFNA delegations visited Nicaragua on six occasions between 1986 and 1992. They were responding to an appeal of American Baptist missionaries Gustavo and Joan Parajón who challenged participants as follows: "Ask what, in obedience to our Lord, can I do to bring reconciliation where there is war, hope where there is injustice, consolation where there is despair?"[5]

Number one on the Contra hit list and vilified as communist revolutionary, Dr. Parajón helped organize in May 1986 a friendship visit and BPFNA steering committee meeting. In a joint effort with Baptist World Aid, an arm of the BWA, the delegation gave the first installment towards $22,000 for the purchase of two four-wheel drive vehicles and an additional $2,000 in medical supplies to PROVADENIC. Founded by Dr. Parajón in 1967 as the medical arm of the Nicaragua Baptist Convention,

---

5. Dekar, "Peacemaking in Nicaragua," 7.

the organization provided primary health care to over 30,000 patients around the country in 1985. As well as curing common illnesses, the project emphasized mass vaccination. Among children treated, the infant mortality rate dropped from 15.74 to 9.93 per thousand over a period of five years.

Baptist leaders with whom participants met in Nicaragua refuted claims by the administration of President Reagan that the Sandinista government opposed the churches. Eugenio Zamora, pastor of the Galilee Baptist Church and Nicaragua Baptist Convention president, said the government very much wanted a collaborative effort to correct past injustices. From his perspective, the Contras, not the Sandinistas were interfering with the spiritual and material outreach of the church. He acknowledged that the Sandinistas had made mistakes, but, when I inquired if the Contras might represent a viable alternative, Pastor Zamora replied, "We have ourselves asked, 'If the Contras are successful, what will be the result?' I can only see a return to Somozism without Somoza. This is unacceptable, a return to dictatorship. I will be in prison or dead."[6]

Twelve people participated in a friendship tour to Nicaragua from May 25–June 5, 1987. They were guests of the Baptist Convention of Nicaragua and met with pastors and doctors, poor and rich, representatives of all political parties, and United States government officials. Sixto Ulloa, a Baptist and a representative of the Sandinista National Liberation Front (*Frente Sandinista de Liberación Nacional*) which governed Nicaragua from 1979 to 1990, said that over a hundred Protestant denominations were thriving in Nicaragua, a country where citizens could own property and freely vote. "If this is communism, we'll take it."[7]

In a statement written at the end of their stay in Nicaragua, tour members stated, "Our lives have been forever changed by the people we have met here, and our faith compels us to share our experiences with others in the hope that the lives of many will be changed by our witness." After describing what they had seen and heard, delegation members expressed concern about the spiritual state of their own nation. "Many Christians in Nicaragua have difficulty understanding why their fellow Christians in the United States [inflict such suffering]. We, too, are troubled by this. We want to state this clearly and unequivocally: The U.S. is lying about

6. Ibid., 10.

7. Whitehead, ". . . to bear witness."

Nicaragua." After describing the lies, participants called for an immediate end to the war. "Finally, we pray that God will forgive our nation for its sins in Nicaragua, and that God will lead us out of darkness into the light of justice and peace.[8]

BPFNA again sponsored delegations to Nicaragua in 1988, 1989, 1990, 1992—years of direct conflict between Contras and Sandinistas— and 2008. Dr. Gustavo Parajón hosted the second international conference, held during July 14–19, 1992 in a thatch-roofed open air conference center at La Boquita, a beach town on the Pacific Coast. Parajón introduced conferees to the revolutionary leader, Daniel Ortega. After the conference, many delegates stood in solidarity in Managua with a hundred thousand Nicaraguans in red bandannas celebrating the Revolution. They then returned to North America and, in many instances, helped their home congregations form active "sister church" relationships with Nicaraguan Baptist congregations.

In addition to friendship visits and the international conference, BPFNA has supported peace workers in Nicaragua. For example, a small grant of $500 from the Gavel Fund in 1996 enabled the Martin Luther King, Jr. Institute of the Polytechnic University (UPOLI) to train people in conflict resolution methods at a time the institute was still assisting former Sandinista and Contra soldiers as they resettled in rural communities.

In 2008, BPFNA again organized a delegation to Nicaragua. Participants in the friendship tour traveled around the country and met with Daniel Ortega who had returned to the presidency of the country the previous year. For Deidre Druk, music teacher, member of University Baptist Church in Minneapolis and a participant in the friendship visit, it was a "sobering experience" to see that the government was unable to meet such basic needs of people as medical care, food, or basic services like water and electricity. "The most troubling aspect of the Nicaraguan experience for me was that the people of the Nemagon camp [in the heart of Managua] met us with love—even after all that has happened to them because of rich American corporations."[9]

El Salvador was also caught up in two struggles during the 1980s. One was a national struggle for freedom, for better living conditions, and for respecting human rights. The other was a war between the national army

8. "1987 Friendship Tour to Nicaragua," *PeaceWork* (May–August 1987) 6.

9. Druk, "Reflections from Nicaragua" 15.

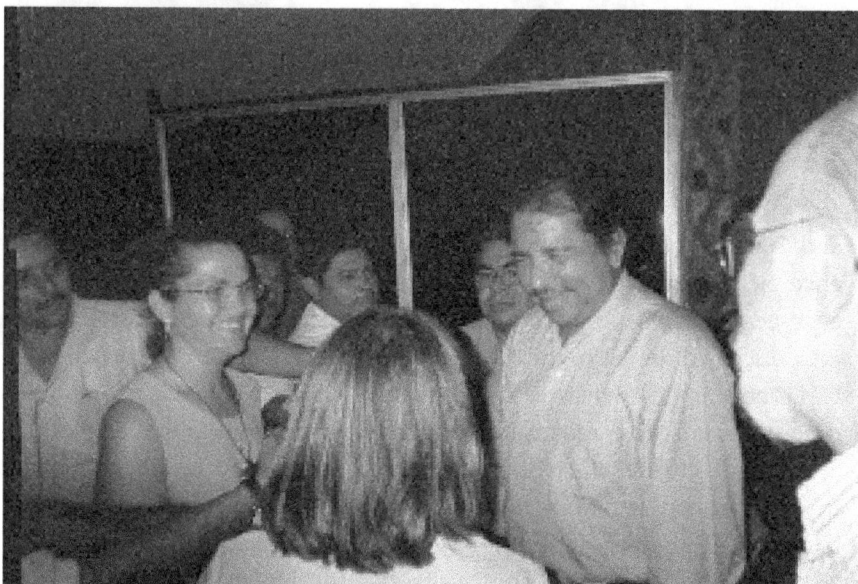

*LeDayne with President Daniel Ortega
during Friendship Tour to Nicaragua August 2008.*

and a guerrilla force, *Frente Farabundo Martí para la Liberación Nacional* (FMLN), in English, Farabundo Martí National Liberation Front. Formed as an umbrella group in 1980 from several left wing groups, FMLN demobilized their armed units after peace accords were signed in 1992. FMLN became one of the two major political parties in the country.

Emmanual Baptist Church, a congregation of two hundred in the capital city of San Salvador, was deeply involved assisting victims of the war. On a Sunday in October 1984, the National Guard arrested one of its pastors, Miguel Tomás Castro. After three days of torture and interrogation, he was sent with his family into exile in Hamilton, Ontario, Canada. Many other members of the congregation, as well as pastors and members of other Salvadorean Baptist congregations also went into exile in Canada, the United States, or other countries.

In advance of the May 1986 friendship visit to Nicaragua, George Williamson, Jr., and I and traveled to El Salvador. At the time, there were some 800,000 internally displaced persons around the country. We visited several of Emmanuel Baptist Church's projects including schools, orphanages, and a program called *Ser Con Mi Hermano*, which means "to be with my brother." Between 1982 and 1986, *Ser Con* had increased the number of communities in which it distributed food and clothing from four to forty-five. The program was expanding into other areas such as agriculture, health, and literacy.

Emmanuel Baptist had established centers for preaching, Bible study, and mutual assistance around the country by 1986. Each program was to engender self-sufficiency on the part of the people. The idea was in keeping with a common development stratagem, "Give a person a fish, and you've given a meal. Teach the person to fish, and you have provided food for a lifetime." By providing training in new skills, the programs validated people and ensured that they not become dependent on external aid. In each context, program animators gave attention to the spiritual needs of the people as well as to their material needs. However, Emmanuel did not insist on helping Christians alone. A worker explained, "The food is for people who need it. It is not only for church members, nor for those who have accepted Jesus Christ. Food is given as a testimony of the love of God."

Peace negotiations were under way under United Nations auspices by 1990. The promise of a transition from war to peace enabled Miguel Tomás Castro and his family to return to San Salvador to participate in the rebuilding of the country. Castro was a primary resource for BPFNA friendship visits to the country in 1991 and 1992. The warring parties signed the Chapultepec Peace Accords in Mexico City on January 16, 1992.

Nine North Americans participated in the first friendship visit during January 22–30, 1991. One of the members of Emmanuel Baptist Church asked, "Don't you see the light of hope in our midst, the flame of courage from which we warm ourselves? Do you see the signs of the Kingdom?"

The signs were plentiful. Many projects of the projects running in 1986 continued including work with orphans, preparation of candidates for baptism in the face of threats, ecumenical efforts among Roman Catholics, Lutherans, and others committed to the poor, formation of community groups for Bible reflection and action, a training center for women, a school for pre-kindergarten children, and literacy programs.[10]

In a 1990 speech at Berkeley, California, Edgar Palacios, a Baptist minister who led the Permanent Committee for the National Debate for Peace in El Salvador summarized the urgency of the hour, "There can

---

10. Siler, "Therefore, Love Truth and Peace."

be no transformation of history without the changing of people and of structures."[11]

In July 1992, another BPFNA-sponsored friendship group visited El Salvador after the International Baptist Peace Conference in Nicaragua. The situation was more hopeful. Earlier that year, an accord had brought twelve years of a civil war to a close. Nevertheless, over 75,000 human beings had died. An additional 8,000 had disappeared. More than 1.5 million persons were displaced, internally or outside the country. The economy was devastated. The countryside was in ruins.

I was a member of the delegation. We journeyed around the country talking with ex-combatants, members of popular movements, educators, pastors, and peacemakers. We heard stories of past terrors and present fears. We visited places of mourning. We worshiped with *hermanos* and *hermanas* of Emmanual Baptist Church. Swept up into the mood of celebration and hope of these Salvadoran wagers of peace, forged in suffering, we came to understand that God had heard their cries. Living into the Reign of God, they allowed no time for despair. When we asked, "How can we be your compañeros on the road?" they replied, "Do not forget us. Be present with us in your prayers, in your petitions to your governments; and be present with us here, witnesses to our reality. Tell our stories."[12]

Sixteen persons from the Philadelphia area, including several from a BPFNA partner congregation, Central Baptist Church in Wayne, traveled to El Salvador in March 2000 to commemorate the twentieth anniversary of the assassination on March 24, 1980 of Óscar Arnulfo Romero y Galdámez, commonly known as Monseñor Romero. The group found evidence of progress such as new home construction, plentiful food, water, and other essentials of life, and restored infrastructure. They also observed that prevailing economic policies—the creation of free trade zones and the establishment of sweatshops (*maquiladoras*)—ensured that the poor were forgotten, cast aside as worthless, martyred at the hands of the very culture of wealth that Archbishop Romero had critiqued shortly before his death.

In a letter to the churches of North America, Romero observed that the idolatry of wealth and private property inclines people toward *having* more and lessens their interest in *being* more. This absolutism supports

11. James Gamble letter to *Baptist Peacemaker*, 11:4 (1991) 30. In 2007, Palacios was elected to BPFNA's board.

12. Purchase, "Caught between Hope and Horror."

structural violence and oppression. He wrote, "The god of money forces us to turn our backs on the God of Christianity. Because people want a god who turns his back on them, instead of the true God—therefore many criticize the church. They kill every movement that tries to destroy false idols and give us the true God."[13]

The BPFNA board of directors announced in February 1991 plans for a new program focus. Timed to coincide with the 1992 quincentenary of Columbus's historic voyage to the "new world" the campaign would explore the legacy of colonialism in the Americas. Entitled "The Longest War: 500 Years Since Columbus," the program sought first, to educate the dominant European American culture of North America about the history of colonization for which Columbus and his 1492 voyage are the primary symbols; second, to engage in biblical reflection on this legacy; and third, to offer appropriate models of redemptive action in hopes of participating in a process of justice and healing for first peoples of the Americas.

In addition to the 1991 and 1992 peace camps, the *Baptist Peacemaker* featured articles by Native American speakers and a curriculum on first peoples' cultures. Reaves Nahwooks (Comanche/Kiowa) assumed a prominent role as Vice President of the board of directors. Along with members of his community, he hosted the October 1992 board meeting in Anadarko, Oklahoma with Kiowa and Comanche hosts.[14]

The effort sought to extend and strengthen BPFNA work in Cuba, *México*, and Puerto Rico. The BPFNA organized several friendship visits to these three countries, which included opportunities to celebrate the first ordination of women by Baptist conventions in Cuba and México, as well as Nicaragua.

Cuban Baptists ordained their first three women pastors: Ena Garcia, Clara Rodés, and Xiomara Diáz Gutierrez in January 1992. As a result of the collapse of the former Soviet Union, Cuba was in the midst of its most precarious economic situation since 1959 when Fidel Castro came to power. Thirteen women pastors and religious leaders from Canada and the United States representing four Baptist conventions joined the ordinands. The delegation took over $2000 worth of medical supplies as a gift to the Cuban Baptist churches. One of the North Americans, Prathia

13. Romero, *Voice of the Voiceless*, 173; Berrigan, *Steadfastness*, 66; Smith, "Hope beyond Martyrdom."

14. Reaves Nahwooks' obituary appears in *Baptist Peacemaker* 28:2 (2008) 22.

Hall Wynn, a pastor in Philadelphia and an executive of the Progressive National Baptist Convention, delivered the ordination sermon.

About 250 people traveled by bus and bicycles to attend the service, held in the sanctuary of the Ebenezer Baptist Church in Marianao, a commercial and residential suburb of Havana between the elite residential districts of Miramar and Marina Hemingway. Nancy Hastings Sehested, tour participant and pastor of Prescott Memorial Baptist Church in Memphis, Tennessee, recalled, "We prayed for Ena, Clara, and Xiomara and laid our hands on their heads as they knelt down before us. Then we surrounded them with our support through song. The maracas were shaking the beat for us, and we sang, 'Soon and very soon we are going to see the king,' and 'Leaning on the everlasting arms' and some songs in Spanish."

The most significant part of the trip for Judith Webb of the Baptist Women's Missionary Society of Ontario and Quebec was the opportunity to learn something about the churches and to be able to affirm the women pastors. It was obviously a joyous occasion for the church, and a special moment as each individual went and lay hands on the ordinands and prayed for them.

A Cuban television news program noted the ordination service the next day. This marked a new trend in the country's three decades of virtually ignoring religious people and their practices.[15]

The Baptist Convention of Eastern Cuba refused to sanction the ordination of women for several years, a practice consistent with many Baptists around the world. When Second Baptist Church of Santiago de Cuba proposed to ordain Gisela Perez Muños, many expressed indignation. "By women, the earth is cursed," exclaimed one [male] pastor in the presence of Yamina Apolinaris, [female] executive minister of the Baptist Churches of Puerto Rico. A woman in the audience remarked that Puerto Ricans had benefited from woman pastors, prompting the man to retort, "And we have benefited from *not* having them." Gisela Perez was ordained March 4, 1998.[16]

A few years earlier, in January 1993, Baptists in Nicaragua ordained the first woman in pastoral ministry in the country, Carmen Pena Garay of Hebron Baptist Church in Juigalpa. Isobel Docampo, president of the Ministers' Fellowship of the Baptist Convention of Washington DC and

15. Greene, "Cuban Baptist Women Ordained."
16. McKenna, "Like a Stone Cast into Still Waters."

BPFNA board member, represented BPFNA. In a departure from the custom that only ordained ministers of the council participate in the laying on of hands, some of the women who were present were asked to lay hands on the ordinand. "The Spirit of God was breaking free and traditions were tossed aside," said Docampo. At the conclusion of her sermon, Garay said,

> In these past seventeen years of pastoral ministry, time in which God has confirmed the vocation for which he chose me, I have cried, I have suffered, but today there remains within me the great satisfaction that "yes" it is all worth it to serve and to follow the One who gave his life for us. It is worth everything to serve the One who—without questioning us, without questioning who we are and from where we originated, or that we are women—it pleases to call us.
>
> ... without both women and men, the mission of God's kingdom would be incomplete. And like Julia Esquival says in her poem, "Go and tell my brothers that I have overcome death, that there is room for all, over there, where the New World is being forged."[17]

A six-woman delegation of North American Baptists went to Mexico City in March 2000 for the ordination council and ordination of Rebeca Montemayor Lopez. Her congregation, Shalom Baptist Community, became the first Baptist church in México to ordain a woman. Of particular note was the strong presence and participation of Roman Catholic women for whom the ordination was a symbol of hope. One commented, "This is also a great day for Catholic women. We are being encouraged also to hear and to respond to God's call in a new way."[18]

Delegations visited Puerto Rico in 1994 and 2000. The first came as a response to the focus on the legacy of colonialism in the Americas. Like many areas of North America, the original inhabitants of Puerto Rico are now extinct. A combination of conquest, deadly slave labor, and exposure to European diseases for which the Taíno people had no immunity resulted in their extermination. Ken Sehested observed, "The connection between militarism and the destruction of native peoples made those of

---

17. Translated by Isobel Docampo; *Baptist Peacemaker*, 13:1 (1993) 1.
18. *Baptist Peacemaker* 20:2 (2000) 16.

us from the United States and from Canada remember similar realities in our own lands."[19]

A day trip to Vieques, an island off the east coast of the main island, highlighted the friendship tour. Participants met with a Navy information officer and with leaders of the Committee for the Rescue and Development of Vieques, which was trying to reclaim the land. The United States Navy owned two-thirds of the island and used it as a major staging ground for military training, including shelling and strafing by naval ships, airplanes, helicopters, and tanks. United States forces have practiced their invasions before carrying them out in numerous Caribbean and Latin countries.

For several years, Vieques became a focus of protests. The turning point in the struggle to end the occupation of the island came on April 19, 1999. Flying a mile off course, a fighter pilot dropped a 500-pound bomb on a guardhouse, killing security guard David Sanes Rodriguez. This friendly-fire incident was a catalyst for mobilization of the local people, reinforced by a growing international campaign joined by a second BPFNA friendship delegation in 2000.

In May 2000, more than six hundred people entered the Navy firing range at Vieques and were arrested. Hundreds more were arrested in April 2001. Among those charged with trespassing was Damaso Serrano, elected a year before as mayor by 9,100 residents of the island. Before he was sentenced to four months and led away to jail by United States marshals, Serrano said, "I will continue to follow my conscience by defending the rights of my people."[20]

The United States Navy abandoned the base on orders of President George W. Bush in 2003 after more than sixty years of using Vieques as a practice range. Guillermo Ramirez of San Juan, Puerto Rico—a former BPFNA board member—and Bob Paterson-Watt of Toronto—the board's vice president—represented BPFNA at ceremonies marking the official closing of the United States base and its transfer to the United States Department of the Interior to be managed by the United States Fish and Wildlife Service. Decontamination of land and sea as well as other significant problems remained. Paterson-Watt observed, "I was humbled to be part of the celebration of this moment in history, when a small, nonvio-

19. *Baptist Peacemaker* 14:3–4 (1994) 21.
20. *Baptist Peacemaker* 21:3 (2001) 4.

lent collective of disparate people won a victory over the most powerful military force in the world."[21]

BPFNA's board met for the first time in *México* in May 1996. After meeting for two days at the Baptist Seminary in Mexico City, board members attended worship in area churches and participated for two additional days in intensive exchange of ideas with students and local pastors. Leading Mexican human rights activists presented an overview of the country's current reality in the light of an analysis of cultural, political, religious, and social processes.

Six board members continued at the end of this time of dialogue to the state of Chiapas. Chiapas has been torn by armed conflict between the Zapatista National Liberation Army and the Mexican military since January 1, 1994 when the North American Free Trade Agreement (NAFTA) went into effect. Its largely Mayan population was already among the poorest in *México*. Provisions of the NAFTA accord adversely affected life for many peasants.

Lázaro Gonzalez accompanied the delegation to introduce participants to these realities. Gonzalez has served as seminary professor and director of the *Consejo Indígena Campesino Evangélico de México* (CICEM), or Council of Indigenous Campesino Evangelical Churches, an association of forty Baptist, Methodist, Presbyterian, and Pentecostal congregations. Gonzalez facilitated visits to displaced communities. At the end of the friendship tour, participants wrote President Ernesto Zedillo of *México* urging that those most affected by the war be party to negotiations between the government and the Zapatista Army.

The visit engendered a number of BPFNA initiatives. These included meetings with the Bishop of Chiapas, Samuel Ruíz Garcia; support for a ground-breaking dialogue between Roman Catholics and CICEM that began in April 1997 in San Cristóbal de las Casas, cultural center of Chiapas; publication of Spanish language materials; and BPFNA membership in *Servicio Internacional para la Paz (SIPAZ)*, an international observation program created in 1995 to aid in the construction of a culture of peace, through dialogue, nonviolence, and tolerance.

As part of its commitment to be involved in the search for peaceful solutions to the conflict, BPFNA sent Lee McKenna of Toronto and Javier

---

21. Paterson-Watt, "Fall and Rise of Vieques Island," 3.

Ulloa Castellanos of Mexico City to Chiapas for celebrations marking the retirement of Bishop Ruiz Garcia on January 25, 2000.[22]

INTERNATIONAL CONFERENCES

BPFNA and the European Baptist Federation co-sponsored the first international Baptist peace conference in 1988. A hundred and seventy embattled Baptist peacemakers came from five continents to Sjövik, Sweden where they explored the Anabaptist and Baptist heritage, practical strategies to implement peace and justice ministries, and the Final Act of the Conference on Security and Cooperation in Europe, known as the Helsinki Accords.

In an attempt to improve relations between the Communist bloc and the West, thirty-five countries signed the Helsinki Accords. Key provisions called on signatory nations to respect the sovereignty of other nations by not intervening in their internal affairs, to refrain from the threat or use of force, to settle disputes peacefully, and to respect human rights and such fundamental freedoms as freedom of thought, conscience, religion, or belief. The Helsinki Accords provided the backdrop for the flowering of dissident and liberal movements in Eastern Europe and the policy of *glasnost* introduced by Mikhail Gorbachev. People living under Communist rule could claim official sanction to say what they thought.[23]

On the first morning of the conference, a bird flew into the A-frame chapel where participants gathered. Day after day, the gorgeous golden bird with black markings bashed against the apex skylight. Trapped in its own aspiration to be free, it grew visibly weaker. On the last day, Reaves Nahwooks, a Kiowa-Comanche pastor and rancher in Oklahoma, prayed in Comanche, a language full of picture-words that Nahwooks translated into English for conferees (not for God). It was during this prayer that the bird, apparently doomed, fell to one of the lower windowsills. A young pastor from the Soviet Union heard it, gently took it in his hands, and opened the window. The bird escaped. Nahwooks said amen and another conferee, John Sundquist, cried out, "the bird is free! Victor set it free!" Some cheered, some wept, and everyone embraced in expectation that one day all the nations shall be free.[24]

---

22. *Baptist Peacemaker* 16:2 (1996) 4; 17:2 (1997) 3; 19:4 (1999) 15.

23. Bichkov, "Baptists for Implementation."

24. Williamson, "Coming Peace," 209–16.

A government retreat house in La Boquita, Nicaragua, hosted the second International Baptist Peace Conference in July 1992. Delegates from around the world—East and West Germany, North America, Indonesia, the Philippines, India, Cuba, El Salvador, South Africa, Nicaragua, and elsewhere—represented a market place of grassroots communities: Amnesty International, Greenham's Common, the Women's International League for Peace and Freedom, Greenpeace, the Fellowship of Reconciliation, and others. By prayer and song, formal presentations and informal conversation, Baptist peacemakers to glimpse the coming time of freedom for all peoples and nations of the world. Women pastors garbed in liturgical gowns from around the world led communion at the end of the gathering. A rainbow of hope they pointed to a future, reconciled world. Children from the countryside wove their way among people. Mountains moved. People danced. Worshipping God, the community of faith celebrated the length the non-violent God has gone to restore broken community.

In a flash, participants saw coming the time when swords will be hammered into ploughshares and nations shall not even study war when the proud shall be scattered, the mighty pulled down, the lowly ones exalted and the hungry filled with good things, when God will wipe every tear from our eyes. Death will be no more; mourning and crying and pain will be no more. And the holy one of God will give water as a gift from the spring of the water of life, sparkling like crystal, flowing from the throne of God and of the Lamb down the city streets. On either side of the river will be the tree of life. Its leaves shall be for the healing of the nations (Rev 22:2).

I was not alone in understanding this moment as similar to that John experienced when he heard loud voices in heaven saying, "The kingdom of the world has become of kingdom of our Lord and of his Messiah, and he will reign forever and ever" (Rev 11:15). This transitory, ecstatic time did not fade but motivated participants to reclaim their responsibility as earthkeepers, stewards of "the world, and those who live in it" (Ps 24:1).

One night, Daniel L. Buttry stayed up with three others and began to dream new dreams. He experienced a call to a new ministry in international peacemaking. In 1996, he joined BPFNA staff to manage the newly-endowed Gavel Memorial Peace Fund in a part-time position. Lee McKenna succeeded him in 2005 when Buttry accepted a position with International Ministries of the American Baptist Churches USA as Global Service Missionary for Peace and Justice.

I add a note of tragedy. On September 2, 1992 an earthquake occurred off the Nicaragua coast. Located in an active zone of stress and deformation, the quake created tsunamis along the Pacific Ocean coast. La Boquita and other communities were destroyed. At least one hundred and sixteen people were killed and several more were injured.[25]

Whitley College, a Baptist institution in Melbourne, Victoria, Australia, hosted the third international Baptist gathering on the eve of the eighteenth congress of the BWA in January 2000. Under the theme "Hearing the Cry, Acting in Hope," a hundred and forty-one persons came from twenty-six countries. Over 50 percent of participants were from countries of the so-called majority world and nearly 40 percent were women.

Several hundred persons attended an opening service of worship which featured didgeridoo music of Australia's Aboriginal people and an address by Lowitja O'Donoghue, a member of the Yankunjatjara people. Well-known advocate for the rights of indigenous Australians, O'Donoghue was named in 1984 "Australian of the Year."

In her address, O'Donoghue summarized the history of exploitation and painful steps being taken on the journey of healing. She stated, "Reconciliation is not wallowing in guilt" but we must "acknowledge the destructive behavior of the past and how it causes disadvantage today." To move forward, to be reconciled, we must tell the truth about the historical record and initiate public and private policies of restitution.[26]

After three days of Bible studies, workshops, and plenary talks, issue-oriented groups met to develop ideas for response in such areas as environmental degradation, fair trade, gender justice, interfaith dialogue, justice for indigenous peoples, military spending, and conflict transformation training. Conferees approved the text of an "Open Letter" addressed to delegates to the BWA congress. The document concluded by affirming that the God of the Bible manifests special concern for the cries of the poor—of the marginalized, the outcast, indeed all who do not share in the distribution of wealth—and correspondingly wants faithful people to locate themselves in compassionate proximity to those whose lives are battered, bruised, and broken.

25. Background information online: http://en.wikipedia.org/wiki/1992_Nicaragua_earthquake.

26. *Baptist Peacemaker* 20:1 (2000) 8; Dekar, "Australia Apologizes to the Stolen Generation."

At the time of this writing, a fourth International Baptist Peace Conference is scheduled to take place February 9–14, 2009 at Villa Mundo Migliore, outside of Rome, Italy, with the theme, *Vive in Armonia, Vive in Pace* (Live in Harmony, Live in Peace). The gathering will bring together Baptists who are active around the globe in nonviolent struggles for peace and justice. Participants will engage in storytelling, networking, training, spiritual development, encouragement for the sake of strengthening the witness of Baptist peacemakers in various global contexts, and a renewed passion for building a culture of peace.

TRAINING AND OTHER INTERNATIONAL PROJECTS

From the earliest days of the BPFNA, members have discussed the vision of an endowed Baptist peace foundation. Its purpose would be to support both North American and international mediation, conflict transformation training, and nonviolent resistance efforts.

In 1995, the BPFNA brought the dream to reality thanks to a bequest from the estate of Victor and Eileen Gavel. The BPFNA created the Gavel Memorial Peace Fund to support Baptist leaders through training, logistical support, and limited financial resources for strategic peace or justice ventures around the world and named Daniel L. Buttry the first director. Board president Glenda Fontenot, a communications consultant in Houston, Texas, commented, "We are drawing to a close of what will be the bloodiest century in human history. The connection between physical violence and spiritual corruption is clear and we are confident that the Gavel Fund will continue to address violence and corruption in new and empowering ways."[27]

At its October 1996 meeting, the board of directors approved support from the Gavel Fund for six projects and for a major training session on conflict resolution that took place during November 26–29, 1996 in Chiang Mai, Thailand. The specific projects and funding amounts included four in Africa.

In partnership with Nonviolence International, the Gavel Fund provided $2,000 for a month-long training program during February 1997. Nigerian Baptists were the lead organizers of nonviolence training in four cities in Nigeria. The project included special components for women and

27. Press release, October 11, 1996.

youth. Nigerian Baptists have been leading figures in a Christian-Muslim peace movement in the country.

A $1,300 grant enabled Eleazar Ziherambere, BWA Regional Secretary of the All-Africa Baptist Fellowship, to offer training on repentance, forgiveness, and reconciliation in several African countries. He also assisted in negotiations to avert a civil war threatened in an African country. Because of the fragile nature of the process, that country cannot be publicly identified. The BWA assisted in delivering the funds.

A $1,000 grant enabled Ron Ward of the Toronto Baptist Intercultural Services to serve among Oromo who had fled Ethiopia and lived in large numbers in Toronto, Canada. Ward and his family had served in India and East Africa, experience which he brought to the work

As well, the Gavel Fund supported a wider dialogue process among Eritreans and Ethiopians whose conflict has continued on and off for decades. Peace had seemed possible when, in 1991, Ethiopians who had fought beside the Eritreans against the Mengistu regime came to power. However, in 1998, a border dispute erupted and grew into a war that cost over 100,000 lives. The lines of division followed Eritreans and Ethiopians who came to North America.

Eritreans and Ethiopians came together for three days of prayer, structured dialogue, advocacy, and conflict transformation training in Detroit, Michigan in June 2000. This gathering laid foundations for further reconciliation events in Toronto (November 2000) and Washington DC (June 2001) where participants gave public witness to a formal process called the "Ethiopian and Eritrean Reconciliation Prayer Mission.[28]

A $1,000 grant provided seed money to form *Christians United for Peace in Liberia*. The organization brought together people from many tribes, or ethnicities. The team undertook evangelistic efforts, conflict transformation training, and reconciliation workshops in local congregations emphasizing repentance as a first step towards healing a war-torn society.

A $10,000 grant provided funding for an Intensive Training Conference on Conflict Resolution. Growing out of the 1992 International Baptist Peace Conference at La Boquita, Nicaragua, and the 1995 BPFNA friendship tour to Burma (Myanmar), the conference took place November 26–29, 1996 in Chiang Mai, Thailand. The Asian Baptist Federation was

28. Buttry, "Tears of Mutual Repentance" and "Ethiopians and Eritreans Vigil Together for Peace."

lead sponsor, with the BPFNA the largest contributing co-sponsor. Over seventy church leaders from fourteen countries in Asia and the Pacific attended.

Subsequently BPFNA has supported projects around the world. One was a three-year effort to provide books on topics of peace, justice, reconciliation, human rights, and social ethics to the libraries of seminaries, colleges, and universities which are training future leaders in poor and war-torn countries. The idea for the project was conceived when BPFNA staff visited the libraries of key institutions in some conflicted countries and saw collections of books that were small, mostly outdated, and very inadequate on topics related to how to respond in faith to violent conflict. The staff met one student who had done a paper on a major war in which he drew major points from having heard about but never having read *Christian Peacemaking* by Daniel L. Buttry, who headed the effort.

Over a thousand books valued at $15,000 were sent in three shipments in January 1998, April 1999, and January 2000, to a total of forty institutions in twenty-two countries. Donations from several publishers contributed to the success of the project, including: Augsburg/Fortress, Beacon Press, William B. Eerdmans, Herald Press, Judson Press, Orbis Books, Oxford University Press, and Smyth and Helwys. FOR donated books and magazines. Training for Change donated copies of a title on leadership development. The BPFNA added its own publications. The BPFNA also purchased titles which could not be received by donation but were viewed as crucial for inclusion in the collections. One special feature of the second round of shipments was the inclusion of Spanish-language resources for Latin American institutions. National Ministries of the American Baptist Churches, several congregations, and grants from the Mustard Seed Foundation provided financial support to help gather and mail the books.

Letters from recipient institutions confirmed the value of the project. Dr. Tuisem A. Shishak of Patkai Christian College in Nagaland, India, wrote, "I want to thank you for thinking of us. I am sure our faculty, staff and students would be challenged by the books you have sent. Kindly thank the donors on our behalf." Dr. Shishak had already begun reading one of the titles.

Sheila Heneise wrote from the *Instituo Teológico Bautista* in Santiago, Chile, "We received four boxes of books for our Institute library. Thanks so much. What a wealth of materials on peace and justice. We'll have to see how we can work it into the curriculum. It's especially good for the Latin American Reality course."[29]

One of the main areas of Asian Baptist growth has been in Burma (Myanmar), where the American Baptist missionary Adoniram Judson (1788–1850) first found a positive response among some of the minority ethnic groups, including the Chin.[30] A Chin pastor, the Reverend Saboi Jum was among those who attended the first International Baptist Peace Conference in Sweden. Saboi Jum explained that Adoniram Judson had converted the poorer half of his country to Baptist "seat-of-the-pants-dissenter-religion"; that the Chin were trapped, like the bird, in futile violence against the murderous, tyrannical prejudices of the privileged other half. As God's messenger to North American Baptists, Jum pleaded they send another Judson. BPFNA did.

Daniel L. Buttry went on the most improbably impossible of missions, to teach nonviolent resistance to a people confronted by a powerful regime, the State Law and Order Restoration Commission (SLORC). Jum successfully arranged a ceasefire and subsequently launched the Shalom Foundation, which on numerous times has invited Buttry or others to teach conflict transformation to church and community leaders in Burma (Myanmar).

Since 1955, armed conflict has gone on between the army of India and insurgents in Nagaland, a hill state located in north-eastern India. The war has claimed an estimated 200,000 lives. In 1997, the Government of India entered into a cease-fire agreement with the National Socialist Council of Nagalim for peace talks. This created space for the BPFNA to sponsor and facilitate for several years a peace process among Naga insurgent groups and social sector organizations.

Leaders of warring factions met at the Carter Center in Atlanta from July 28-August 3, 1997 and pledged concrete steps to be taken for reconciliation. Read for the first time during Sunday morning worship at Oakhurst Baptist Church in Decatur, Georgia, the "Atlanta Appeal" proposed strategies to promote dialogue among the Naga peoples, a complete cease-fire between Nagas, and adoption of a visual symbol to express the desire of Naga people for peace and unity.

29. Buttry, "BPFNA Ships 1,000 Books," 9; also *Baptist Peacemaker* 18 (Spring 1998) 9 and 19 (Summer 1999) 14.

30. Williamson, "Twenty-five Jubilees" and Buttry, *Christian Peacemaking*, 139–43 for the following.

In November of 1997, a four-day celebration of a hundred and twenty-five years of Christianity in Nagaland gave a clear indication of progress towards a peaceful resolution of the long-standing war. At the opening ceremony, an estimated hundred thousand Christians from different Naga tribes committed themselves to shift from violent to nonviolent struggle.

In addition to facilitating the creation of a united peace front, the Gavel estate supported travel to Nagaland by Ken Sehested (1997) and Daniel L. Buttry (1999) to consult with Naga churches and social organizations in nonviolent methods. In 2000 Daniel L Buttry and Daniel Hunter were denied Restricted Area Permits to travel to Nagaland. Wati Aier, head of Oriental Theological Seminary in Dimapur, Nagaland's commercial center, arranged for the training just across the state border in Assam. These sessions helped Naga leaders develop a comprehensive strategy that gave a constructive expression of Naga aspirations.

In January 2000 I was similarly denied entry to Nagaland. I did, however, meet with several hundred Naga young people at the end of a "Journey of Conscience." This nonviolent people-to-people campaign involved public witness in New Delhi marking the anniversary of Gandhi's assassination on January 25, 1948. For Akum Longchari, an organizer of the journey, this was a significant step marking the culmination of a process by which the Naga people came together as a nation to walk together towards and through the conflict.[31]

Michelle Tooley, at the time on the faculty of Belmont University in Nashville, Tennessee, met with women from across the Northeast—all of which is conflicted—in 2001.

BPFNA has continued to support people-to-people dialogue in India and elsewhere. In 2005 and continuing through 2008, BPFNA has responded to a request to do conflict transformation training in Sudan with the Swedish Fellowship of Reconciliation (SweFOR) and a Sudanese partner organization, Sudanese Organization for Non-violence and Development (SONAD). The effort has continued amidst escalating violence, displacement, starvation, rape, and deteriorating living conditions for millions of Sudanese both in the South, and in the west, a region known as Darfur.

---

31. Longchari, "Sowing Seeds of Peace."

BPFNA has sponsored Lee McKenna's travel to Sudan in 2005, 2006, 2007, and 2008 for training of over forty people from all parts of Sudan—Christians and Muslims, Nubians, Nuer, Dinka, Bor, Furians, Zaghwaw, Baggara, and Beja. She has helped train Ilham, a Sudanese Muslim woman, and Phillip, a Sudanese Christian man, who have served as co-facilitators and translators. In less than three years, they have exponentially multiplied their own learning and trained more than a thousand people, including parliamentarians of the new government of South Sudan, village leaders and providers of health to internally displaced persons, members of the Sudan People's Liberation Movement, teachers and families.[32]

REFLECTIONS

As early as 1956, President Eisenhower argued that educational and cultural exchanges not only foster mutual understanding, but also promote peace. The President saw the potential of international "People-to-People Programs" as limitless, saying, "If only people will get together, then so eventually will nations."[33]

The journey of fifty Baptists to the former Soviet Union in 1983 was an example of citizen diplomacy. Did members of the delegation know they were engaging in citizen diplomacy? Absolutely, although they possibly would not have used that phrase. Did such engagement in citizen diplomacy make a difference in bringing the Cold War to an end? Absolutely. Social movements, non-government organizations, and churches made a huge difference in resisting undemocratic regimes and fostering change.

In many conflict situations, Baptists have been in a strategic position to offer leadership for nonviolent change or mediation. In part, this has been due to the fact that, after Roman Catholics, Baptists are most widespread worldwide among Christian groups.

Organized at a time when Cold War tensions were at a high and intensely brutal regional or internal civil wars were raging in Asia, Central America, and sub-Saharan Africa, the BPFNA was in an excellent position to become an instrument for sustained intervention in situations of conflict. After the collapse of the Soviet Union, BPFNA pulled back from organizing friendship visits to Eastern Europe or Russia and became

32. McKenna, "Sudan: Never Again All over Again."

33. Accessed Human Rights Day, December 10, 2008. Online: http://chennai.usconsulate.gov/uploads/images/TdEmzsGSur6XnIqu2amLVw/intouch08octnov.pdf.

less active in the region. Conflicts continue in the region. The conference scheduled for February 2009 may re-ignite interest in mutual peace work in Eastern Europe and the former Soviet Union. This in turn may lead to the resumption of friendship tours there.

Recently, BPFNA has similarly devoted less attention to Central America. However, members of the delegation who visited Nicaragua in 2008 affirmed an ongoing concern on the part of some North American Baptists for a country which has experienced economic exploitation and United States military intervention not just in the 1980s, but for most of its history.

Formed at a critical moment when the end of the Cold War was imminent, BPFNA was able to contribute to confidence building, cooperation, and fostering a culture of positive peace among the nations. Ever since, the BPFNA has been on the cutting edge of international peacemaking, supporting in practical and effective ways courageous Baptist peacemakers in Eastern Europe, the former Soviet Union, Central America, Asia, and Africa. Through sponsorship of friendship tours, the organization of international conferences, and the funding of crucial projects around the world, BPFNA has created new possibilities for building a culture of peace. How exactly has this happened?

A partial answer rests in a question which I have asked my hosts, every time I have traveled, "What can I do?" With one voice they have answered invariably in the same way. Go back and insist that your government change its policies. I have followed with another question, "What do you need?" Again, invariably, my hosts have answered, go back to your country and speak at the board meetings of the multi-national companies that have a grip on our local economies. Tell your governments to stop the flow of arms to our government and military. Do not bring our military personnel for training in yours in methods of counter insurgency. Support the United Nations and other organizations that promote peace and justice.

I have sought to be faithful to those affected adversely around the world by the way we North American live. It has been life changing for me and for participants generally in delegations around the world to see that people who raise coffee or cocoa or work in factories that produce cheap clothing marketed in a Wal-Mart or Target store in North America do not receive a living wage. Seeing has led to small and still tenuous efforts to support Fair Trade plantations and to lobby for improved working conditions on the part of multi-national corporations.

In a church in El Salvador, I saw a poster, *Todos niños son Cristo con nosotros*, in English, "all children are Christ with us." Without denigrating any contribution I may have made in terms of material assistance or encouragement, I have experienced Christ with me not only in prayer, but also in the eyes of new friends. I have seen Christ in the children and others I have met.

Reflecting on his own experience in El Salvador with a BPFNA friendship visit, Mahan Siler, at the time pastor of Pullen Memorial Baptist Church in Raleigh, North Carolina, observed that these believers in a poor country imparted hope amidst his sense of helplessness. "How like God to do it that way."[34]

As a participant in the international work of BPFNA, I have wrestled with the tension of being a Christian and a dual-citizen of the United States and Canada, both part of the rich North. In 2000, on behalf of BPFNA, I joined the Naga Journey of Conscience in New Delhi, India. We met at the site where Gandhi died in 1948. There, I copied words from a marker which not only summarizes Gandhi's deepest social commitment, but also offers guidance for giving birth to a culture of peace.

> I will give you a talisman. Whenever you are in doubt, or when the self becomes too much with you, apply the following test. Recall the face of the poorest and the weakest man [person] whom you may have seen, and ask yourself, if the step you contemplate is going to be of any use to him [or her]. Will he [or she] gain anything by it? Will it restore him [or her] to a control over his [or her] own life and destiny? In other words, will it lead to *swaraj* [freedom] for the hungry and spiritually starving millions? Then you will find your doubts and your self melt away.[35]

---

34. Siler, "Therefore, Love Truth and Peace."
35. Online: http://www.mkgandhi.org/gquots1.htm.

6

Building Blocks for a More Inclusive Vision

INTRODUCTION

CHARLES KIMBALL, BAPTIST SCHOLAR and former FOR staff member, has explored the complexities and dangers of global conflict after the sobering events of the September 11, 2001 attacks by Al Qaeda on the World Trade Center in New York City and the Pentagon in Washington DC. In *When Religion Becomes Evil* Kimball addresses the question, "Is religion the problem?" Kimball identifies five warning signs of corruption in religion: absolute truth claims, blind obedience, establishing the "ideal" time, the end justifies any means, declaring holy war. "Nevertheless," he concludes, "in my view, people of faith offer the best hope both for correcting the corruptions leading to violence and for leading the way into a more promising future."[1]

To provide a "compass for the journey ahead," Kimball refers to God as a "direction, not an object."[2] By this metaphor, he likens our journey to God to the needle of a compass. Pointing to the magnetic north rather than the geographical north, the needle can deviate by several degrees of variation, or magnetic declination, depending on where you are on earth. On flight charts, lines of equal magnetic variation, called isogonic lines, are plotted in degrees of east and west variation. Calculating the difference in locations of the geographic and magnetic poles, pilots must re-plot these lines periodically while in flight and correct for any needed change of course.

With Kimball, I believe there are many paths to God. Each of us must locate that Center we name Holy and move towards it along what-

1. Kimball, *When Religion Becomes Evil*, 187.
2. Ibid., 191.

165

ever path the Spirit inclines us. As long as our pathway does not inflict harm to self or others, and vice versa, respect and tolerance for another person's walk are among the greatest gifts we can offer her, or him. As children of Abraham, we would do well to look towards a shared future. The scriptures of Islam provide wisdom to guide humanity on the path: "If God had willed, He would have made you one nation; but [He has not done so] that He may try you in what has come to you. So be you forward in good works; unto God shall you return, all together; and He will tell you of that whereon you were at variance."[3]

In the 1990s, the BPFNA entered intentionally into arenas of "variance" within society at large, and especially among Baptist Christians. The ultimate aim remained unchanged, to foster, create, and inhabit a culture of peace. To journey in that direction, BPFNA members had to make allowance for differences within the movement and to necessary adjustments along the path.

This chapter explores three arenas of variance: homosexuality, economic justice, and interfaith relations. By addressing each creatively, BPFNA members affirmed that justice and love are two faces of a single reality, two dimensions of human life needing to be mutually integrated in order to establish true peace on earth. In the process of joining an uprising on behalf of those oppressed or wounded when religion becomes evil, BPFNA members gave attention to such conditions for a culture of peace as tolerance, development, eco-awareness, and interdependence.

BECOMING WELCOMING AND AFFIRMING[4]

Among several themes on which Christians in the late twentieth and early twenty-first centuries have differed, the question of justice in relation to sexual orientation remains the most contentious. Especially glaring is the failure of many Christians to dialogue individually or corporately with people who differ not simply in their views with respect to homosexuality, but in their very being. A friend (intentionally not named) observes, "For me, it's not an issue; it's my life. And it's like fingernails on the chalkboard every time I hear anything about "the issue," since it's about real people."

3. *Koran* 5 (The Table) 136.

4. This section draws on "Statement on Justice and Sexual Orientation" in *Baptist Peacemaker* 15:1–2 (1995); letters in *Baptist Peacemaker* 15:3–4 (1995); and a review of the controversy in *Baptist Peacemaker* 16:1 (1996).

Around 1992 the BPFNA board of directors began a process of becoming fully affirming and welcoming of homosexual persons. Three years followed of dialogue within the BPFNA family. In February 1995, the board approved a fully affirming statement regarding homosexual persons.

The following month, the executive committee of the Board of National Ministries (BNM) of the American Baptist Churches USA voted to "sever ties" with the BPFNA. In July, the Coordinating Council of the Cooperative Baptist Fellowship (CoBF), an organization founded by so-called moderate Southern Baptists, similarly voted to remove the BPFNA from its cycle of funding through its Ethics and Public Ministry Group (EPMG). The recommendation approved originally by EPMG, for consideration by its governing body, was two-fold: that the BPFNA be removed from regular funding, which had averaged $3,600 annually for several years; but that the BPFNA be encouraged to submit funding proposals for specific projects for consideration by the EPMG. However, the Council's Administration Committee withdrew the second part of that recommendation before it reached the Council floor.

In May 1995, the board of directors responded to two points of contention, namely, that the original statement on sexual orientation contained inflammatory language, and that it implied improper meddling in denominational decision-making processes. The board rejected both accusations. With the intent of clarifying its inclusive vision, the board approved and published a revision of the original statement.

As printed, the statement opened with two affirmations: God creates and loves all human beings, the BPFNA welcomes into the movement all persons of faith who desire to be peacemakers and workers for justice, regardless of sexual orientation. The statement continued,

> Sexual orientation is a matter of significant conflict within the church and the larger culture. In welcoming gay and lesbian people into our movement, we do not intend to break relationship with those who disagree with our position, but rather seek to deepen dialogue. Even within our leadership it has taken more than two years of dialogue—with the Scripture, with each other, with gay and lesbian Christians—to reach agreement among ourselves. We believe, though, that this process has been a productive one, enabling us to practice the disciplines of reconciliation, which

include listening to and respecting those with whom we disagree, while resisting the temptation to intimidate or coerce.

The statement stressed that welcoming gay and lesbian people into the life of the BPFNA was and remains a matter of justice for the BPFNA. The board committed itself to work on several initiatives including the following:

- To work with homosexual brothers and sisters to secure their full civil and human rights within the larger culture and full participation within the body of Christ;

- To advocate on behalf of anyone who has been excluded because of sexual orientation;

- To encourage the wider Baptist family of faith, particularly within local congregations;

- To engage in open and vigorous dialogue—which includes the testimonies of gay and lesbian believers, along with the study of Scripture—in seeking to discern the mind of Christ;

- To oppose any action, statement, or policy leading to discrimination or violence against people based on sexual orientation.

The statement concluded,

> In welcoming all persons into the life of the BPFNA, we trust that the purposes of God in creation and in redemption will be fulfilled and that, ultimately, only grace—not merit, not correct opinion— assures us of a seat at the coming banquet of our Lord.

There are different and conflicting opinions as to whether the BPFNA board "backed off" from the convictions of the earlier statement. Members of the board did not think that they had done so. In an article, Executive Director Ken Sehested elaborated,

> We find ourselves in the midst of a major public controversy. And my heart is heavier than it's ever been. Why such anxiety? There have been other controversies. We took a very public stand against a very popular war in the Persian Gulf. We've engaged in acts of civil disobedience when convinced that holy obedience was at stake. There have been overseas trips involving a level of physical danger. So why the fearful heart now?

Because this subject is different. Simply raising the subject of homosexuality for discussion dredges up some of the most volatile passions in the human soul. Baptist journals that have rarely mentioned the BPFNA in 11 years now devote full editorials to our actions for gay and lesbian justice. Long-term friends threaten disaffiliation.

I've had nightmarish visions of 11 years of patient network building run aground and splintered, not to mention ambitious new plans for the future. It's not so much the withdrawal of financial support from the American Baptist Churches that poses a danger. From the beginning, we chose to develop a financial base of member support rather than rely on institutional funding. More threatening is the prospect of losing the confidence of mainstream Baptist leaders around the world with whom we work.

Given the tension often accompanying the question of sexual orientation, and the admittedly tenuous nature of our organization, it's fair to ask, "Why did the BPFNA board choose to wade into these troubled waters?" We have been interrogated both by those with principled convictions and those with pragmatic considerations. The latter warn us that we can't take on every issue; that we will lose the solid core of our constituency for involvement on issues of broader consensus.

Each of these objections and a few more, have been mental wrestling partners worthy of Jacob's angel at the Jabbok. Each has had not just one but several nights to work me over. Moreover, my personal passion rests in other arenas. Domestically, our cities are being wrecked by violence, often with racial overtones. Virtually every leading social indicator of human health in the African American community is lower now than when in the U.S. riots scorched our conscience a generation ago. Our addiction to guns needs attention from communities of faith. Fully one-fifth of U.S. children live in poverty.

The struggle of Cuba to be free of U.S. imperial designs has a grip on my imagination. Additionally, we have privileged conversation with Baptists in a dozen countries involved in leadership to mediate civil strife and in movements of nonviolent resistance to injustice.

Isn't all this at risk when you address the question of justice in relation to sexual orientation? Yes. Aren't you in danger of losing your credibility across the board for the sake of this one point of attention? Could be. And what about your efforts to show the connection between biblical faith and matters of justice and peace? Aren't you

*in danger of undermining that influence when you take a position in
apparent opposition to that of the Bible? That is a possibility.*

Then why take the risk? Don't all these other involvements
stretch your resources and threaten your existence enough, without adding the most volatile issue of all?[5]

Responding to the composite portrait of actual criticism, Ken argued, first,

[This] is, simply, the right thing to do. Matters of justice cannot be
segregated. Of course we have to make choices, live within time
and resource limitations. Often the hardest thing about our work
is deciding what not to do, for there are so many points at which
we could make a difference. Many of us, myself included, have resisted for too long speaking out on matters of simple human and
civil rights for gay/lesbian people.

Second, Ken argued that the controversy offered a "ready-made opportunity to practice our calling as reconcilers within our own household." Finally, he explored the issue of biblical authority and concluded
that the questions, "Is homosexuality compatible with Christian faith?" or
"Is heterosexuality compatible with Christian faith?" like "Uncircumcised,
or circumcised?" are not relevant. "To quote sacred Scripture, 'We believe
that we will be saved through the grace of the Lord Jesus, just as they will'"
(Acts 15:11).

Letters poured in to the BPFNA office in Memphis, Tennessee.
Several of these appeared on the pages of the next few issues of *Baptist
Peacemaker*. Writing "in the bond of peace," John F. Anderson, pastor
of Third Baptist Church in St. Louis, Missouri, affirmed, "our churches
should be welcoming and affirming places to all persons. . . . But we cannot call good what Scripture calls evil—not even with the pressures of gay
and lesbian persons at the end of the 20th century."[6] With less discussion
of biblical authority, Jeffrey W. Roop of China Spring, Texas, felt that the
BPFNA board had strayed from its main focus, "I'm disappointed in the
path taken by the BPFNA. It seems that the main thing is no longer the
main thing. Only in Christ is true peace found, not in agendas. I pray the

5. Sehested, "St. Peter and the Jerusalem Protocol." Highlighted sections in original.
See Appendix twelve for the full text.

6. *Baptist Peacemaker* 15:1 and 2 (1995) 11.

Fellowship will return to the source of peace."[7] With yet a third focus of objection, Gordon C. Bennett of Paoli, Pennsylvania worried, "I don't see why the BPFNA has to 'meddle' in the homosexuality issue when there are so many issues on the traditional peace agenda . . . [by spreading] yourselves thin and offending so many you lose effectiveness. There are others lobbying for the rights of gays and lesbians. The BPFNA doesn't have to cover everything."[8]

Others affirmed the board's statement and reacted negatively to the initial decisions of the American Baptists and Cooperative Baptists. Brenda J. Moulton of Attleboro, Massachusetts, wrote, "I have been meaning to join and *officially* participate in your efforts for peace. When I heard of your statement on justice for lesbian/bisexual/gay persons I pulled out an application form I had tucked away somewhere. When I heard about the action of the National Ministries Executive Committee I pulled out my *checkbook*! You're in my prayers!"[9] Another letter expressed disappointment by the action of the CoBF which continued to nurture a "homophobic mindset." For this writer who asked to remain anonymous, "I care little about anyone's sexual orientation. I am concerned only that we advance the cause of our Lord Jesus Christ by acts of social justice. If we do not come to terms with the true meaning of "love" and "justice," we will have missed the point entirely! Will Southern Baptists ever come together to vote a resolution of apology to gays and lesbians? I doubt it."[10]

In August, the Alliance of Baptists weighed in. Like BPFNA a progressive body, the Alliance of Baptists is a group of congregations and individuals who seek to listen for, and respond to the continuing call of God in a rapidly changing world. The board of directors of the Alliance unanimously adopted a resolution in which they noted, "our continuing support of the BPFNA. We join you . . . in encouraging dialogue . . . on issues of discipleship, justice, and peace, including human sexuality."

In October of 1995 the BNM's executive committee unanimously approved a motion to reestablish ties with the BPFNA, based on the May revisions. In January of 1996, a motion was introduced at the CoBF's Coordinating Council to reverse the July 1995 vote to rescind funding for

7. *Baptist Peacemaker* 15:3 and 4 (1995) 10.

8. *Baptist Peacemaker* 15:3 and 4 (1995) 11, emphasis in original.

9. *Baptist Peacemaker* 15:3 and 4 (1995) 10, emphasis in original.

10. *Baptist Peacemaker* 15:3 and 4 (1995) 11.

the BPFNA. That motion failed. A substitute motion was then approved that opened the door for case-by-case funding of specific projects.

The only other reaction received from leaders of Baptist mission bodies came from David Phillips, general secretary of Canadian Baptist Ministries. While BPFNA had received no direct funding from Canadian Baptist Ministries, there have been cooperative ventures, and Canadian supporters are allowed to make contributions designated for the BPFNA through that organization. In a November 1995 letter, Reverend Phillips wrote, ". . . you have made a statement on sexual orientation to which we as an organization can not agree. . . . To honor our constituency, we feel we need to register our disagreement in writing. . . ." He also indicated, "we want to continue our relationship with you."

The strategy of extensive dialogue over a number of years meant that several years passed before BPFNA became fully welcoming of all persons in the movement and affirming of them in every respect. Nonetheless, the dialogue was necessary as a prerequisite of bringing to birth a more inclusive movement, excluding nobody because of her or his sexual orientation or gender identity.

In keeping with a key provision of the May 1995 statement, the board encouraged dialogue by developing resources on the subject. Regularly, articles on the theme have appeared in *Baptist Peacemaker*. In 2004 the Associated Church Press commended the periodical for its "editorial courage" in publishing reflections by a heterosexual man who stood up for gay and lesbian brothers and sisters, people generally condemned by the church. "Reflections on Lynchburg II: The Return of Soulforce to 'Falwell Territory'" by Doug Donley, pastor of University Baptist Church (UBC) in Minneapolis, Minnesota, received an Award of Merit.[11]

LeDayne McLeese Polaski, newly appointed as BPFNA managing director, and Millard Eiland, member of the Alliance of Baptists, BPFNA, and BPFNA partner Covenant Church in Houston, Texas, co-edited *Rightly Dividing the Word of Truth. A Resource for Congregations in Dialogue on Sexual Orientation*, co-published with the Alliance of Baptists in 1997. Developed to assist clergy and lay leaders in leading healthy and respectful dialogue and discernment, *Rightly Dividing the Word of Truth* features wisdom distilled from thirteen congregations who have struggled with the questions of sexual orientation and Christian faith, Bible study and

---

11. *Baptist Peacemaker* 24:2 (2004) 16. Appendix thirteen reprints the article from the Summer 2003 issue.

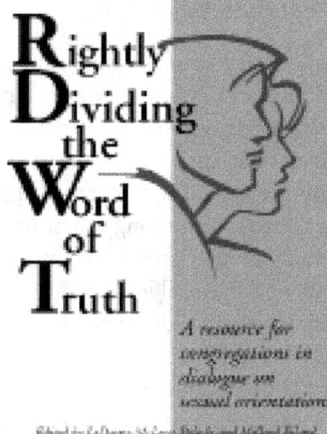

R ightly
D ividing
the
W ord
of
T ruth

*A resource for
congregations in
dialogue on
sexual orientation*

Edited by LeShawn McCray, Felicia and Michael Blount

theological reflection, studies from scientific, medical, and psychological perspectives, stories from gay and lesbian Christians, their families, and congregations, and an extensive, annotated bibliography.

At the time, the outcome was costly in terms of loss of finances, of members, and of key support within several partner bodies, as well as of stress on the staff. BPFNA lost nearly all connection to former Native American leaders and members, and some African Americans.

The controversy subsided, but hostility towards the BPFNA, and hatred of homosexual persons have not disappeared. Local Baptist associations have expelled BPFNA partner congregations because of their welcoming and affirming stance, while other congregations that might support BPFNA either by giving money, or by becoming a partner congregation do not because of BPFNA's proactive, inclusive stance. Once or twice every month, staff members have a conversation around this point.

Often, controversy surrounds possible BPFNA participation in gatherings of the wider Baptist family. In 2005, the Alliance of Baptists invited April Baker to preach at the start of its annual gathering. At the time, Baker was BPFNA board vice president and co-pastor of Glendale Baptist Church in Nashville, Tennessee. The Alliance asked Baker to share how the partnership model shapes her ministry with co-pastor Amy Mears and with Glendale's sister congregation in Santa Clara, Cuba, *Iglesia Bautista Alberto J. Díaz*. Members of the host congregation, First Baptist Church in Greenville, South Carolina, protested because of Baker's sexual orientation. Members of Glendale Baptist Church wrote the Greenville congregation. An excerpt of the letter follows:

> Upon learning the news that some in your congregation had reservations about opening your pulpit to our pastor . . . we were disheartened and sad. However, as we considered the situation more carefully, we imagined that surely there must be more at stake than we could see on the face of it. We sensed this because many of us have also been through the long, often painful, and heart-wrenching discernment about matters pertaining to the nature of Christian community and pastoral leadership. As you likely know we recently found ourselves struggling as a congregation regarding the role of gay and lesbian persons in the community of faith. This challenge faces many churches in our time, and none that we know have found any easy way to navigate the path. . . . We trust that your actions were not intended toward our pastor in any personal way, but rather were the consequence of your struggle as a congregation as you wrestled with large and very complex issues.[12]

In a statement, Baker asked for all voices to be heard. Jeff Rogers, pastor of the Greenville congregation, expressed gratitude for sensitivity by all the parties. The Alliance of Baptists moved its meetings to the campus of Furman University. Baker preached at the opening convocation and led a workshop.

In 2007, former President Jimmy Carter called on Baptists to discuss the importance of work Jesus holds up for followers to do in Luke 4:18–20. This led to planning a conference called the New Baptist Covenant to be held January 30–February 1, 2008 in Atlanta, Georgia. BPFNA members were to be involved, including Glen H. Stassen and me. The BPFNA asked if it could contribute as a partnering organization. The Alliance of Baptists made a similar proposal. On July 18, 2007, planners informed both organizations that their policy of including all persons irrespective of their sexual orientation threatened the unity of the New Baptist Covenant.

The BPFNA board responded by seeking to ensure that many voices were heard on crucial justice issues of the time. In a statement, the board encouraged its members and partner congregations to attend the event. Many did. As well, the board encouraged BPFNA members and other partners to participate in other programs in Atlanta that overlapped with the New Baptist Covenant.

12. *Baptist Peacemaker* 25:1 (2005) 6.

An estimated 15,000 people from eighteen Baptist denominations and organizations attended the New Baptist Covenant. Participants explored commonalities, developed new partnerships, and provided resources on ways by which Christians might impact the world from the perspective of the Bible's concern to promote justice by feeding the hungry, clothing the naked, sheltering the homeless, caring for the sick, welcoming the strangers among us, and promoting religious liberty and respect for religious diversity. Along with other exhibitors, BPFNA and the Alliance of Baptists both had displays.

A year later, controversy over BPFNA's welcoming and affirming spilled over to plans for the February 2009 international Baptist conference in Rome, Italy, of which the BPFNA is a co-sponsor. Because several of those planning the event have BPFNA ties, at least one person has indicated a desire to attend to disrupt the proceedings.[13]

Homosexual persons have achieved equality greater in Canada than in the United States. After 1999, Canada extended most legal benefits commonly associated with marriage to cohabiting same-sex couples. With the approval of the Civil Marriage Act on July 20, 2005, Canada became the fourth country in the world to legalize same-sex marriage nationwide. But Baptist groups in Canada have threatened to expel pastors who solemnize same-sex marriages or congregations which allow the blessing of same-sex marriages.

In *México*, neither same-sex marriage, nor civil unions are recognized by the federal government. Civil unions between same-sex couples are currently legal in Mexico City and in the State of Coahuila. Other states are considering a similar measure.

The controversy over welcoming into the BPFNA all persons of faith regardless of sexual orientation has engendered tens of thousands of words. For all the words, there is a deed floating somewhere, head down, and unborn. In themselves words do not make anything happen, no, not one prophetic word prayed, preached, or otherwise pronounced.

At numerous gatherings and in myriad publications peace and justice advocates call Baptists and others to action on grave issues such as child poverty, global warming, ending religious conflict and war, and food insecurity on the part of the world's poor majority. Such appeals will make

13. The person who apparently had that intent did not register after all. There were no problems at the conference. Email, Paul Hayes, July 29, 2009. For articles on the New Baptist Covenant, *Baptist Peacemaker* 27:4 (2007) 8; 28:1 (2008) 10; and 28:2 (2008) 8.

not one iota of difference unless people recognize their web of mutuality and show their love for God by loving self and neighbor. Every single one. Period.

ECONOMIC JUSTICE

"The foundation of peace is justice." This line in its statement of purpose has led the BPFNA to address in publications, workshops, and other venues actionable ideas by which Baptists could make the connection between economic justice and peace. As early as 1984, the idea of creating a "Gleaner's Fund" surfaced during an Executive Committee brainstorm that generated proposals for the newly-formed BPFNA. A passage in Leviticus provided a name for the suggestion: "When you reap the harvest of your land, you shall not reap to the very edges of your field, or gather the gleanings of your harvest; you shall leave them for the poor and for the alien: I am the Lord your God" (Lev 23: 22).

In 1996, Ken Sehested introduced a special issue of the *Baptist Peacemaker*. In an "admittedly modest" way, Sehested explored why people of faith should be concerned about scarcity and abundance. At a time when wealth is flowing from the poor and to the rich at a histori-cally unprecedented rate, Sehested wrote, many Baptists benefit from the paradigm of free-market capitalism. To seek to understand a world of ex-treme disparities between the poor and the rich is to confront a spiritual challenge. "We may discover that our religion, instead of being character-altering, is actually character-altered."[14]

In the United States during the mid 1990s, the administration of President Clinton introduced major legislation impacting public assis-tance programs. To find out how these changes were affecting people—particularly children—already living in poverty—BPFNA staff decided, instead of going to policy analysts and social workers, to ask the impov-erished people themselves how they were faring under the new system. Sixteen-year-old David Lane went to Caritas, an emergency assistance agency in Waco, Texas, to talk with recipients and get an idea from them about what it's like "out there." His report appeared in *Baptist Peacemaker*.[15]

14. Sehested, "Character-Altered Religion."

15. Lane, "How Grace Gut-Punched Me in English Class," Appendix fourteen. In 1998 the article was singled out for an Associated Church Press award. David now lives and works in New York City.

At the time David was a junior at Midway High School, an editorial assistant for *Seeds Magazine,* and a member of Seventh and James Baptist Church in Waco, Texas.

Ancient Israel developed this element of their faith. In Leviticus 25, the Jubilee codes mandated a profound redistribution of wealth every fifty years. The prophets and writers of wisdom literature affirmed God's special concern for the poor. In Luke 4:18–19 and elsewhere, Jesus spoke of a direct link between spiritual and social renewal. And Luke indicated that the earliest Christian community, in Jerusalem, held "all things in common; they would sell their possessions and goods and distribute the proceeds to all, as any had need" (Acts 2:44–45).

In October 1999, Sehested invited his former associate at *Seeds* magazine, Andy R. Loving, to make a presentation to BPFNA's board regarding community development investing. Sehested and Loving advocated advancing economic justice by crafting a mechanism by which BPFNA's constituency could invest in institutions which loan money to poor people. After discussion, the board authorized Sehested to explore the feasibility of developing a loan fund as a BPFNA project. The following spring, Sehested circulated a formal plan of action.

In June 2000, first the global networks committee and then the entire board discussed and approved the Gleaners Project. In creating the Gleaners Project, the board did not move into the finance business. Rather, it sought to offer one way by which BPFNA members might leverage a small portion of their assets to promote economic justice, articulate the outrage felt about the current ordering of values in the world, and partner with the poor who aspire to provide good nutrition, health care, and safety for their children.

Anyone could participate in the Gleaners Project by making an investment through one of several agencies, including Oikocredit which promised a return up to 2 percent on a minimum investment of $1000. Founded in 1975 by the World Council of Churches, Oikocredit has funneled more than $70 million of investments to worker-owned cooperatives and micro credit institutions. According to information BPFNA provided its membership, several factors contributed to its success. Oikocredit only financed productive investments which led to sustainable, income-generating activities. They financed groups, mostly cooperatives, not isolated individuals. They financed projects chosen by the borrowers, not by overseas consultants or government agencies. They financed activities which are feasible. They financed only when there is a grassroots commitment and a sense of ownership of the project. They emphasized women's participation at all levels, including management.[16]

By the time of the board's next meeting, Sehested reported that the Gleaners Project was projected to reach its initial goal of $200,000 before year's end.[17] During its first year, United States folk invested almost $1,000,000 with a variety of financial institutions. These included Oikocredit, based in Europe, and the Self-Help Credit Union, based in North Carolina. Another partner, the Calvert Foundation, provided a conduit for capital to a variety of non-profit organizations in the United States and around the world. In sum, the project focused on granting loans to low income residents for housing and economic development as well as working nationally on low-income housing mortgage markets.

Because of regulations, BPFNA could not provide to its Canadian and Mexican members a direct mechanism for this kind of investing. However, Oikocredit had representatives in Canada and in *México*. Staff provided information on how to contact these offices or other community development organizations in both countries.

Despite tangible support on the part of nearly two hundred individuals and several congregations, the project engendered controversy. Some of the concerns related to financial oversight, timelines, what could be viewed as mission, rather than a peacemaking project, and the relative merits of several community development agencies which have long histories of making strategic loans for maximum impact.

After the end of 2002, when Ken Sehested left the office of Executive Director, the Gleaners Project ceased to have a board or staff champion for the project. Still, contributing BPFNA members have continued to invest in their accounts. These funds are seeds of peace. The fund enables poor people to get micro enterprise loans, small business loans, and non-profit financing. The project also advances human rights and democracy.

In 2006 the Norwegian Nobel Committee awarded the Nobel Peace Price to Muhammad Yunus of Bangladesh and Grameen Bank "for their efforts to create economic and social development from below." In making this award, the Nobel Committee affirmed that lasting peace can not

---

16. BPFNA, *Gleaners Project*, Brochure.
17. Press release, November 2, 2000.

be achieved unless large numbers of people find ways to break out of poverty.

> Every single individual on earth has both the potential and the right to live a decent life. Across cultures and civilizations, Yunus and Grameen Bank have shown that even the poorest of the poor can work to bring about their own development.
>
> Micro-credit has proved to be an important liberating force in societies where women in particular have to struggle against repressive social and economic conditions. Economic growth and political democracy can not achieve their full potential unless the female half of humanity participates on an equal footing with the male.
>
> Yunus's long-term vision is to eliminate poverty in the world. That vision can not be realized by means of micro-credit alone. But Muhammad Yunus and Grameen Bank have shown that, in the continuing efforts to achieve it, micro-credit must play a major part.[18]

The Gleaners Project is one of several economic-justice initiatives which the BPFNA has supported. Lee McKenna has done economic literacy training with a focus on health care at Oakhurst Baptist Church in Decatur, Georgia and at Pullen Memorial Church in Raleigh, North Carolina. Since the mid-1990s the BPFNA has lifted up the Jubilee campaign. Jubilee 2000 was a global, ecumenical effort focused not only on convincing developed countries to forgive debt owed by poorer nations. Even with the progress made on debt relief in the past dozen years, the JubileeUSA network continues to advocate on behalf of the majority of the world's poorest nations which are still mired in a debt crisis.

During an August 2000 board meeting, BPFNA endorsed the "Covenant of Poverty." A coalition representing a wide range of denominations and faith-based organizations in the United States, Call to Renewal, developed the document. *Baptist Peacemaker* published the text and encouraged *all* readers—but especially those in the United States—to endorse and use the document for discussion and education in local congregations. The Covenant of Poverty read, "The persistence of widespread poverty in our midst is morally unacceptable. Just as some of our religious forbears decided to no longer accept slavery or segregation, we decide to

18. Online http://nobelprize.org/nobel_prizes/peace/laureates/2006/press.html.

no longer accept poverty and its disproportionate impact on people of color."

In the biblical tradition, by entering into this covenant, signatories resolved to give priority to people who are poor through prayer and action. Financial choices were to be decided in ways which promote economic justice, evaluate public policies and political candidates by how they impact people who are poor, nurture the bonds of family and community and protect the dignity of each person, and organize across barriers of race, denomination, and social boundaries in common commitment and action to overcome poverty in local communities, the nation, and the world.[19]

The BPFNA board and staff have encouraged the membership to work for economic justice in yet ways. For example, the board created a mechanism in the spring of 2008 for United States taxpayers to give part of their tax refunds away. The board urged United States taxpayers to take a Jubilee Pledge for economic justice. It read, "As a disciple of Jesus, I pledge to participate in God's Jubilee economics by returning half my U.S. tax rebate to the poor."

The project grew out of a United States government economic stimulus package. Adult taxpayers received a rebate of up to $600 ($300 per dependent children). Some 130 million families and individuals received tax rebate checks from the Internal Revenue Service. Those who signed the Jubilee Pledge called BPFNA offices or registered at www.bpfna.org/jubilee. This enabled the office to track responses. Individuals gave to a veterans group, the Judicial Process Commission, a Food Bank, a program for low-income people, a homeless shelter, a Catholic Worker House, a group which holds a six-week summer day camp for low-income neighborhood children, a group which offers housing for homeless people.

A number of partner congregations took up the pledge. For example, Lake Avenue Baptist Church in Rochester, New York suggested people designate their checks to the church for their refugee work. Members of First Baptist Church in Madison, Wisconsin gave over $20,000 to the church. These funds were used to house three local families and to provide support for ABCUSA International Ministries, for those returning to their communities from incarceration, and for rebuilding the Gulf Coast following Hurricane Katrina.

19. *Baptist Peacemaker* 20:3 (2000) 17; a presidential election was taking place at the time in the United States.

In Minneapolis, UBC members supported a visit to the United States of six members of their partner congregation, Second Baptist Church, in Leon, Nicaragua. This relationship was established in 1992. Over the years, members of the two congregations sent letters and pictures back and forth. UBC established a Godparent program by which they "adopted" students by providing scholarships for their primary school. In 2003, a delegation of six from UBC spent ten days in Leon as guests of the sister congregation. In 2008, UBC members donated portions of their economic stimulus checks to enable six members of the Leon congregation to visit the United States. UBC pastor Doug Donley observed,

> We worked hard to give them a balanced (and enjoyable) view of US American life. We took them to a feeding program—a very important thing for them to do as they packaged food for people in third world countries suffering from malnutrition, like so many of them have. We also took them on our church retreat, giving us all a good opportunity to know each other. The retreat was on their second weekend and toward the end of the visit. They saved up their hardest questions of us for that experience. They wanted to know about our Welcoming and Affirming status, how we got there and how they could be as inclusive as we were in a culture of such machismo as Nicaragua. It was a fascinating discussion that we wanted to have happen but didn't know how to facilitate. I guess the Holy Spirit intervened and gave us an opportunity to see each other and celebrate each other. As they left us, loaded down with donations for their church and school, we also gave them a quilt that we had created during their stay to remember the ways that our lives intertwine and shelter each other from the storms of our lives. That quilt is now on the wall of their church . . . We are a richer community because of the trip. We look forward to the next trip, possibly in the winter of 2010.[20]

BPFNA partner congregation Binkley Baptist Church in Chapel Hill, North Carolina, has supported Jamkhed, a Comprehensive Rural Health Project in rural communities in the State of Maharashtra in Western India. The project builds the capacity of communities for sustainable development in such areas as education, health, organizing women to combat

20. Donley, "Welcoming Guests: A Sister Church Delegation Experience." The full *Model Ministry* is part of Appendix eleven.

domestic violence, watershed management to conserve water and reduce soil erosion. One village has planted a million trees.[21]

In keeping with its role of nurturing action for a culture of peace, the board has promoted myriad other concrete economic-justice ideas such as purchasing fair-trade products, or using a popular resource which draws on a sermon of Dr. Martin Luther King, Jr., "Why Jesus Called a Man a Fool," delivered at Mount Pisgah Missionary Baptist Church in Chicago, Illinois on August 27, 1967,

> Maybe you haven't ever thought about it, but you can't leave home in the morning without being dependent on most of the world. You get up in the morning, and you go to the bathroom and you reach over for a sponge, and that's even given to you by a Pacific Islander. You reach over for a towel, and that's given to you by a Turk. You reach down to pick up your soap, and that's given to you by a Frenchman. Then after dressing, you rush to the kitchen and you decide this morning that you want to drink a little coffee; that's poured in your cup by a South American. Or maybe this morning you prefer tea; that's poured in your cup by a Chinese. Or maybe you want cocoa this morning; that's poured in your cup by a West African. Then you reach over to get your toast, and that's given to you at the hands of an English-speaking farmer, not to mention the baker. Before you finish eating breakfast in the morning you are dependent on more than half of the world.[22]

In terms of aligning its annual budget of over several hundred thousand dollars with its commitment to justice, the BPFNA moved its funds nearly ten years ago into a deposit account of the Self-Help Credit Union. The institution is headquartered in Durham, North Carolina. Since its founding in 1980, Self-Help has reached out to female, rural, and minority borrowers across North Carolina, in Washington DC, California, and many other states. Providing financing, technical support, and advocacy for those left out of the economic mainstream, the Credit Union has had long-term relationships with religious organizations, non-profits, and other socially responsible individuals and institutions. In accord with its mission statement, the Credit Union provides funds to low-income, supposedly high-risk borrowers for local community development organiza-

21. Gates, "Jamkhed."

22. King, *Knock at Midnight*, 151–52; *Baptist Peacemaker* 23:3 (2003) 10; http://www .forusa.org/fellowship/may-june_06/GlobalBalance2.html.

tions, such as Habitat for Humanity which helps provide homes for the working poor. As well, the Credit Union has also waged a fight against predatory lending. Self Help is now opening a federal credit union in California so they can help out with the mortgage disaster there.[23]

WORKING WITH PEOPLE OF OTHER FAITHS

BPFNA friendship visits, development projects, and opposition to several wars in eastern Europe, Africa, and the Middle East have created opportunities over a period of nearly twenty years for engaged Baptists to form relationships with Muslims. In 2002, BPFNA launched the Christian-Muslim Peace Initiative, a pioneering venture to nurture cooperative efforts among Baptists and Muslims.

BPFNA and the Muslim Peace Fellowship (MPF) share a common history of relationship with FOR. Founded in 1994, the MPF represents a gathering of Muslims of all backgrounds who are dedicated to making the beauty of Islam evident in the world. MPF members believe,

> that personal example is the only convincing argument for the truth of any religion. Since the particular business of Muslims is to emulate the model of the Holy Prophet (peace and blessings be upon him), who was sent as *a mercy to the worlds*, our main concern must be to learn and teach the integrity and kindness that were his chief characteristics. And since the Creator of the Universe asks us, at the beginning of every act, to call to mind God's benevolence and compassion, we know that these qualities must be the primary hallmark of any full realization of Islam. We are consciously devoting ourselves to work toward that realization.[24]

According to Mas'ood Cajee, a writer living in Stockton, California and a MPF board member, "There are over a dozen places around the world where either Muslims or Christians [are being] killed in some form of Muslim-Christian conflict." This sobering fact challenges the conscience of adherents of all religions alike.

In North America, the Muslim community rejected the ideology of Al Qaeda that led to the events of September 11, 2001. Muslims and Baptists open to dialogue began collaborating in two initiatives. The first

23. Broadway, "A Report on the Self-Help Credit Union." Email, Evelyn Hanneman, December 8, 2008. Update at www.self-help.org.

24. MPF brochure; also, *Fellowship* 60 (May 1994) and http://mpf21.wordpress.com/about-2/.

was to organize jointly workshops and gatherings at which members of the two faith communities could begin to listen to each other. MPF and BPFNA co-sponsored the first joint training workshop in conflict transformation at Dearborn, Michigan. During April 12–14, 2002, participants learned skills for conflict transformation and cross-community bridge-building, explored the roots of peacemaking in the Koran and Bible, and began to develop meaningful relationships across religious lines.[25]

Participants and leaders of both organizations are planning additional joint conflict transformation sessions. Also in 2002 the BPFNA and MPF jointly published *Peace Primer*, a collection of quotes from Christian and Islamic Scriptures and tradition edited by Ken Sehested and Rabia Terri Harris.

The Olive Branch Interfaith Peace Partnership (OBIPP) and the Tent of Abraham, Hagar and Sarah, a group of Jews, Christians, and Muslims who have met together since 2003, are the principal settings within which BPFNA and MPF members continue to work together. OBIPP has united several organizations in working together to end the United States led war and occupation of Iraq, to support the troops, to support an Iraqi-led peace process and peace with Iran, to say NO to torture, and to say YES to justice. According to an OBIPP statement, "Together we can end the war in Iraq and bring our troops home. Together we can stand against fear and violence, and live into a longing for wholeness that unites us across all boundaries. Together we can offer a path toward reconciliation. Together we can learn to build security through right relationships[26]

OBIPP has partnered with an interfaith group called "The Tent of Abraham, Hagar, and Sarah" to initiate a dialogue through common study of a guide, *Rebirthing King, Rebirthing America: Celebrating the 80th Birthday of Reverend Dr. Martin Luther King Jr. as a New American Government Takes Office*. The immediate goal is that over a hundred congregations across the nation will use this resource for four weeks in anticipation that the first hundred days of the new government in the United States will see significant progress against the "giant triplets of racism, extreme materialism, and militarism" identified by Dr. King in his April 4, 1967 Riverside Church speech "A Time to Break Silence."[27]

25. Buttry and Cajee, "Christian/Muslim Peace Training Initiative Launched."
26. Online: http://olivebranchinterfaith.org/.
27. Washington, *Essential Writings*, 240; OBIPP, *Rebirthing King*, 19.

BPFNA is a member of the Christian Peace Witness for Iraq, a coalition of various Christian peace fellowships and other peace groups. This is from the first event on March 16, 2007 when participants worshipped at the Washington National Cathedral and then walked to the White House for a candle light vigil. About 4,000 people gathered in Washington DC despite a major snow storm that hit the East Coast of the United States.

One of the extraordinary fruits of the Christian Muslim Peace Initiative launched in 2002 is that BPFNA and MPF members are now working out an action proposal for multi-religious visioning of the future. Success or failure will ultimately determine if we humans abandon sharing life together on our planet earth.

In a powerful scene in the 1937 film *Shall We Dance?* Fred Astaire and Ginger Rogers wonder if they should call off their relationship. They dance on rollerskates and sing about their differences pronouncing certain words. Is it neether, or niither, tomahto or tomeyto? They conclude, "We need each other so, it doesn't matter."[28]

To overcome intolerance, to fight the greed and inequality brought on by economic globalization, and to respond to terrorism, we need each other so much. It really does matter that BPFNA members have expanded

28. Online: http://www.youtube.com/watch?v=s0ce1agpBVM.

their understanding of peacemaking to include not only gender identity and economic justice, but also working together for peace and justice with interfaith partners. In each arena, BPFNA has encouraged people of faith to relate biblical texts to concrete reality and to act not on the basis of fear, but with nonviolent strategies and lifestyles.

REFLECTIONS

Peacemaking entails willingness on the part of several parties to enter into situations of conflict rather than withdrawing passively trying to calm troubled waters, save face, or refuse to fight. Makers of peace must commit themselves to several practices of reconciliation: absorbing assault without resort to revenge, dialoguing empathetically with people who have views which are poles apart, welcoming these differences, listening with openness to having one's mind changed, and partnering with them.

In 1693, a member of the Religious Society of Friends, or Quakers, described "true religion" as inclusive, albeit rooted in many traditions. William Penn (1644–1718) wrote:

> The humble, meek, merciful, just, pious, and devout souls are everywhere of one religion; and when death has taken off the mask they will know one another, though the divers liveries they wear here makes them strangers. The world is a form; our bodies are forms; and no visible acts of devotion can be without forms. But yet the less form in religion the better, since God is a Spirit: for the more mental our worship, the more adequate to the nature of God; the more silent, the more suitable to the language of the Spirit.[29]

I was raised in a family of mixed Orthodox Christian and Jewish backgrounds. In the spring of 1958, I heard Billy Graham preach at the Cow Palace, made a faith-profession, and joined Valley Baptist Church, a congregation which became, after several mergers and moves, Shell Ridge Community Church Walnut Creek, California. Upon graduation from high school, I attended the University of California at Berkeley, returning to Walnut Creek some weekends in order to worship at Valley Baptist Church.

Through those years, especially after Bishop Robinson wrote about being "honest to God" and other theologians received attention for writ-

29. Online: http://thinkexist.com/quotation/the_humble-meek-merciful-just-pious_and_devout/332483.html.

ing about the "death of God," I wrestled with faith issues and connected faith with politics. I disagreed, for example, with a Sunday school teacher who asserted that capital punishment is an instrument of divine punishment or, in 1960, that a Catholic president would be an abomination.

Our college and careers group discussed peace and war and several of us, students at U.C. Berkeley, refused to participate in drills practicing how we would survive in the event of a nuclear attack. We also protested mandatory Reserve Officers' Training Corps.[30] We opposed the growing presence of the United States presence in Vietnam.

We did not, however, talk about sex or money, nor did we seek dialogue with people of different religions. At least in my memory. Was that in fact the case? Or was I selective in how I received a Gospel word which might prove embarrassing or life-changing in values?

In 1965 I participated in a summer project in Chad through Operation Crossroads Africa. Founded in 1958 by Dr. James H. Robinson, the organization encouraged participants to "make a difference for others, see the difference in yourself." One of the inspirations for creation of the Peace Corps, Operation Crossroads has continued to enable young people to build bridges of friendship to Africa, with Africans.[31]

The experience of participating in Chad in a work camp expanded my understanding of fundamental principles for building a just, sustainable, and peaceful global society. Three years later, I returned to Africa. Indirectly, the experience also led me to seek out FOR and the BPF. Since 1967 when I joined both organizations, I have sought to integrate teaching, research, and practical action as essential elements of engagement to eradicate war at its root causes: intolerance, racism, economic injustice, post-colonial colonialism, environmental injustice, and other seeds of violence.

Much remains to be done to overcome homophobia, economic injustice, and lack of mutual understanding among peoples of different faiths. In these and so many other areas, we must repent, as Dr. King wrote in his *Letter from Birmingham Jail*, "not merely for the vitriolic words

---

30. In 1965, the Board of Regents finally abolished compulsory ROTC. Accessed December 10, 2008; Online: http://www.alumni.berkeley.edu/Alumni/Cal_Monthly/September_2004/Recalling_Cal.asp.

31. Online at http://www.operationcrossroadsafrica.org/indexI.and.php.

and actions of the bad people, but for the appalling silence of the good people."[32]

Members of FOR and BPFNA have been in the forefront of efforts to address these roots of violence and war. With Robert Kennedy, who addressed an audience at the University of Capetown in South Africa on June 6, 1966, I resonate with his affirmation that,

> It is from numberless diverse acts of courage such as these that the belief that human history is thus shaped. Each time a man stands up for an ideal, or acts to improve the lot of others, or strikes out against injustice, he sends forth a tiny ripple of hope, and crossing each other from a million different centers of energy and daring those ripples build a current which can sweep down the mightiest walls of oppression and resistance.[33]

As we move to conclusion of this study, chapter seven assesses an observation that the coupling of *Baptist* and *peace* is an oxymoron. God is love (1 John 4:8). Made in God's image, love is the reason for our existence. Affirming this fundamental biblical insight, Baptist peacemakers do "seek peace and pursue it" (Ps 34:14), through building blocks for a culture of peace.

32. Washington, *Essential Writings*, 296.

33. Online: http://www.mtholyoke.edu/acad/intrel/speech/rfksa.htm.

7

Where Do We Go From Here?

WHERE DO WE GO FROM HERE?

T HE TITLE OF THIS last chapter derives from the last book by Dr. Martin Luther King, Jr. In the subtitle of the book Dr. King suggested two possible alternative futures, *chaos or community*. He argued that the nations of the world could continue to refuse to work with unshakable determination to wipe out the last vestiges of racism. They could continue to ignore those conditions of poverty, insecurity, and injustice which are the fertile soil in which seeds of totalitarian governments and revolutionary movements grow. Likewise they could continue to spend more money on military defense than on programs of social uplift. Alternatively, people could come together and construct a "world house," his phrasing for a culture of peace.

For Dr. King, building a world house was not simply a matter of strategy or rhetoric. He envisioned an effort radically to restructure the architecture of society. Such an undertaking could not occur it grew out of a revolution of values. To overcome the evils of racism, poverty, and militarism, economies around the world would have to become more person-centered than property- and profit-centered. Governments would need to depend more on their moral power than military power. Ordinary people would learn to accept limitations, both personal and structural, work within them, and come to understand that we are all interdependent. Dr. King cited what changes would be needed for humankind to begin to move in the right direction:

> . . . In the final analysis . . . [an] intelligent approach to the problems of poverty and racism will cause us to see that the words of the Psalmist—"The earth is the Lord's and the fullness thereof;"

[Ps 24:1 KJV] are still a judgment upon our use and abuse of the wealth and resources with which we have been endowed.

A true revolution of values will soon cause us to question the fairness and justice of many of our past and present policies. We are called to play the Good Samaritan on life's roadside; but that will be only an initial act. One day the whole Jericho road must be transformed so that men and women will not be beaten and robbed as they make their journey through life. True compassion is more than flinging a coin to a beggar; it understands that an edifice which produces beggars needs restructuring.[1]

Fast forward to 2009, the year in which this book first appears. Ours is a time of multiple challenges not unlike those faced by Dr. King. In North America, these include the need for changing lifestyles, healing the land, arresting climate change, and addressing the realities of hunger, poverty, and war.[2] Dr. King's vision of a world house and his call for a revolution of values are as relevant as ever. If humanity is to survive the clear and present dangers that exist, we must mobilize for change and create something new, a culture of peace.

The edifice on which the prosperity of some in North America depends is crumbling as if hit by a powerful earthquake such as that which occurred on December 26, 2004, with its epicenter off the west coast of Indonesia, triggering a devastating tsunami along the coasts of most landmasses bordering the Indian Ocean and killing more than 225,000 people in eleven countries, or by a powerful hurricane such as Katrina which, on August 29, 2005, caused severe destruction along the Gulf coast from central Florida to Texas.

We are not able to ignore the problems. Nor can we surrender to the status quo. What specific changes in lifestyle and values are needed if we going to live after the crumbling of empires? After oil supplies have peaked and other natural resources are no longer available? After the effects of global warming no longer adversely affect simply the polar bear population of the Arctic and a few islanders in the South Pacific?

In words of the World Social Forum, another world is possible. Since 2001, community organizers, trade unionists, young people, academics, and others have been meeting to rethink and recreate globalization for the

---

1. King, *Where Do We Go from Here*, 187–8; also King's April 4, 1967 address in Washington, *Essential Writings*, 241.

2. For a summary, see Worldwatch Institute, *State of the World 2009*.

benefit of all people. Having attended one forum in Caracas, Venezuela in 2006, I am strengthened in my conviction that civil society organizations such as BPFNA and FOR have a crucial place in building a culture of peace on foundations Dr. King and others have characterized as positive peace. Describing a certain kind of peace, which is not merely the absence of war, Toni Morrison has offered, in a 1996 speech accepting the National Book Foundation medal for her distinguished contribution to letters, the arresting image of the dancing mind:

> The peace I am thinking of is not at the mercy of history's rule, nor is it a positive surrender to the status quo. The peace I am thinking of is the dance of an open mind when it engages another equally open one—an activity that occurs most naturally, most often in the reading/writing world we live in. Accessible as it is, this particular kind of peace warrants vigilance. The peril it faces comes not from the computers and information highways that raise alarm among book readers, but from unrecognized, more sinister quarters.[3]

Rather than being gripped by fear or overwhelmed with despair at threats in sinister quarters, we can begin to address the challenges. We can construct a world house. We can build a culture of peace. Fortunately, the work is not mine to do alone. I am part of the church and an even larger company of peacemakers worldwide. We need each other for inspiration, nurture, and glimpses of God's power to open windows into a new world in which humans concentrate on learning ways to dwell together in peace.

Throughout its history, the BPFNA has formed strategic partnerships with numerous organizations committed to peace and justice. These partnerships have proven mutually beneficial for both organizations and have enhanced our efforts to build a culture of peace rooted in justice. In a recent statement, the BPFNA board reaffirmed its intentional and longstanding relationships with organizations with common mission and values. The board expressed the expectation that partner organizations will collaborate on projects that are consistent with the mission and core values of both organizations. They will continue to share resources and information mutually beneficial to the shared work of the partner organizations, exchange information and recommendations regarding potential

3. Morrison, *Dancing Mind*, 7–8.

staff, board or committee members, and inform the respective membership about resources available through the partner organizations.

The BPFNA currently recognizes several partner organizations: Christian Peacemaker Teams, Churches Supporting Churches, the Fellowship of Reconciliation (FOR), Christian Peace Witness for Iraq, and the Olive Branch Interfaith Peace Partnership. At times the BPFNA chooses to engage joint initiatives with these, and other organizations. As well, routinely the board endorses various peacemaking projects, events, and initiatives of these, and other organizations. These endorsements do not require any type of collaboration or work by the BPFNA, but are consistent its core values and mission. Examples include the New Baptist Covenant or Pace e Bene, whose workbook *Engage* is intended to help readers to tap into their own power and make the positive changes needed to improve one's own life, and that of the community of which you are a part.

What ingredients are essential to the work of building a culture of peace? Glen Anderson heads Olympia chapter of FOR. A colleague on the governing body of FOR in North America, Glen suggests three pathways by which to move forward. First and with specific reference to the United States, we must stop antagonizing other people. Second, we must practice the values which we preach. And finally, we must create more justice in the world.[4]

STOP ANTAGONIZING OTHER PEOPLE

It would be a sobering exercise for citizens of the three countries which form the core constituency of BPFNA to reflect on what it would mean for members of our countries to end enmity which other members of our countries feel towards some of our compatriots. How quickly a nation which depended on one enemy to fuel its sense of purpose replaced it with another: Iraq for the former Soviet Union, the world of Islam for the Communist world. How engraved in our mental DNA are the attitudes Anglophones and Francophones in Canada have for each other. How infrequent it is that aboriginal and non-aboriginal people in each country come together on the basis of genuine mutuality.

In the period after Iraq invaded Kuwait in August 1990, peacemakers around the world sought to avert escalation of the Gulf crisis right up to

4. Email, November 24, 2008.

January 16, 1991, the day the United States began bombing Iraq. The day before, January 15, the BPFNA organized a service of prayer for peace in the Middle East at First Baptist Church in Washington DC. Among speakers, the Reverend Jesse Jackson offered this prayer:

> Forgive us for our sins and our foolish ways. In this dreary hour of cynicism and fear, be a light unto our paths. And through it all make us a better people, not a bitter people. Lead us forward by hope and not backwards by fear. Bless the prophetic urgency embodied by those who called this meeting. Bless all who have ears to hear and a will to come together, as we seek to bring the Kingdom right here on earth—a peace without end, as it is in heaven.
>
> Touch the hearts of Presidents Bush and Hussein today. Steer them away from the tragic night of war and terror. There is a way. There is a balm in Gilead. There is possibility. Let us choose this hour to take the high road that lives might be spared, that we might have a sense of redemption and renewal. We know, as we fast and pray as you have taught us to do, that if we have the faith, you have the power. Amen.[5]

Through the duration of the war, I lived in Oxford, England, where a group of us formed the Oxford Movement for Peace in the Middle East. We reached out to Muslims and sought to develop joint, culturally-sensitive approaches to several initiatives. These included attempts to negotiate the release of westerners detained in Iraq, organizing public demonstrations, and efforts to lobby British government officials.

One action was to mail a film canister to the White House. Made to look like a 55-gallon drum of oil, the canister featured the words "no blood for oil." The oil canister idea came out of FOR staff discussions about graphic ways to oppose the war. FOR adopted and widely disseminated it through the religious peace fellowships, including BPFNA, and local chapters. It was featured in news stories about opposition to the war.[6]

In response, I mailed a photo canister and a postcard to President George H. W. Bush, and the card to Saddam Hussein. Provided by BPFNA, the card appealed for a negotiated settlement and offered the following prayer, which I prayed daily:

> O God, you fill the universe with light and love. In you we live and move and have our being. We pray for Saddam Hussein and

5. *Baptist Peacemaker* 11:1 (1991) 1.
6. Richard Deats, email, December 4, 2008.

George Bush. Enlighten their minds and fill their hearts with the power of your creative love. Guide their actions so that all civilians and soldiers in the Persian Gulf area are protected from the sufferings of war. Inspire their decisions so that the crisis in the Middle East is resolved peacefully, and all people of the world learn to walk in ways of justice, love and peace. Amen.

None of these undertakings had any discernible impact on the march towards war. As a result, when the war broke out in January 1991, I experienced tremendous despair and isolation. My wife Nancy, son Matthew, and I came up with a simple idea. We set a candle of peace in a window. Daily, I lit it and prayed for the war to end.

One day, the Spring 1991 *Baptist Peacemaker* issue arrived. It included the remarks of Jesse Jackson, a "Call to Prayer and Fasting," and other action suggestions. Around the same time, Nancy and I received a letter from Beverly Donald, a colleague on the board and a dear friend. Beverly brought us up to date on family news and then asked,

> What must it have been like being "over there" during the Gulf war? I can't imagine. We seem so far removed over here—a quick, clean swat for a nasty pest. Will we ever know the havoc we have wrought? I have been so depressed about it. I marched around the Federal Building carrying a "no blood for oil" placard. I mailed film canisters made to look like a 55 gallon drum of oil with the same words on it to Bush, Foley, whomever—all to no avail. Now it's over and we will probably never know of all the "collateral damage." We first guess at it and the numbers are so high we can't comprehend. How many miles will the Iraqi (Vietnam) War Memorial Wall extend to include all the names?[7]

In a powerful way, Nancy and I realized that we were not alone. Before, during, and after the war, we were part of one of the largest social movements in history. With millions and millions of people around the world, we sent a clear message to our governments in London, Ottawa, Washington DC, and elsewhere that we did not want war and, after the war broke out, that we wanted the war to end.

Were our protests all to no avail? If the only basis of measuring our efforts as successful had been achieving our initial goal, we failed. We did not prevent the war. Thousands of civilians and soldiers were killed in the immediacy of war. The conflict has continued for years, first through

7. Beverly Donald to Nancy and Paul Dekar, April 6, 1991.

application of sanctions against Iraq, and then, after September 11, 2001, in an invasion that toppled Saddam Hussein and resulted in the occupation of Iraq by western countries. What began with a response to the invasion of Kuwait on August 2, 1990 by the military forces of Iraq has morphed into a war against terror seemingly without an end in sight.

Again in October 2002, citizens of the United States said no war in my name. Again on February 15, 2003, people around the world joined one of the largest coordinated global demonstrations in the history of the world. Ten million people from more than sixty countries sent a clear message to Washington DC and other capitals of the world to say no to war against Iraq in our name. Again, the voice of the global peace movement seemed irrelevant as the second Bush administration appeared to ignore us.

However much governments have ignored, ridiculed, or actively subverted the "no" of millions of ordinary people around the world, time and time again activists have insisted that we stop antagonizing those with whom we need to find a way to at peace one with another. If indeed we are bound up together, we can only walk together along one pathway into a shared future. This much we can do in response to a challenge in our sacred text, the Bible, to love neighbor as self and God. We can accept each other's rights. We can respect even those whom culture characterizes as enemy. We can purge whatever fear, racism, or stereotypes we have of the other from our being. We can work mutually to find durable solutions to challenges facing all our communities. We can be peace. There is no way to peace. Peace is the way.

PRACTICE THE VALUES THAT WE PREACH: BUILD COMMUNITY

In North America, many of us inhabit cultures marked by values of consumption, accumulation, and endless economic growth. These values ultimately are the root cause not only of many wars, but also of our deepening environmental crisis. We cannot easily abandon our "culture of more" without some form of community.

Recent, insightful analyses identify the loss of community as a fruit, or consequence of extreme individualism and run-away materialism rampant in North American society. *Bowling Alone*, a sociological study by Robert D. Putnam, reports that from 1980 to 1993, the total number of

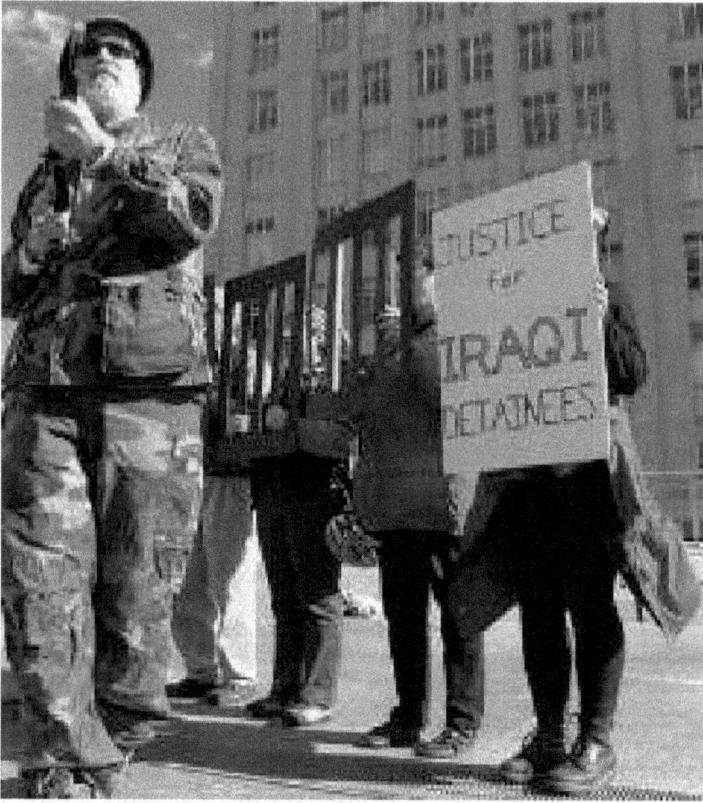

*Canadian BPFNA members participated in Toronto street theater in
opposition to the continuing detention without due process
of Iraq detainees*

bowlers in the U.S. increased by 10 percent. But league bowling decreased
by 40 forty. This is not trivial. In 1994, 80 million Americans bowled at
least once weekly, nearly a third more than voted in congressional elections that year. About the same number attended church regularly. For
Putnam, people bowling by themselves signals the decline of connec-
tional or associational life, seen as the heart of civic culture in the United
States ever since Alex de Tocqueville reported in *Democracy in America*
in the 1830s.

Putnam's findings raise four questions. First, what has happened to
civic engagement and social connectedness since the 1960s? Putnam reports that it has declined, as evidenced by the loss of community, compassion, a sense of civic culture, and a commitment to the common good.

Second, why has this happened? Putnam argues that changes in family structure, time pressure, suburban sprawl and, especially, television are the main culprits. Since he first published his findings, another factor has been the use of internet.

Third, so what? I believe Putnam's findings reveal patterns in our society which are damaging to our health and to the well-being of our communities.

Finally, what is to be done? My answer to this final question entails a very simple strategy: build community. We can create secular intentional communities which are sustainable at the local level, for example eco villages or cohousing neighborhoods which combine the cultural given that we occupy private homes with some of the benefits of cooperative living such as common facilities and many connections with neighbors.[8]

We can also create spiritually-grounded intentional communities. An example of a new wave of intentional Christian communities is Rutba House in Durham, North Carolina. Part of a network of communities of Christians who think that Christians in Western society have accommodated too easily or too completely to the consumerist and imperialist values of North America, the members of Rutba House have responded to a call to enter more deeply into the pain of the world.

In June 2004, Rutba House hosted a gathering of friends from around the country to discern the shape of a radical movement called the New Monasticism. Out of the gathering came a book. Introduced by Jonathan R. Wilson, who holds the Pioneer McDonald Chair in Theology at Carey Theological College in Vancouver, British Columbia, the book offers strategic guidance for the movement. The new monasticism is diverse in form and characterized by these twelve marks:

1. Relocation to the abandoned places of Empire.

2. Sharing economic resources with fellow community members and the needy among us.

3. Hospitality to the stranger.

4. Lament for racial divisions within the church and our communities combined with the active pursuit of a just reconciliation.

5. Humble submission to Christ's body, the church.

8. One website http://www.cohousing.org/.

6. Intentional formation in the way of Christ and the rule of the community along the lines of the old novitiate.

7. Nurturing common life among members of intentional community.

8. Support for celibate singles alongside monogamous married couples and their children.

9. Geographical proximity to community members who share a common rule of life.

10. Care for the plot of God's earth given to us along with support of our local economies.

11. Peacemaking in the midst of violence and conflict resolution within communities along the lines of Matt 18.

12. Commitment to a disciplined contemplative life.[9]

Participants in the network which has birthed the New Monasticism are not unified by a shared theological tradition, or denomination, but rather by the wisdom of a shared legacy, and a vision of a spirituality which can shape the Christian life in postmodern society. Another New Monastic community is the Community of the Transfiguration in the State of Victoria, Australia. The Resolve of the Community of the Transfiguration states,

> Being perfectly assured of your salvation, with your whole life proclaim your gratitude to the non-violent God.
> Reject nothing, consecrate everything.
> Be the good of love, for God, for neighbor, for all creation.
> Judge no one, not even yourself.
> Love beauty.
> Maintain inner-silence in all things.
> Show hospitality, err only on the side of generosity.
> Speak truth to power, especially power without love.
> Let your only experience of evil be in suffering, not its creation.
> To breathe peace into the world, first disarm your own heart.
> For us there is only the trying, the rest is none of our business.[10]

9. Rutba House, School(s) for Conversion, xii–xiii; Wilson-Hartgrove, New Monasticism; Claiborne, Irresistible Revolution; www.newmonasticism.org.

10. Dekar, Community of the Transfiguration.

Where Do We Go From Here?

On my filing cabinet is a magnet which explains how to build community, a crucial value that has been, over the years, central to members of BPF and BPFNA

Turn off your TV
Leave your house
Know your neighbors
Look up when you are walking
Greet people
Sit on your stoop
Plant flowers
Use your library
Play together
Buy from local merchants
Share what you have
Help a lost dog
Take children to the park
Garden together
Support neighborhood schools
Fix it even if you didn't break it
Have pot lucks
Honor elders
Pick up litter
Read stories aloud
Dance in the street
Talk to the mail carrier
Listen to the birds
Put up a swing
Help carry something heavy
Barter for your goods
Start a tradition
Ask a question
Hire young people for odd jobs
Organize a block party
Bake extra and share
Ask for help when you need it
Open your shades
Sing together
Share your skills
Take back the night
Turn up the music
Turn down the music
Listen before you react to anger

Mediate a conflict
Seek to understand
Learn from new and uncomfortable angles
Know that no one is silent though many are not heard. Work to
change this.[11]

Over the years, through its gatherings, programs, publications, and other resources, BPFNA has made available resources for community building. *Shalom for the Earth*, a guide for making ecological decisions about lifestyle and the environment, appeared in the November-December 1989 issue of *PeaceWork*. *Giving Good Gifts,* an issue of *PeaceWork* with ideas and resources for avoiding the malls, appeared in 1993. Those with access to the BPFNA website can purchase books such as a *The Better World Shopping Guide* by Ellis Jones.

CREATE MORE JUSTICE IN THE WORLD

In 1985, reflecting on their travels in the USSR, Dawn Kirk Butler and Michael Butler asked, "In our efforts to prevent a nuclear holocaust, we must ask ourselves: Hasn't World War III already begun? As long as people are dying of hunger, poverty, and other needless reasons, a war is being waged. The money which could feed and clothe people is buying weapons."[12]

How can we create more justice in the world? Drawing on words of Baptist peacemaker Howard Thurman in a BPFNA bookmark, one place to start is to pursue the work of Christmas,

> When the song of the angel is still, when the star in the sky is gone, when the Kings and princes are home, when the shepherds are back with their sheep, the work of Christmas begins: to find the lost, to heal the broken, to feed the hungry, to release the prisoner, to rebuild the nations, to bring peace among people, to make music in the heart.

This quote is offered not as a rhetorical flourish, but a simple insight. We need not re-invent the wheel. We simply need to keep on doing what BPFNA members, along with millions of peacemakers around the world, have been doing all along: saying no to war, creating community, working for justice, finding the lost, healing the broken, feeding the hungry,

11. Online: http://blog.perfectspace.com/2008/08/10/how-to-build-community/.
12. Butler and Butler, "Peace Mission to USSR," 5.

releasing prisoners, rebuilding the nations, bringing peace among people, and making wonderful music, as at BPFNA peace camps and other gatherings.

As part of their commitment to building a culture of peace, world leaders adopted on September 8, 2000 a "United Nations Millennium Declaration" which made problems engendered humans the object of broad and sustained efforts to create a shared future, based upon our common humanity in all its diversity. Not only did the UN Millennium Summit create goals for the global community, but it also set up the deadlines of 2015 to achieve these goals. These are the Millennium Developments Goals:

Goal 1:   Eradicate extreme poverty and hunger

Goal 2:   Achieve universal primary education

Goal 3:   Promote gender equality and empower women

Goal 4:   Reduce child mortality

Goal 5:   Improve maternal health

Goal 6:   Combat HIV/AIDS, malaria and other diseases

Goal 7:   Ensure environmental sustainability

Goal 8:   Develop a Global Partnership for Development

These lofty goals are the aspirations of leaders who realized that they were facing the harsh realities of a crowded planet. We can turn these fragile—and as yet unfulfilled—global commitments into real solutions. Yet three huge challenges make realization of these goals by 2015 unlikely. First, lofty statements notwithstanding, the full cooperation and commitment of world leaders to achieve these goals are lacking. Second, market capitalism as an economic system is inadequate. Finally, a radical transformation—the building of a tradition of peace spirituality—is only beginning to emerge needed to underpin or motivate creation of a new kind of economy and governance which are sustainable and can serve the needs of all creation.[13]

In the immediate aftermath of September 11, 2001, Tama Ward Balisky former BPFNA board member and a pastor in Vancouver, British Columbia wrote an article, "So that All May Lie Down in Safety." First

---

13. Sachs, *Common Wealth*, 12; Galtung and MacQueen, *Globalizing God*, 184–87.

published in the *Social Concerns Newsletter* of the Baptist Union of Western Canada, the article appeared in 2002 and again in 2005 in *Baptist Peacemaker*. Reflecting on the example of Jesus, no pie-in-the-sky idealist, Balisky offered several suggestions. We must live more simply. We must love our enemies. We must hang out with a praying community which has the courage to follow new pathways in building a culture of peace.[14]

REFLECTIONS

In his introduction to *For the Healing of the Nations, Baptist Peacemakers*, historian Martin E. Marty observed that the coupling of *Baptist* and *peace* is an oxymoron. Yet BPFNA is a reality. Its work is a source of great hope. Along with its birth-mother the FOR and civil society organizations around the world, the BPFNA is contributing to a global movement of limits, of deep dependence on God, and of a culture of peace.

Newly-formed in 1984, the BPFNA charged Ken Sehested to find Baptist peacemakers around North America. Sehested discovered that Baptist peace and justice groups were active around the world. Speaking in Sweden in 1988 at the first international Baptist peace conference, he asked, "Are we facing a new moment in Baptist history?" Was the time ripe for Baptists not simply to hold conferences or to create an informal global Baptist peace network, but to be open to a tremendous outpouring of the Spirit at a pivotal moment in history.[15]

In January 1990, just two months after the fall of the Berlin Wall on November 9, 1989, I participated as a Canadian Council of Churches delegation similar to those sponsored by the BPFNA. I listened as a pastor from the German Democratic Republic (East Germany) expressed sentiments of East Europeans generally, "We want to share our joy and our challenge. This is a time not for slogans but for hard work. The road ahead is difficult. We need a new vision for the people. We need a new vision for the world."[16]

Along with these witnesses, I believe that people of God—by which I mean *all* people of God, not just Baptists, not just Christians—need to be enlisted to help end regional wars, to control, reduce, and eliminate nuclear stockpiles, to overcome racism and economic injustice, to address

14. Balisky, "So That All May Lie Down in Safety," *PeaceWork* 4–5 (1999).
15. Sehested, "Are We Facing a New Moment in Baptist History?"
16. Dekar, "For Peace and Reconciliation."

the dire threat humanity confronts with climate change, and to respond to these and other challenges with a new spirituality for the work.

Nearly three decades after the first Baptist friendship tour to the Soviet Union, nationalism and intolerance are once again on the rise in the region. The Doomsday Clock, which conveys how close humanity is to catastrophic destruction—the figurative midnight—and monitors the means humankind could use to obliterate itself is set at five minutes to midnight, the closest since 1984. This recognizes, first and foremost, that the United States, its European allies, and the former Soviet Union retain vast arsenals of nuclear weapons, but the danger also encompasses climate-changing technologies and new developments in the life sciences which could inflict irrevocable harm.[17]

Through its ongoing commitment to organize friendship visits, to organize peace camps, conferences, and other gatherings, to print excellent publications, and to sustain other projects, BPFNA is able not only to support peacemaking efforts around the world, but also to inspire future peacemakers with a new vision for building a culture of peace, not slogans, but practical skills and a deep spirituality. Both are needed to address the challenges of the next generation.

The future of the world rests squarely in our hands. We cannot wait for divine intervention. We cannot wait for the world leaders. We cannot even expect others to take the lead. We have to do something ourselves. In the words of Gandhi, "We must be the peace we want to see in the world."

There is an inscription dating around 1100 of the Common Era on the tomb of an Anglican Bishop in Westminster Abbey. It reads as follows:

> When I was young and free and my imagination had no limits, I dreamed of changing the world. As I grew older and wiser I discovered the world would not change—
> So I shortened my sights somewhat and decided to change only my country, but it too seemed immovable. As I grew into my twilight years, in one last desperate attempt, I settled for changing only my family, those closest to me, but alas, they would have none of it. And now I realize as I lie on my deathbed, if I had only changed myself first, then by example I might have changed my family. From their inspiration and encouragement I would then

17. Online: http://www.thebulletin.org/content/doomsday-clock/timeline.

have been able to better my country. And who knows, I might have even changed the world.[18]

No less than in 1939, when formation of a BPF was being discussed, or in 1984 when Baptist members of two denominations, the Southern Baptist and American Baptist Conventions, came together to talk about creating a new organization, Baptist peacemakers are needed to put on whatever sandals or shoes are available to enable us to proclaim the Gospel of peace (Eph 6:15).

There are limits to what we can do. Some singularly harebrained ideas have not worked out. During May 7–9, 1987 in Granville, Ohio, BPFNA steering committee and the planning committee of the New Call to Peacemaking, a cooperative program of the Historic Peace Churches, met together. It was a joyous and productive meeting. This little circle of Christian peacemakers dared to think of the year 2000 as being a time free from war and nations directing their resources to eradicate poverty, hunger, and injustice in the world.

Fired up, I shared the idea with my family, with members of MacNeill Baptist Church in Hamilton, Ontario, and with classes. In my own wildest dreaming, I thought that, if BPFNA could attract one half of 1 percent of North American Baptists, perhaps 300,000 Baptist peacemakers, we could make significant progress towards marking the year 2000 as a year of peace for a millennium of peace. I could imagine our singing something equivalent to "Solidarity Forever," Ralph Chaplin's union song

> When the Union's inspiration through the workers' blood shall run,
> There can be no power greater anywhere beneath the sun.
> Yet what force on earth is weaker than the feeble strength of one?
> But the Union makes us strong.
>
> Chorus...
>
> In our hands is placed a power greater than their hoarded gold,
> Greater than the might of armies, magnified a thousand-fold.
> We can bring to birth a new world from the ashes of the old
> For the union makes us strong.

Not one part of the vision has worked out. At no time has the BPFNA ever attracted the kind of numbers which would have supported a broad movement of people transforming war-making society in which I live

18. Online:http://robbinquotes.blogspot.com/2007/01/inscription-on-tomb-of-angli can-bishop.html.

into a culture of peace. Especially discouraging, the end of the Cold War with the collapse of the former Soviet Union and its empire was not accompanied by a corresponding move to creating a culture of peace. The first Gulf War and the wars in Afghanistan and Iraq have further restored my healthy sense of reality.

Despite promising steps at the end of the Cold War to reduce the number of nuclear weapons, many thousands of weapons are still deployed, and doctrines allowing for the first use of nuclear weapons still exist, including the possible use of nuclear weapons against non-nuclear countries. Perhaps we need to move towards creation of a Baptist development and relief organization, as once proposed by Robert Broome. He had in mind something like the American Friends Service Committee, the Mennonite Central Committee, or Brethren Service Committee. More recently, Gary Percesepe, Coordinating Director from 2004–2006, advanced the idea of creating a Baptist Peace Institute.[19]

Are these idle dreams? What could have been more hair brained than the dream of BPFNA founders seventy years ago that two world wars should give way to a time of peace and reconciliation? In those days of a so-called "great war" and "good war," those who said no to violence were cursed and jailed, scorned, and avoided by many. That has always been the fate of prophets.

Back in the 1960s, churches did not necessarily support the Civil Rights movement. In the last year of his ministry Dr. King faced enormous opposition within the very movement he had led to unexpected success. Similarly, one of BPFNA's greatest success stories—support for the Naga and Burma peace processes—has been conspicuous for the fact that the role of the churches in both contexts has been far less than it could have been. The voices of the prophets have been ignored by the majority of their own peoples.

Fear for the future should not hold us back. In *A Return To Love: Reflections on the Principles of A Course in Miracles*, Marianne Williamson writes,

> Our deepest fear is not that we are inadequate. Our deepest fear is that we are powerful beyond measure. It is our light, not our darkness, that most frightens us. We ask ourselves, Who am I to be brilliant, gorgeous, talented, fabulous? Actually, who are you *not*

19. Gary Percesepe, "Three Ways BPFNA Partner Congregations Can Make a Difference."

to be? You are a child of God. Your playing small doesn't serve the world. There's nothing enlightened about shrinking so that other people won't feel insecure around you. We are all meant to shine, as children do. We were born to make manifest the glory of God that is within us. It's not just in some of us; it's in everyone. And as we let our own light shine, we unconsciously give other people permission to do the same. As we're liberated from our own fear, our presence automatically liberates others.[20]

Essential to our work to end the scourge of war and to build a culture of peace is a deep spirituality of justice and peace. Writing at a time when North Americans faced oil shortages, hostage-taking, and economic turmoil, Baptist theologian E. Glenn Hinson observed,

> It is in prayer, in the true sense, that God breaks through the cloud of covetousness and greed which hovers over human civilization and reorders our priorities and commitments. The frightening economic recession which looms ahead of us may be the opportunity God will seize to shake westerners free from the mindless self-indulgence and to slap them awake from their pitiless unconcern about starving masses on the rest of the globe. It may provide also the occasion for all of us to find that prayer is a friend on whom the future of mankind depends.[21]

It has been a half a millennium since 1527 when our South German and Swiss Anabaptist foremothers and forefathers declared, concerning the sword,

> Christ . . . Himself forbids the violence of the force of the sword when He says: "the princes of this world lord it over them etc., but among you it shall not be so." [Matt 20:25] Further Paul says, "Whom God has foreknown, the same he has also predestined to be conformed to the image of his Son," etc. [Rom 8:30]. Peter also says: "Christ has suffered (not ruled) and has left us an example, that you should follow in his steps." 1 Pet 2:21[22]

At the end of *Radicals*,[23] George Williamson, Jr., suggests such work is costly, sometimes boring, often bruising and painful, usually risky, nearly always discouraging, and certainly opposed by the mainstream of society,

20. Williamson, *A Return to Love*, 165. Emphasis in original.
21. Hinson, "Prayer in an Economy of Abundance," 93.
22. Yoder, *Schleitheim Confession*, 15.
23. Williamson, *Radicals*, 72.

now and historically. Peacemakers trying to follow Jesus more faithfully know all about that. But they also know in the certainty of conscience that they are linked arm to arm with the great ones in their eternal march toward the coming day when,

> They shall beat their swords into plowshares,
> And their spears into pruning hooks;
> Nation shall not lift up swords against nation,
> Neither shall they learn war anymore. (Isa 2:4; Mic 4:3)

Asking who or what we picture as needing to be done to achieve this vision of the ancient prophets, can BPFNA continue to sustain Baptist peacemakers in their work of creating a culture of peace? Wendell Berry answers this question in a poem, in which he suggests that we honor those whose stories we become not by going back. Rather, we have become like a tree standing over a grave. And so, he concludes,

> Now more than ever you can be
> generous toward each day
> that comes, young, to disappear
> forever, and yet remain
> unaging in the mind.
> Every day you have less reason
> not to give yourself away.[24]

However small in numbers or reviled, Baptist peacemakers have for seventy years been building a new world of forgiveness, respect for human rights, and the practice of nonviolence. While we have a long way to go before we see this dream become reality, Baptist peacemakers are building a culture of peace through a truly interracial and international community. On this journey, we not only imagine peace. We seek to be peace.

24. Berry, *Collected Poems.*

AFTERWORD

LILIANE KSHENSKY BAXTER

O**N THE SECOND FLOOR** of the Martin Luther King, Jr. Center for Nonviolent Social Change in Atlanta, where I worked for over a dozen years, sat a table-sized matchstick diorama composed of bridges and suspended walkways that curved and twisted around each other ultimately converging at the top into a display of symbols from the world's religions: a cross, a crescent, a star of David, a spinning wheel, and so on. I loved to follow with my eyes these matchstick bands to their triumphant ends, as much for their playfulness as for their careful crafting, and would nod each time I read the title on the side: "The Many Roads to Heaven."

Reading this book gives me that same pleasure. As a Jewish pacifist and member of the Jewish Peace Fellowship (JPF), reading about the Baptist Peace Fellowship of North America (BPFNA), its history and accomplishments, fills me with great enjoyment and spiritual sustenance. For, despite our different religious practices, we hold in common what matters most, I believe. We share a commitment to activism rooted in the values of nonviolence, and have reached, through our separate paths and distinct religious traditions, a similar vision of a just and peaceful world created and sustained by just and peaceful means.

"We make the road by walking," a wise person once said. That is particularly true of practitioners of nonviolence. For a few thousand North American Baptists committed to pacifism, this has meant charting a course where none existed before, not only within the Baptist faith itself but also in the realm of social change. In association with the interfaith Fellowship of Reconciliation-USA, it exists in ongoing engagement with a broader community of practical mystics that spans the Americas, Europe, Asia and Africa through the International Fellowship of Reconciliation (IFOR).

Indeed, the BPFNA, the JPF, and other religious peace fellowships associated with FOR-USA and IFOR are all members of a larger global movement composed of thousands of non-governmental organizations that, in service to a global vision of peace and reconciliation, have harnessed their imaginations, energies and hearts to connecting across what seem to many others as insurmountable differences in religion, ideology, ethnic identity, nationality, and race. How fortunate for us that they exist.

What glad memories are evoked when reading about Ken Sehested and his good work in formally establishing the BPF at Oakhurst Baptist Church in Atlanta. When white folks were a rarity, Ken was at the King Center at Mrs. King's side. I remember many King Week commemorations where his spry and gracious presence added so much to the programs and activities.

Most recently, the Atlanta Fellowship of Reconciliation (FOR-Atlanta) was revived at Oakhurst, with its senior pastor, Lanny Peters, giving us his blessing. Lucas Johnson, a member of the national council of the Baptist Peace Fellowship and a pastoral intern at Oakhurst, was one of the chief organizers.

My first visit to Ramallah, on the West Bank, was with Lanny Peters. We were both members of an interfaith group from Atlanta—eleven Christians, eleven Muslims, and eleven Jews, World Pilgrims as the group is called—travelling together through the Holy Land and charged with bringing back to our hometown insights and understandings from our collective journey to the birthplace of each of our religions.

Ramallah was hot, dry, dusty; even the few trees were gray. Lanny and I sat together on the touring bus as it wound its way through the narrow streets. From the bus window we saw broken buildings, idle men and ragged children. Lanny and I had used the ride from Jerusalem to talk about our work, our hopes, and our dreams. We had learned, to our mutual delight, that we were both members of the Fellowship of Reconciliation.

The day before, our group had visited Yad Vashem, the Holocaust memorial and museum in Jerusalem—a more recently-established holy site in a country replete with sacred buildings, groves, rocks, and waters. I had been asked to speak about my family, since both my parents were Holocaust survivors from Poland, and I had been born in a displaced persons camp in Sweden after the war. So, I recounted something about my parents's happy lives in Krakow before the war, about their little son, Daniel, and about the close-knit family within which they both had lived and thrived. Then, the war came and the terrible Nazi persecutions. At the age of three, Daniel was torn from my mother's arms and herded, along with my grandmother and two young cousins to Auschwitz. She never saw them again. My mother survived countless concentration camps, as did my father, who was saved by the Red Cross from Bergen Belsen at the end of the war, and nursed back to health in Sweden.

The next day our group was in Ramallah, former home to Yasser Arafat, his PLO headquarters now in ruins. Equal claims to the same small parcel of land had, over the years, escalated into an intractable conflict between two otherwise sage and noble religious cultures. The cycle of killings had left both populations traumatized, violated, distrustful and defensive, with most people on both sides increasingly convinced that a lasting peace was but a naïve and distant dream.

Despite these intractable conditions, the peace activists on both sides—too often reviled and misunderstood, especially by their own—continue their courageous work. They promote contact and friendship between people from all sides of the conflict. They provide ongoing humanitarian relief, monitoring of human rights abuses, early warnings of potentially violent conflicts, nonviolence training, and conflict resolution. They are my own, our own, true heroes.

War is not the answer; neither is violence. There's got to be a better way. For those of us who feel the weight of our times, who have known intimately, *familialy*, the horrors of war, working for cultures of peace in our homes, our towns, our nations, and the world has become a powerful antidote to despair and a major motive for being. In partnership with each other, we experiment with truth, and struggle together across racial, religious, ethnic and national boundaries to the greater truths of nonviolence. Yes, working for peace can be dangerous sometimes, tedious sometimes, but always transformative. As Martin Luther King Jr. understood, working for the Beloved Community is never for naught, for "the arc of the moral universe is long, but it bends towards justice."

Naomi Goodman, *may her memory be a blessing*, served for many years as the secretary of the Jewish Peace Fellowship. Her description of its work—"bringing pacifism to the Jewish community, and Judaism to the peace community"—captures equally well the role played by the Baptist Peace Fellowship within the greater Baptist tradition, as the book in your hand amply illustrates. May our Fellowships long flourish.

Happy reading. Hopeful futures. Peaceful tomorrows. Thank you, Paul Dekar, for bringing this important history to us all.

Appendix 1

Officers

Years	President	Treasurer	Secretary
1940–1941	Edward C. Kunkle	Al Hassler	Ruth E. Murphy
1941–1942	Edwin T. Dahlberg	Ruth E. Murphy	
1942–1944	Lilburn B. Moseley	Dorothy Hassler	
1944–1946	Gene E. Bartlett	Ronald V. Wells	
1946–1947	Ronald V. Wells	Bruce G. McGraw	
1947–1948	John W. Thomas	not a matter of record	
1948–1949	Lee A. Howe, Jr.	Margaret G. Macoskey	
1949–1953	not a matter of record		
1953–1954	Philip G. Van Zandt	William M. Hammond, Jr.	
1954–1958	Harold V. Jensen	William M. Hammond, Jr.	
1958–1961	Charles R. Bell, Jr.	William M. Hammond, Jr.	
1961–1962	Edwin T. Dahlberg	Lillian Robertson	
1962–1964	Carl W. Tiller	Lillian Robertson	
1964–1966	Victor H. Gavel	Martha Beardsley	
1966–1968	John W. Laney	Martha Beardsley	
1968–1970	John C. Zuber	Martha Beardsley	
1970–1972	A. E. Lacy, Jr.	Martin England	
1972–1973	Jerry Catt	Beverly Donald	
1973–1975	Robert W. Tiller	Beverly Donald	
1975–1977	Dona M. Reddy	Beverly Donald	
1977–1981	Olive Tiller	Beverly Donald	
1982–1983	Richard Newell Myers	Beverly Donald	
1984	George Williamson, Jr.	Beverly Donald	
1985	George Williamson, Jr.	Beverly Donald	
1986	George Williamson, Jr.	Beverly Donald	

1987	George Williamson, Jr.	Beverly Donald	
1988	George Williamson, Jr.	Beverly Donald	
1989	George Williamson, Jr.	Beverly Donald	
1990	George Williamson, Jr.	Beverly Donald	
1991–1992	George Williamson, Jr.	Beverly Donald	Rachel Gill
1993–1994	George Williamson, Jr.	Beverly Donald	Eugene McLeod
1995–1997	Glenda Fontenot	Beverly Donald	Eugene McLeod
1998	Glenda Fontenot	Beverly Donald	Eugene McLeod
1998–1999	Steve Hammond	Beverly Donald	Isobel Docampo
2000	Steve Hammond	Beverly Donald	Daniel Hunter
2001	Lindsay Penn-Matheson	Beverly Donald	Paul R. Dekar
2002	Lindsay Penn-Matheson	Beverly Donald	Amy Coursen
2003	Lindsay Penn-Matheson	Beverly Donald	
2004–2005	Bob Paterson-Watt	Beverly Donald	Jeanette Quick
2006	Leslie Withers, Wendy Scott	Tom Bryson	Karen Hilliker
2007	Wendy Scott	Tom Bryson	Karen Hilliker
2008	Stephen D. Jones	Tom Bryson	Karen Hilliker

APPENDIX 2

Peace Camps

Dates	Location	Theme
June 30–July 5, 1986	Green Lake, Wisconsin	Announcing the Reign of God
July 6–11, 1987	Asheville, North Carolina	Be of Good Cheer
July 4–9, 1988	Atlanta, Georgia	Love Your Enemies
July 10–15, 1989	Keuka Park, New York	Prisoners of Hope
July 2–7, 1990	Ottawa, Ontario	Justice and Peace Will Embrace
July 1–6, 1991	McMinnville, Oregon	Be Not Afraid
June 29–July 4, 1992	Roanoke, Virginia	The Earth Is the Lord's
July 26–31, 1993	Birmingham, Alabama	Walk Together Children
July 4–9, 1994	Granville, Ohio	We've Come This Far by Faith
July 10–15, 1995	Redwood City, California	Fools in the Eyes of the World
July 8–13, 1996	Waterloo, Ontario	And a Child Shall Lead
July 21–26, 1997	Harrisonburg, Virginia	Disarming the Heart
July 27–August 1, 1998	Richmond, Indiana	Proclaim Jubilee
July 19–24, 1999	Vancouver, British Columbia	Building a Culture of Peace
July 10–15, 2000	Winston-Salem, North Carolina	On Earth as It Is In Heaven
July 9–14, 2001	Oberlin, Ohio	For Such a Time as This
July 22–27, 2002	Wolfville, Nova Scotia	To Sing among the Peoples
July 14–19, 2003	Keuka Park, New York	With Such a Cloud of Witnesses
July 19–24, 2004	Towson, Maryland	The Stones Will Cry Out
August 1–6, 2005	McMinnville, Oregon	For the Healing of the Nations
July 10–15, 2006	Atlanta, Georgia	Becoming the Beloved Community
July 23–28, 2007	Berea, Kentucky	As the Powers Fall
July14–19, 2008	Ste. Anne de Bellevue, Quebec	The Way that Leads to Peace
July 20–25, 2009	Ogden, Utah	When There Is Justice, Then Peace Will Come!

Appendix 3

Friendship Tours

Dates	To	Led by	Report
1984	Soviet Union	Priscilla Inkpen, E. Glenn Hinson	BP 4, 3 1984
1985	Soviet Union	Paul Hayes, Chuck Mercer	BP 5, 3 1985
1986	Nicaragua	Doug Donley	PW 5–8 1986
1986	Soviet Union	Kaye Cooper, Howard Roberts	PW 9–10 1986
1987	Nicaragua	Doug Donley	PW 5–8 1987
1987	East Europe	Paul C. Hayes	PW 1–4 1988
1988	Nicaragua	Sandra George and John Detwyler	PW 7–10 1988
1988	East Europe	Dick and Beth Myers	PW 7–10 1988
1988	Estonia, Latvia, USSR	William Apel and Mark Trumbo	PW 7–10 1988
1989	Nicaragua	John Detwyler	PW 3–4 1990
1989	Southwest Virginia	Kim Christman and Stan Dotson	BP 10 1–2 1990
1990	Cuba	Roger and Ruth Crook	BP 1–2 1990
1990	Soviet Union	Cliff Cain and Gene Ton	BP 10, 3–4 1990
1990	Panama, Guatemala	Jim Lowder	
1990	South Africa	G. McLeod Bryan	
1990	Nicaragua	Mary Anne Forehand	
1991	El Salvador	M. Mahan Siler, Jr.	BP 11, 2 1991
1992	Cuba	Jualynne Dodson	BP 12, 2 1992
1992	El Salvador	LeeAnn Purchase	BP 12, 3–4 1992
1992	Nicaragua	John and Sandra Detwyler	BP 12, 3–4 1992
1994	Puerto Rico	Luis Collazo	BP 14, 3–4 1994
1995	Burma/Myanmar	Paul C. Hayes	BP 15, 1–2 1995
1996	*México*	Lázaro Gonzalez	BP 16, 2 1996

Friendship Tours

1997	Liberia	Napoleon Divine	BP 17, 2 1997
1998	East North Carolina	LeDayne Polaski	BP 18, 3 1998
2000	*México*	LeDayne Polaski	BP 20, 2 2000
2000	Puerto Rico	LeDayne Polaski	
2005	Israel/Palestine	Fellowship of Reconciliation	
2008	Nicaragua	LeDayne Polaski	BP 11–12 2008

Appendix 4

International Projects

1. May 1996: sponsored dialogue in between grassroots peacemakers in Chiapas, Mexico and Nicaragua and subsequently supported *SIPAZ*

2. September 1996: sponsored nonviolence/reconciliation training in Rwandan refugee camps in Zaire (now the Democratic Republic of Congo).

3. November 1996: organized an Intensive Training Conference on Conflict Resolution held in Chiang Mai, Thailand. Over 70 church leaders from 14 countries in Asia and the Pacific attended this training sponsored by the Asian Baptist Federation.

4. December 1996: sponsored and provided nonviolence training for Chin refugees from Burma (Myanmar) living in India.

5. 1996 through 2001: provided funding for two mediation initiatives related to ethnic insurgencies in Burma (Myanmar) and to launch in 2001 a church-based peace center, the Shalom Foundation in Burma (Myanmar).

6. February 1997: sponsored and funded nonviolence training in through the Christian Center for Peace and Reconciliation in Oyo State, Nigeria.

7. April 1997: sponsored and organized grassroots dialogue in southern Mexico, including the state of Chiapas, between Catholics and evangelicals to expose the issues leading to violence and to explore paths of reconciliation. The process sparked the formation of a joint Protestant-Catholic theological institution doing grassroots education related to the southern Mexican context.

8. May 1997: led conflict transformation training workshops in Liberia for over 125 participants and facilitated founding of the Liberian Baptist Peace Fellowship.

9. 1997 through 2001: sponsored and facilitated peace talks between Naga insurgent groups and civil society groups in Northeast India. In November 1999, the development of a comprehensive strategy led to the "Journey of Conscience," a nonviolent people-to-people campaign that took place in January 2000. BPFNA maintains ties with key parties.

10. 1997: provided scholarships for students enrolled in the Peace and Conflict Studies Program at the Diakonia College, Nairobi, Kenya.

11. 1997: provided funding support and consultation services to a mediation team seeking to negotiate a peaceful settlement to a brewing political crisis that threatens civil war in an African country.

12. 1997: provided support for conflict resolution courses at the Martin Luther King Institute of the Polytechnic University in Managua, Nicaragua and funding for a gathering of grassroots conciliation commission members for dialogue and training through *CEPAD*.

13. 1998: provided assistance to the nonviolence training projects of the *Institut de Recherche pour la Paix* in Kinshasa, Congo.

14. 1998: sponsored a seminar for over 50 participants on conflict transformation in conjunction with the Union of Baptists in Latin America in Guatemala City, Guatemala.

15. January 1998, April 1999, and January 2000: over a thousand books valued at $15,000 were sent in three shipments in to a total of forty institutions in 22 countries.

16. June 2000: sponsored and led conflict transformation and reconciliation training for the Ethiopian-Eritrean Peace Conference in Michigan followed by similar events in Toronto, Ontario in November 2000, and Washington DC in June 2001. Participants were Ethiopians and Eritreans living in the United States and Canada.

17. March and April 2000: led training of church and community leaders in conflict transformation in Northeast India.

18. Jan 200l: a grant enabled the Shalom Foundation of Burma (Myanmar) to organize six trainings on conflict transformation throughout the country.

19. January 2001: led trainings on conflict transformation with pastors and youth leaders in Indonesia.

20. March 2001: sponsored and financed conflict resolution and reconciliation training of Rwandan pastors.

21. May 2001: led and funded training on conflict transformation for church leaders from across Africa in Cameroon.

22. 2001: sponsored conflict transformation training in Indonesia.

23. 2003 and 2004: sponsored conflict transformation training in Philippines.

24. 2003: funded consultation in Ghana of Christians participating in peace talks for Liberia.

25. 2005–2008: supported conflict transformation training in Sudan.

26. 2006: assisted Ruth Mooney, serving in Costa Rica with International Ministries of the American Baptist Churches USA, in the publication of a multi-leveled curriculum entitled *Building a Culture of Peace*.

27. 2007: Lee McKenna represented BPFNA at the graduation of the first class from the new indigenous seminary in Chiapas and led conflict transformation training.

28. In addition, BPFNA staff and members have participated in delegations to Croatia (1992), Iraq (1989, 2001), Cuba (1990–2008), and other countries.

APPENDIX 5

Two Prayers

"A PRAYER FOR THE WORLD" by Lee McKenna[1]

Oh Holy One, Spirit God,
You, who satisfies the hungry heart
You, who provides words to poets:
Oh God of the Exiles

We are your people;
we feel that this is no longer our home
we're not sure at all that we like life
on the edge . . .
We know too well the threat of the cross;
we have glimpsed the danger of the resurrection;
we have taken tentative steps on Jubilee's road to costly liberation.
And . . . we're not sure we like it.

How can we sing the Lord's song?

The happy tunes of a gospel of certitude
and privilege
have long been dissonance to our ears.
Yet still we feel the urge to hang our harps on trees:
Jubilee is hard saying!
Who can hear it? Who can accept it in this culture of Seinfeld and
SUVs and self-cleaning appliances
and not feel offence?
But yet, we know, deep in ourselves,
that you do hold the words of life.

1. In October 1999, Lee McKenna, a member of the BPFNA board, international organizer for peace and justice, and an interim pastor in Toronto, Ontario delivered this prayer at Oakhurst Baptist Church, Decatur, Georgia. It appeared on the cover of *Baptist Peacemaker* in the Spring of 2000.

APPENDIX 5

We see your church in fetal position,
desperate to protect what it used to be
its running after order
in a disordered world,
its race for Easter without Good Friday ...
And your poets yearn.
Widows and orphans die in the streets ...
canaries in coalmines;
The IMF and the World Bank and the WTO organize our debts
oblivious to Jubilee.

We stand in the 49th year:
The people of Kosovo and of East Timor cry
for their return
to the lands of their ancestors
The people of Aceh and West Papua dream of life
out from under the hand of oppression
The children of Sierra Leone learn the craft
of war and dismemberment,
their childhood the stolen property of overlords
Boatloads of Chinese laborers, indentured,
sold into slavery in their search
for the Golden Mountain,
sweating out their lives so that we can enjoy cheaply
the benefits of the "free" market.

The people of Sudan and Nagalim die
in their hundreds of thousands,
silent to our ears.
Ugandans, Zambians and Malawians
bury entire generations of AIDS victims
never dreaming of life-extending drugs

Women, children and men ...
God! How can you can stand it!?
wander homeless in the streets
of the cities
of the richest countries
in the world.

We lie shackled to Empire that invites us
into denial, despair, amnesia
and when that happens,
your people become
shoppers.

Two Prayers

Empire's mantra tells us to
GO ALONG
if we want to
GET ALONG;
Our churches sit dormant under the narcotic of liturgies
designed to accommodate the people to Empire, producing
custodians of the dominant power, making them feel good
enough to carry on, but not guilty enough to do anything
dangerous.

In the face of the demands of Jubilee,
we sometimes find ourselves
acting and believing that there is
no one greater than Nebuchadnezzar.

O God of the Exiles,
give words to your poets

For poets make no concessions to Babylon;
They write poetry that undermines
the prose of Empire;
They dance;
Poets speak the ordinary things of faith
that the Empire considers outrageous.

Give strength to your people who believe—
that we are saved for the world, not from it;
that peace, like war, is waged;
that discipleship means being redemptively involved in the world's pain
at some cost to ourselves;
that, if not outrageous,
poetry has no power to give life;
that the principalities and powers are not
in charge of this world.

Give words to your poets
these repairers of breaches
and restorers of streets to live in
your poets
who know that, while words of release
are dangerous,
they emancipate.
They give life.

Because of Christ
in whose name we pray. Amen

APPENDIX 5

"THE VOICE IN THE TEMPLE" by Katie Cook[2]

This is the year that King Uzziah died.
There is brokenness and death all around us.
There is violence and injustice and hunger.
We have hatred in our hearts,
And we dwell in the midst of a people with hateful hearts.
We fear that our dreams and hopes are dying.
We believed that we were supposed to dream along with God,
But we wonder sometimes if it's worth all the pain.
We see evidence that the work is not in vain,
And we cling in the midst of our fatigue to those glimpses of truth,
We cherish those rumors of glory.

This is the year that King Uzziah died,
And we have come to the temple to weep.
We wait now to hear that word that will keep us going.
We wait to taste of the holiness of God,
The vision, high and lifted up.
We wait to hear that voice that we love so much.
Somewhere in the middle of our weeping we hear a question:
"Who will go out into a world such as this,
Where people suffer and die
And infant hopes are dashed against the rocks?"
And we search our hearts.
Are we ready for this task?
Are we worthy to go where God sends us?
Can we do this?
We feel too young. We feel too old.
We tend to stammer. We tend to fall down.
We each feel unfit in different ways.
But we have heard a voice, a beloved voice,
In the temple, where we went to weep.

This is the year that King Uzziah died,
And we have heard a voice in the temple.
May God give us grace,
May God give us courage,
May God keep us on the journey,
For we must go and tell the people what the voice has told us.

2. Katie Cook is the editor of *Baptist Peacemaker*, *Hunger News & Hope*, and *Sacred Seasons*. This meditation appeared on the cover of *Baptist Peacemaker* in the Winter of 2002. A missions group at Oakhurst Baptist Church, Decatur, Georgia used the prayer in worship.

Appendix 6

For Such a Time as This[1]

Jerene Broadway

Leader: Perhaps *you* were brought to the kingdom for such a time as this...

People: FOR EVERYTHING THERE IS A SEASON, AND A TIME FOR EVERY PURPOSE UNDER HEAVEN

L: A time to be born and a time to die. A time to plant and a time to harvest what is planted

P: A TIME TO KILL AND A TIME TO HEAL. A TIME TO BREAK DOWN AND A TIME TO BUILD UP

L: A time to weep and a time to laugh. A time to mourn and a time to celebrate

P: FOR EVERYTHING THERE IS A SEASON, AND A TIME FOR EVERY PURPOSE UNDER HEAVEN

L: A time to hold each other and a time to refrain from embracing. A time to seek what we long for and a time to lose what we love

P: FOR EVERYTHING THERE IS A SEASON, AND A TIME FOR EVERY PURPOSE UNDER HEAVEN

L: A time to fast and a time to share a feast with the hungry. A time to hold silent vigil and a time to dance in a conga line

P: FOR EVERYTHING THERE IS A SEASON, AND A TIME FOR EVERY PURPOSE UNDER HEAVEN

---

1. Litany written by Jerene Broadway for Peace Camp 2001. It appeared in *Baptist Peacemaker* in the Fall of 2001.

L: A time to raise our fists in anger and a time to let go of our anger. A time to take up the fight and a time to lay our weapons down

P: A TIME TO SOAR LIKE EAGLES AND A TIME TO MUDDLE THROUGH. A TIME TO KEEP SILENT AND A TIME TO SPEAK UP

L: A time to love and a time to hate. A time for war and a time for peace

P: FOR EVERYTHING THERE IS A SEASON, AND A TIME FOR EVERY PURPOSE UNDER HEAVEN

L: Perhaps our own ancestors—our own cloud of witnesses—have gathered around us for such a time as this. If we are alert to moments of possibility, we will see bushes burning

P: ARMIES CAST INTO THE SEA, SWORDS BEATEN INTO PLOWSHARES, CAPTIVES SET FREE

L: The paralyzed picking up their beds and running through the streets, Kings dancing before the Lord with all their might, A child leading the way

P: FOR EVERYTHING THERE IS A SEASON, AND A TIME FOR EVERY PURPOSE UNDER HEAVEN

ALL: PERHAPS *WE* WERE BROUGHT TO THE KINGDOM FOR SUCH A TIME AS THIS.

Appendix 7

Two Reflections on the School of the Americas

"WHY I CROSSED THE LINE AT FORT BENNING" BY RICK AXTELL[1]

In 1994, I stood in the rose garden at the University of Central America in San Salvador. Five years earlier, the bodies of six Jesuit priests who were professors at the university were dragged into that garden after being shot in the head by members of the Atlacatl battalion of the Salvadoran army.

Most of the battalion members cited by the United Nations Truth Commission report for these grisly murders were trained at the U.S. Army School of the Americas. Last November, more than 10,000 people showed up at the SOA in Georgia to commemorate the tenth anniversary of the massacre of the priests, their house-keeper, and her daughter.

On that same trip, I stood in the chapel where Archbishop Oscar Romero was assassinated while saying mass at the altar. Graduates of the School of the Americas were responsible for the death of this dedicated champion of peace and justice.

I talked to dozens of civilians that summer who were victims of violence perpetrated by Salvadoran forces trained and armed by the United States. At the church where I was staying, a woman named Laura told me about the gruesome death of her child. The soldiers tortured him while she watched helplessly. She will never be the same.

---

1. *Baptist Peacemaker* 20 (Spring 2000) 6–7. Twenty-one people from Centre College in Danville, Kentucky, where Rick Axtell teaches ethics, accompanied him to Fort Benning in November 1999. Nineteen of twenty-six Salvadoran army officers cited by a UN Truth Commission as responsible for the assassination on November 16, 1989 in San Salvador of six Jesuit priests, their housekeeper Julia Elba Ramos, and her fifteen-year-old daughter Celina Ramos were trained at the School of the Americas.

So where else could I have been on November 21? I went to Fort Benning because of Laura.

I went to Fort Benning for Juan Castro Chibalan of Ximbaxuc, a Quiche village in Guatemala. This summer, Juan told me about the torture and murder of his two brothers when Ximbaxuc was attacked and destroyed.

I went to Fort Benning for Emilia Garcia of Guatemala City who has been looking for her disappeared son Edgar since 1984. Edgar's picture was one of hundreds on the wall of the office where Emilia spoke to our group this summer.

I went to Fort Benning for Valdemar, my host in a community of returned refugees on the south coast of Guatemala, who told me shocking stories of the violence that drove him from his village and into a refugee camp in Mexico. Valdemar lost everyone in his family.

I went to Fort Benning for Pasqual and Micaela of Union Progreso in Chiapas, Mexico, who told us what their lives have been like since the murder of their sons Lorenzo (18) and Bartolo (21). They were among the five young men killed in their fields when the Mexican military attacked on June 10, 1998.

Every one of these people knew that the U. S. Army trains their military officers and soldiers at Fort Benning's School of the Americas. Most of them knew that the School of the Americas used training manuals in some courses (now declassified) that advocated infiltration of opposition groups, collection of bounties for bodies of opponents, use of psychological warfare, and other "counter-insurgency" techniques against advocates for social justice.

Graduates of the School have been the architects of the horror that killed, displaced, and terrorized tens of thousands of civilians in Latin America's dirty wars in the 1970s and 1980s. I crossed the line for Laura and Juan and Emilia and Valdemar and Pasqual and Micaela. They believe the school should be closed. So do I.

CINDY WEBER, "REVOLUTIONARY LONGINGS"[2]

"He will turn many of the people of Israel to the Lord their God. With the spirit and power of Elijah he will go before him, to turn the hearts of the parents to their children...." (Luke 1:16–17)

---

2. This article, published in *Baptist Peacemaker* 25 (Winter 2005) 10, received an Associated Church Press Award of Excellence for Personal Experience.

Two Reflections on the School of the Americas

Dear Francisca Clara:

I don't know anything about you, really, except that you are the daughter of Julia Clara, that you lived somewhere in Central America, and that you were 11 years old when you and other members of your family were killed by soldiers who were trained at the School of the Americas in Fort Benning, Georgia.

That's where I learned your name: at Fort Benning, Georgia. I was there with more than ten thousand other people from my country to ask that the school be shut down. It was quite a sight to behold: pierced noses, bare feet, dreadlocks, and nuns everywhere. One of the nuns, Sister Lucille, was 91 years old.

I met up with friends from the Baptist Peace Fellowship of North America. Jane Esdale had made crosses for our group to hold, white wooden crosses, and out of the thousands of names of persons slaughtered by graduates of the School of the Americas, she had, for some reason, chosen yours. There it was, written on the cross, black on white, "Francisca Clara, *años* 11, daughter of Julia Clara." I'm not sure why Jane chose your name, but I chose your name, I chose your cross, I chose you, Francisca, because you were 11 years old when you died, and because I have sons who are close to your age.

I had said goodbye to my sons in the wee hours of the day before. They were still asleep, and as I touched them goodbye, I felt a jolt in my heart at leaving them. But then I said to myself, "But there are other children." I was thinking of you, Francisca, though I didn't know your name at the time.

We gathered there in lines of ten abreast, and as the funeral procession began, the leaders would read the names of the dead, and we would raise our crosses, I would raise your cross, and say, "*Presente.*" *Presente*: here, present, remembered. The sky was blue and the Georgia pines were green and the sun was shining—and, up ahead, the American flag was flying, red, white and blue. And every few seconds, thousands of white crosses would be raised into the blue sky, raised before the American flag, *presente, presente, presente.* Juan Rodriquez, 35 years old, they would read. *Presente.* White crosses raised before the flag. Unnamed baby, 15 months old, they would read. *Presente.* White crosses raised before the flag. Maria Cortez, 72 years old, they would read. *Presente.* White crosses raised before the flag. I cried for the first fifteen minutes or so, listening to the names. Two hours later, long after I had stopped crying, the names were still coming. *Presente. Presente. Presente.*

I listened for your name, Francisca. I listened for over an hour, name after name after name. Then, "Francisca Clara, 11 years old." *Presente*.

I left your cross on the fence at Fort Benning, there with thousands of others. I knelt there for a while before it, and remembered you, prayed for you, prayed for a different world, for a world where the hearts of the parents are truly turned towards their children, and not just their children, but all the children.

I tell you this, Francisca Clara, because I want you to know that you matter. You were *presente*, present, remembered and revered that day, and you are present today, and I will carry you in my heart.

I write this on the first Sunday of Advent. In our culture, Advent is a time when we prepare for the coming of the Christ, a time of watching and waiting. It is a time when we prepare for and hope for the new thing that God is doing, when we long for God's revolution to be birthed in our hearts and in our world.

This is what I long for, little Francisca, this is the revolution that I want to see: I long for the day when children like you are still alive at the age of 11, and at the age of 18, and at the age of 35, and on into old age. I long for a world where you would be alive somewhere, a young woman by now, dancing, laughing up into your partner's face, your brightly colored skirt spinning, spinning, spinning to the music.

This is the revolution that I long for, Francisca Clara, the revolution that I will work for. And as I do, I will remember you. Francisca Clara, 11 years old. *Presente*.

Your sister,

Cindy Weber
November 30, 2003

APPENDIX 8

With Such a Cloud of Witnesses[1]

With such a cloud of witnesses,
How can we turn from trust aside?
So let us run this race with joy,
And come what may, in love abide.

Strong light You cast across the years,
In human souls we still recall
These gave their lives to testify
The rising grace that frees us all.

Some had no place to call their home
Some died in chains, some faced the sword!
Yet to the end, they walked in faith,
Held by Your promise, living Word.

For all whose steps we slowly trace,
We give You thanks, still dawning Sun!
Till comes the day when love rules earth,
In Jesus' name, we'll carry on.

With such a cloud of witnesses,
We dare not throw their hope aside!
We'll stay Your course till night is done,
And come what may, in love abide.

1. Written by Peter J. B. Carman, *Baptist Peacemaker* 23 (Fall 2003).

Appendix 9[1]

Let us Seek Justice

A Reflection Following the Death of Amadou Diallo

Following the jury's decision in the trial of the four New York City police officers charged in the shooting death of the Amadou Diallo, an African American, many people have voiced their opinion that justice was not done. As painful as it may be, it is important for them to take a step back from their emotions and realize that, in our criminal justice system, justice is simply a determination of whether a law of the State has been broken and, if so, who has broken it.

The jury decided that, given the facts as presented at the trial, no law had been broken by the actions of the officers. From the statements several jurors have made, it appears that they made a careful review of the facts and presented a thoughtful decision based on the law as instructed by the judge. This, however, does not mean that justice, as demanded by the family of Amadou Diallo and the community, occurred.

It is my belief that this justice can occur only when the focus changes from whether a law of the State has been broken to concern about the harm done by the actions of one person against another. This type of justice, called restorative justice and based on biblical principles of Shalom, declares that crime causes harm which must be acknowledged and addressed.

In the death of Amadou Diallo definite harm has been done, harm which the recent trial and verdict did not address at all because the system was not established to address such concerns. The emerging paradigm of restorative justice does address these concerns and, if allowed to be a part of the process in this and other cases, could lead to a sense of justice having been achieved.

Looking at the harm that was done by the shooting and death of Amadou Diallo opens us up to new ways of thinking about this

---

1. Evelyn Hanneman, "Let Us Seek Justice," 13. This article received an Associated Church Press award.

crime and moves us on to new responses. Not having been a part of this case, I am well aware that I do not have all the details and, therefore, probably do not understand the total situation. However, the three questions of restorative justice developed by Howard Zehr can be presented and, with broad strokes, applied here.

"What harm was done by the crime?" Obviously, Amadou Diallo was harmed in that the actions of the police caused his death. His parents and friends were also quite directly harmed in the loss of a loved one. But in order to see the totality of the harm done, we have to broaden our sights.

The community in which Amadou Diallo lived also experienced harm. Those who witnessed the killing may continue to have flashbacks to the event. Those who live in the building and have to enter though the bullet-riddled vestibule may be "re-harmed" each time they enter their own homes. And any African American in the United States may be harmed because of experiencing, once again, the sense that they are not safe in their own country. They may also experience a greater sense of fear surrounding the police who are supposed to be, and in many cases will be, there to protect them.

But let's broaden the picture even more. Let's look at the police who may really have thought Amadou Diallo had a gun and was going to use it. They may be experiencing a sense of guilt for having taken a person's life under a false presumption. Yet in the moment a decision was necessary and they made one, one that only after the fact did they know to be wrong.

And it is probable that their defense attorneys, working under the rules of our criminal justice system, would not allow them to express any remorse that they may feel directly to the family of Mr. Diallo. They had to plead "not guilty" so that the system could play out its usual scenario to the end. This end determined that they had not broken any laws, even though great harm has been done by their actions.

We can continue to broaden the picture by looking at the harm done to the police officers' families who have their own anguish and, possibly, conflicting emotions to deal with, and to their colleagues who may now be second-guessing themselves every time they think about drawing their guns. When will they make a similar bad decision?

The two other restorative justice questions are, "What needs to be done to repair the harm?" and "Who is responsible for repairing it?" Many possibilities come to mind. Mr. Diallo's family needs support at this time from friends and from counselors who can help them work through their grief. They may also need financial assistance in obtaining such assistance. Are there organizations that can supply this?

An apology could be made by the police officers to Amadou Diallo's family, perhaps given directly during a victim-offender mediation session, should the family wish to participate, or through a written letter. However, the system continues to grind on and the four police officers are, no doubt, prevented from doing this lest it be held against them in the next phase of civil trials and internal police investigations.

The Chief of Police and the Mayor of New York City could also lead the way through apologies to the family and by promising better training for all police officers regarding responses to such situations. And by also truly working to root out those police officers who exhibit racist tendencies; they have no place on a police force charged with the protection of all citizens.

New York City could also offer support and counseling for all those who witnessed the event and are traumatized by it. The city could work with the people in Amadou Diallo's building to discover what they need to have done with the bullet-riddled vestibule to make living there tenable once again and then assist the landlord in making any necessary repairs.

The families of the police officers need support during this time. Not support that tells them that the officers are being railroaded and misused but that helps them to acknowledge what actually happened and then learn to live with those facts. Where can this support come from? Certainly from friends, but also from pastors and other professionals who can help them find their way through these difficult times.

This is just a short list of ways in which the harm caused by this event could be addressed. There are many more; the only limit is the boundaries we all too often put on our thinking.

Our criminal justice system has made its determination in this case. It is now time for the search for true justice to be made. The tear in the fabric of society caused by the shooting of Amadou Diallo will remain for the individuals directly involved, and for society as a whole, unless actions are taken to address the real issues of justice by seeking ways to repair the reality of the harm that has been done.

The biblical witness declares that justice can, indeed, roll down like water. Ask yourself the three questions of restorative justice. Then ask yourself what your part in this restorative system is to be. And then resolve to take action to help bring the peace of Shalom.

Appendix 10

Selections from Peace Soup—
Baptist Peacemaker 20 (Summer 2000) 13

"A PARABLE ABOUT CONSUMERISM" by Van Darden[1]

A warning: Once you purchase any object, you've started down the slippery slope of secular consumerism.

For instance, you buy the pair of $80 designer jeans and you think, "Oh, wonderful."

Then you get to thinking, "Wouldn't these jeans look cute with that $100 pair of shoes?"

Then you realize that you need the white silk shirt and the nifty little handbag and . . .

Well, you get the picture. Eventually you're putty in the hands of effete little designers living in Miami and Paris.

So it is with the equally deadly Spiral of Christian Consumerism.

For example, you're given a WWJD bracelet and think, "Boy, I'm really gonna spread the Word now!"[2]

But nobody notices.

So you buy the WWJD polo shirt.

When nobody notices that, you then buy the WWJD shoelaces . . . and the gimme cap . . . and the coozie.

Then you go for the heavy stuff: WWJD bumper stickers, the fish thingie for the back of your car.

---

1. At the time of writing, Van Darden was a 15-year-old member of the youth group at Seventh and James Baptist Church in Waco, Texas.

2. For readers who have not encountered the "WWJD" phenomenon that is rampant in the United States and possibly elsewhere, various clothing accessories and countless knickknacks, with "WWJD" engraved or affixed on them somehow, are on sale almost everywhere. The initials stand for "What would Jesus do?"

It's too late to stop now. You start answering the phone "Heaven-o!" instead of "Hell-o."

You leave Kiwanis and join Promise Keepers.

You pull your kids out of their expensive, exclusive college prep high school and place them in the expensive, exclusive Christian high school.

You pray at the flagpole.

You buy a "Pray at the Pole" t-shirt.

You're at the bottom rung now.

You start buying the Christian "Lose weight fast pills" from advertisements in *Charisma Magazine*.

It's only now that you realize you're putty in the hands of effete little Christian designers living in Colorado Springs, Colorado, and Lake Mary, Florida.

You've spent all of your money on Christian consumer items, including Carmen CDs.

Your family leaves you.

There is an intervention.

You go to Christian 12-step programs.

Then you go to regular 12-step programs.

And then, one bright day, you're cured.

You walk home.

And the first store you pass features a photograph of a beautiful supermodel wearing a pair of $80 designer jeans—and very little else . . .

"INTERVIEW WITH GRACE"[3]

Question: What's the biggest thing you've learned out in North Dakota? Is there anything we talked about that has changed (i.e., you no longer believe in something you once did, etc., so I don't misrepresent your current state of mind.)

Initial Answer: Ooh. All I can really say is I know a lot less then I thought I did, and now I know a lot of different things. I don't know what to say except that I needed this and I can't possibly explain what is different but everything and nothing is.

---

3. Grace chose to finish high school a semester early so that she could volunteer at an elementary school on the Standing Rock Sioux reservation in North Dakota. At press time in 2000 she was about to go through commencement ceremonies at her high school. Below is her response to one of a number of questions she was asked as a graduating senior.

Later Answer: Okay, I went and thought about it. Here's what I know:

1. That I know so much less then I thought I did.

2. That you can always, always run away. Not in the conventional scary sense, but that, no matter what happens, I know that I am capable of packing up my bags and heading wherever, (out West preferably, but pretty much anywhere will do) and making my own life. Knowing that I can do this means that I am strong. I guess maybe running away isn't exactly the bravest thing to do, but striking out with nothing and making your own way is amazing. I had a lot of people behind me, true. But now I know that as long as I have my writing and my dance then I can find my way from there. Whether I stay or go.

3. You don't give service out of pity, but out of respect. Don't help someone just because you feel sorry for them, because that places you on a pedestal. If you are going to volunteer or whatnot, do it because you respect human life and human rights, and remember that you don't necessarily know at all what you are doing. We're all just grown up kids. Everybody is guessing in this life and it's beautiful and just the truth. I like people, that's what.

4. Only what you fight for will you value.

5. I have learned a lot about money. Money is everything. I'm not saying being rich is everything, but money, on this earth, determines quality of life. Everything is all messed up and there is no solution at this point, but I know now that where we put our money is crucial to who we are as people. I didn't know what I have, and I have so much good in my life, and I don't want to hoard it. I didn't do anything to deserve my family, no one deserves anything they get, good or bad, as far as I can tell. But if you have a lot, it is not just a bonus but a responsibility to live consciously and to be socially aware. Basically I think we need to start taking better care of each other.

6. I learned that there is no solution to history. I learned that there are a lot of things with no solution as far as I can see.

7. I learned a lot about my country and it is more complicated than I imagined.

8. I learned a lot about how things once were and still are.

9. I saw what I had been sheltered from.

10. I know that I am only watching and could have left if it got too hard. I know that I am coming from an incredibly easy place and I DON'T know what that means, but it means that I am glad to be here but I don't think it makes me good. (I don't know how else to explain.)

Appendix 11

Model Ministries for November 2008

A Newsletter for Partner Congregations of the Baptist Peace Fellowship of North America

This issue of *Model Ministries* offers two models of bringing the world home to our local congregations.[1]

THREE CUPS OF TEA: CONNECTING COMMUNITY, FAITH, AND PRACTICE[2]

During the month of August, First Baptist offered four discussion sessions on the book *Three Cups of Tea: One Man's Mission to Promote Peace . . . One School at a Time* by Greg Mortenson and David Oliver Relin. The idea came from our Mission Council chairperson, Susan Chambers, who also is a faculty member at Linfield College. Given that Linfield was requiring the book for Freshman Colloquium and had scheduled the author to speak for Convocation in early September, a book study at First Baptist seemed timely and worthwhile.

We chose to go with the theme of sharing three cups of tea, so each of the first three sessions included tea room delicacies. Church members who formerly owned a tea room provided the refreshments so that we could indeed share "three cups of tea" as we discussed the book. Our final session included a tea luncheon and reflection upon the author's address at Convocation. We were able to compile discussion questions by using resources from Linfield, the book's publisher, and the organizers' reflections about how the book impacted our faith.

---

1. This issue of *Model Ministries* was originally published on November 28, 2008.

2. For more information, contact Shelley Varner, Associate Pastor of First Baptist Church, McMinnville, Oregon, USA at 503/472-7941 or shelley.varner@gmail.com.

The book study has had a number of positive outcomes. First, we were able to make use of local resources (Linfield's Convocation, former tea room owners, college professors as facilitators) to engage our church's members and friends in dialogue about pertinent global issues. Secondly, we were able to personalize the book's message, such that events occurring continents away from our own have an impact on the way we interact with our community. Thirdly, we engaged a number of participants who were not affiliated with a faith community; the book study provided a port-of-entry for newcomers. Some of these people may continue attending First Baptist; others may have come only for the book study. Either way, we presented an opportunity to engage in meaningful dialogue about our faith and ways it impacts our everyday decision-making. To me, engaging in dialogue and offering educational opportunities about global events is a meaningful way to connect faith and practice. Dialogue and education synthesize the local and the global in such a way as to make a "glocal" perspective, which is how we respond to global need by acting in parallel ways in our own community.

WELCOMING GUESTS: A SISTER CHURCH DELEGATION EXPERIENCE[3]

In 1992, University Baptist Church (UBC) established a sister church relationship with the Second Baptist Church of Leon, Nicaragua. Over the years, we sent periodic letters and pictures back and forth. UBC established a Godparent program by which we "adopted" students by providing scholarships for their primary school. In 2003, a delegation of six from UBC spent ten days in Leon as guests of our sister church. We were immersed in their lives and their profound ministry. Our eyes were opened, and we experienced their faithfulness, their struggles and their unique way of doing and being the church. Although many UBC folk wanted to go to Leon in subsequent years, we decided it would be more faithful to bring a delegation of six people from Leon to Minnesota. This finally happened in September of 2008.

We were lucky enough to have had our delegation facilitated by Nicaraguan representatives from Project Minnesota/Leon. This is a sister-city project and the coordinator, a U.S. citizen, traveled with the delegation

3. Doug Donley, Pastor, University Baptist Church, Minneapolis, Minnesota, USA. pastor@ubcmn.org.

and served as the primary translator. We immediately realized that there was a significant cultural difference between us, not only in the way we lived and the language we spoke, but also the way we did church. Things that we take for granted like food, transportation, health care, and the relatively short length of our worship services were all major differences for us. We had to find out for ourselves what things we really wanted to share with our guests.

We worked hard to give them a balanced (and enjoyable) view of U.S. American life. We took them to a feeding program—a very important thing for them to do as they packaged food for people in third world countries suffering from malnutrition, like so many of them have. The delegation wanted to go shopping (a lot). We balanced this very real need with a housing activist who explained to them about the foreclosure crisis. We took them to our schools and they marveled at the fact that we have libraries and that the classrooms that feel overcrowded with 28 students would hold 80 in Nicaragua. They were here on two Sundays. The first Sunday, the two pastors of the sister churches co-celebrated communion in two languages. The last Sunday, the Nicaraguan pastor preached the sermon and we sent the delegation off with a tearful service of laying on of hands.

We also took them on our church retreat, giving us all a good opportunity to know each other. The retreat was on their second weekend and toward the end of the visit. They saved up their hardest questions of us for that experience. They wanted to know about our Welcoming and Affirming status, how we got there and how they could be as inclusive as we were in a culture of such machismo as Nicaragua. It was a fascinating discussion that we wanted to have happen but didn't know how to facilitate. I guess the Holy Spirit intervened and gave us an opportunity to see each other and celebrate each other. As they left us, loaded down with donations for their church and school, we also gave them a quilt that we had created during their stay to remember the ways that our lives intertwine and shelter each other from the storms of our lives. That quilt is now on the wall of their church.

It was a great trip, and we learned a lot about ourselves and our guests as the trip progressed. We agreed to pay for the entire trip. Our church came up with the money, in part thanks to a fund established to honor long-time UBC member, world traveler and BPFNA board member Tai Shigaki. It's called the Shigaki Mission Travel Fund, and it helped make the trip possible. Many people also donated portions of their economic stimulus checks to the cause.

There was a lot of unpredictability about who would receive visas. The decisions seemed to be at the whim of the U.S. Embassy, so the size of the delegation was not set until a month before they were to arrive. We had to improvise on the spot when a key meeting got canceled. But this is no different than it was when we visited their community in 2003. We are a richer community because of the trip. We look forward to the next trip, possibly in the winter of 2010.

UPCOMING OPPORTUNITIES TO SHARE WITH YOUR CONGREGATION: REBIRTHING KING, REBIRTHING AMERICA

On Tuesday, January 20, 2009, a new U.S. President will be inaugurated. The day before, Monday, January 19, is Martin Luther King's Birthday. This confluence of dates offers an extraordinary moment of transformation.

On January 19, the Olive Branch Interfaith Peace Partnership will hold a celebratory service and teaching at which Vincent Harding of Iliff School of Theology, one of Dr. King's closets advisers; Rev. Michael Kinnamon, general secretary of the National Council of Churches; Dr. Sayyid Syeed, general secretary of the Islamic Society of North America; Sammie Moshenberg of the National Council of Jewish Women; Mubarak Awad of Nonviolence International; and Rev. William G. Sinkford of the Unitarian Universalist Association are already scheduled to speak at All Souls Church, Unitarian, in Washington DC.

A study guide to King's April 4, 1967, speech given at The Riverside Church, NYC, where he spoke of the three evils of militarism, racism, and poverty will soon be available online. Watch for a link on our website at www.bpfna.org.

BPFNA ELECTION DELEGATION TO MONITOR SALVADORAN ELECTIONS

A Baptist delegation will to travel March 10–17, 2009 to El Salvador, under the auspices of the SHARE Foundation, as a team of international elections observers for the Salvadoran presidential elections in March 2009.

The team will include representatives from BPFNA Partner Congregation Central Baptist of Wayne, PA and is open to any and all interested members of the BPFNA.

Mission: Delegates will join other international elections observers to ensure free and fair participation and reporting of the election results, and will meet with members of SHARE partner communities who are advocating for social and economic justice through women's empowerment, leadership development and citizen participation.

Activities Will Include:

- Electoral observation training and accreditation by the Supreme Electoral Tribunal
- Briefings on the 2009 Salvadoran elections
- Election observation on Election Day
- Visits to historical sites in San Salvador
- Meetings with beneficiaries of SHARE-supported programs in the areas of women's empowerment, food security, and human rights

Cost: $950.00, NOT including airfare. You are responsible for airfare to San Salvador. The delegation fee includes lodging, meals, travel, translation in El Salvador, set-up and facilitation of meetings, orientation, and reading and preparation materials.

Questions: Contact Rev. Andy Smith, member of BPFNA and Central Baptist at 610/644-1504 or ASTheRev@aol.com. A downloadable file of additional information about SHARE's election delegation, including FAQs, is available at www.share-elsalvador.org/MunicNatlAssemElectionsPacket.pdf.

Application and Registration: Please visit the SHARE web site for an application—www.share-elsalvador.org. A first payment of $50 is due by January 15, 2009. The remaining $900.00 is due by January 31, 2009.

LOOKING FOR A GIFT THAT GIVES TWICE?

Visit www.bpfna.org/catalogue for a wide variety of resources that will delight children, youth, and adults on your gift list. Every purchase supports the Baptist Peace Fellowship of North America's work to create peace rooted in justice.

CONFLICT TRANSFORMATION: GOING DEEPER?

A training opportunity in Charlotte, North Carolina, USA following the annual convocation of the Alliance of Baptists April 19-20, 2009. This special intensive training in the theory and skills of transforming conflict will be of use to anyone who experiences conflict at home, church, work, school, or elsewhere. (Hint: This means all of us!) We'll be led by the very talented and experienced trainer Dwight Lundgren, the Coordinator of Intercultural Ministries and Reconciliation of the American Baptist Churches USA. Cost is $100 per person. Spaces are VERY limited so e-mail ledayne@bpfna.org today to reserve your space.

CHRISTIAN PEACE WITNESS FOR IRAQ IN WASHINGTON!

Washington DC, USA. April 29–30, 2009. On the 100th day of the new administration, come to Washington DC for the third national Christian Peace Witness for Iraq event. Join us in the U.S. capital for witness and worship Wednesday evening and nonviolent action and advocacy on Thursday to call on the President and Congress to end the war and occupation in Iraq, support a comprehensive peace process, end the policy and practice of torture and meet human needs at home. Can't make it to Washington? Then plan your own local event for one or both dates. Resources will be available on the Christian Peace Witness for Iraq website at www.christianpeacewitness.org. Lift your voice and witness for peace!

WE'D LOVE TO HEAR FROM YOU!

Do you have a project or program that emphasizes Peace and Justice in the season of Advent? We'd love to share it with others! E-mail LeDayne McLeese Polaski at ledayne@bpfna.org to share your idea. If you know someone who might find "Model Ministries" useful in their work for peace with justice, please forward it on to them! If you received this copy of "Model Ministries" from a friend, please sign up online to start your own free subscription.

Model Ministries is sent to staff and leaders of BPFNA Partner Congregations and others who request it. This edition was published November 28, 2008. To change delivery options, please email johnny@bpfna.org, call 704/521-6051, or send a note to BPFNA, 4800 Wedgewood Dr., Charlotte NC 28210 USA.

Appendix 12[1]

"ST. PETER AND THE JERUSALEM PROTOCOL"
by Ken Sehested

Culturally speaking, nothing seems to divide people more than the question of sexual orientation. At the center of this cultural wrestling match are the Christian churches. Much of the rationale for condemning homosexual behavior, even in secular institutions, is anchored in appeal to the Bible. Even the language of jurisprudence is affected by biblical tradition, with so-called "sodomy laws" criminalizing homosexual activity.

We Baptists are on the verge of devouring ourselves in this dispute. But we're not alone: virtually every mainline Protestant body along with the Roman Catholic church is embroiled in the controversy at the highest levels. Though the debate is less widespread within the "evangelical" side of the Protestant spectrum, the topic is sufficiently threatening to prompt preemptive maneuvers, as with the Southern Baptist Convention's recent constitutional amendment-the first in its 150-year history-prohibiting membership to congregations which condone homosexuality. (Voting "messengers" to this year's convention [1995] must attest to that article of faith with their signature during registration.)

In the public arena, "the gay agenda" has replaced the "communist threat" as the battering ram of reactionary politics. Instead of a commie behind every bush, there's now a queer in every classroom, in every congressional committee room, in every battleship wardroom. Many have predicted that questions around sexual orientation will divide churches more severely than at any time since the debate over slavery a century and a half ago.

We find ourselves in the midst of a major public controversy. And my heart is heavier than it's ever been. Why such anxiety? There have been other controversies. We took a very public stand against a very popular war in the Persian Gulf. We've engaged in acts of civil disobedience when convinced that holy obedience was

1. Sehested, "St. Peter and the Jerusalem Protocol," 10–11.

at stake. There have been overseas trips involving a level of physical danger. So why the fearful heart now?

Because this subject is different. Simply raising the subject of homosexuality for discussion dredges up some of the most volatile passions in the human soul. Baptist journals that have rarely mentioned the BPFNA in 11 years now devote full editorials to our actions for gay and lesbian justice. Long-term friends threaten disaffiliation.

I've had nightmarish visions of 11 years of patient network building run aground and splintered, not to mention ambitious new plans for the future. It's not so much the withdrawal of financial support from the American Baptist Churches that poses a danger. From the beginning, we chose to develop a financial base of member support rather than rely on institutional funding. More threatening is the prospect of losing the confidence of mainstream Baptist leaders around the world with whom we work.

Given the tension often accompanying the question of sexual orientation, and the admittedly tenuous nature of our organization, it's fair to ask, "Why did the BPFNA board choose to wade into these troubled waters?" We have been interrogated both by those with principled convictions and those with pragmatic considerations. The latter warn us that we can't take on every issue; that we will lose the solid core of our constituency for involvement on issues of broader consensus.

Each of these objections, and a few more, have been mental wrestling partners worthy of Jacob's angel at the Jabbok. Each has had not just one but several nights to work me over. Moreover, my personal passion rests in other arenas. Domestically, our cities are being wrecked by violence, often with racial overtones. Virtually every leading social indicator of human health in the African American community is lower now than when in the U.S. riots scorched our conscience a generation ago. Our addiction to guns needs attention from communities of faith. Fully one-fifth of U.S. children live in poverty.

The struggle of Cuba to be free of U.S. imperial designs has a grip on my imagination. Additionally, we have privileged conversation with Baptists in a dozen countries involved in leadership to mediate civil strife and in movements of nonviolent resistance to injustice.

Isn't all this at risk when you address the question of justice in relation to sexual orientation? Yes. Aren't you in danger of losing your credibility across the board for the sake of this one point of attention? Could be. And what about your efforts to show the connection between biblical faith and matters of justice and peace? Aren't you in danger of undermining that influence when you take a position in apparent opposition to that of the Bible? That is a possibility.

Then why take the risk? Don't all these other involvements stretch your resources and threaten your existence enough, without adding the most volatile issue of all?

WHY TAKE THE RISK?

My response to this composite portrait of actual questions is three-fold. First, this is, simply, the right thing to do. Matters of justice cannot be segregated. Of course we have to make choices, live within time and resource limitations. Often the hardest thing about our work is deciding what not to do, for there are so many points at which we could make a difference. Many of us, myself included, have resisted for too long speaking out on matters of simple human and civil rights for gay/lesbian people.

And while we can never be free of the need to make calculated choices, there comes a point when such calculation becomes compromise. After long hours of sometimes painful discussion, the BPFNA board has become convinced that the time for us is now. We hope our members and readers will join us in active and public opposition to gay-bashing—or, at least not abandon our larger mission in disputing our discernment at this one point.

Second, we have a ready-made opportunity to practice our calling as reconcilers within our own household. Gay and lesbian brothers and sisters are among our fellowship. We have listened to their stories. We know something of their pain. To continue formal silence in this regard would involve us in a profound level of hypocrisy.

Nonviolence is more than refusing to shoot someone. Nor is it to be confused with passivity or with sectarian withdrawal (in the name of moral purity). Rather it involves a commitment to willingly enter a situation of conflict, to absorb the assault (in this case, mostly of the verbal and emotional variety) without resort to revenge, to listen with empathy to the "enemy," which involves the willingness to have your mind changed. In occasions like ours, no amount of voting will bring healing. Parliamentary procedure must give way to the discipline of reconciliation.

Finally, there is no way to dodge the question of biblical authority. Although homophobia is a virulent force within the church and the larger culture, and although appeals to "biblical authority" often mask prejudice, there are those for whom genuine fidelity to Scripture is at stake. It also is for me.

WHAT THE BIBLE DOES, AND DOES NOT, SAY

Homosexual behavior is mentioned in seven texts, four in Hebrew Scripture, three in the New Testament. The first text, Genesis 19, is the most common text of reference. It's the story of Sodom and Gomorrah, of Lot and the visit of the three angels. (The second of seven texts, in Judg 19:22–25, is a parallel retelling of this story.)

The narrative is familiar. The angels approach Sodom, when they encounter Lot sitting in the gate of the city, and accept his invitation of hospitality. After a meal, "the men of the city . . . both young and old, all the people to the last man" come banging on the door.

The Sodomites demand to see the newly-arrived guests, demanding to "know" them. Lot refuses, offering to send out his two virgin daughters instead. Just as the crowd gets unruly, the angels rescue Lot from their midst, shut the door and strike the mob blind. Lot and his kin are commanded to leave immediately because of the impending destruction. They flee, instructed not to look back. Brimstone and fire rain over the cities. But in the escape, Lot's wife looks back and turns into a pillar of salt.

Three things are especially important here. First, Sodom and Gomorrah are already under sentence. In chapter 19, the heavenly messengers reveal that their mission is to destroy the cities. They want Abraham to know so that "he may charge his children and his household after him to keep the way of the Lord by doing righteousness and justice" (v. 19). The condemned cities obviously have not done so. Second, the context does make clear that the men of Sodom have sexual intentions with regard to the guests in Lot's house. But the intention is not so much homosexual activity as it is rape. And the principle impulse in rape—whether homosexual or heterosexual—is not about sex. It is about power. Homosexual rape was a common form of humiliation and domination committed against defeated armies in the ancient world, as it is in modern prisons today.

Third, you would assume that if Sodom and Gomorrah's sin was homosexual activity, other authors in the Bible would make that connection. But nowhere does that happen! Listen to Ezekiel: "This was the guilt of your sister Sodom: she and her daughters had pride, excess of food, and prosperous ease, but did not aid the poor and needy. They were haughty and did abominable things before me" (16:49–50).

Amos warns that Israel will be overthrown just as God over-threw Sodom and Gomorrah (4:11) and for the same general reason: the poor are oppressed and the needy are crushed (4:1). Also in Isaiah: the people of Jerusalem and Judah "proclaim their sin like Sodom" (3:9). The charge? "Your hands are full of blood" (1:15); "the spoil of the poor is in your houses" and for "grinding the face of the poor" (3:14, 15). Indeed, "the daughters of Zion are haughty" and are "glancing wantonly with their eyes" (3:16). Also in Zephaniah: "Moab shall become like Sodom, and the Ammonites like Gomorrah" (2:9), for these have filled houses "with violence and fraud" (1:9).

The only New Testament reference to Sodom and Gomorrah comes from Jesus, who predicts a similar judgment in his own day (Matt 10:14–15). Who will receive it, and why? Those towns which do not provide welcome and sustenance to his appointed mission-aries who travel the countryside preaching and healing.

In all these references to the sin of Sodom and Gomorrah, the issue is wantonness. It is about domination of others, about malignant power, about God's intended shalom-harmony, right-relatedness. In each, God-relatedness and just relations among God's creatures are intimately linked. Spiritual realities and socio-economic realities are mirror images.

The second pair of texts in the Old Testament that mention homosexual behavior, in Lev 18:22 and 20:13, are nearly identical commands forbidding a man to lie with another man "as with a woman." Both judge such activity (as in Gen 19) as an "abomina-tion." Note here that the word "abomination" is not a moral/ethical term. Rather, it is always used to indicate a serious breach of ritual purity law. Other "abominations" before God include eating pork, misusing incense and intercourse during menstruation. These and many other prohibitions are connected to questions of what is clean and what is unclean in the eyes of God. The issue of clean and unclean becomes important in the final section of this article.

The dilemma in making this Levitical text normative for faith is what we do with other prohibitions in this same material. Wearing garments made of two different materials is also pro-hibited, as are sowing a field with two kinds of seed, cutting one's hair where it meets the temple of a human face-among a host of other commands, commands which the church has never declared normative.

The remaining three biblical references to homosexual activ-ity appear in the Pauline letters. The Gospels, oddly enough, are utterly silent at this point. "Sodomites" are mentioned in lists of "wrongdoers" (1 Cor 6:9–10) and "the lawless and disobedient" (1 Tim 1:9–10). In both these listings, however, there is considerable evidence that the language used indicates a condemnation of pederasty—the sexual and/or economic exploitation of children, particularly young boys—rather than against homosexual activity per se. In a similar way, Paul's description of women who "exchanged natural relations for unnatural" and of "men committing shameless acts with men" (Rom 1:26–27) is set within a larger context of idolatry. Pagan temple cult prostitution, using adult men and women as well as young boys, was common in that day.

Even if you discount these contextual factors, even if you disregard all alternative explanations set out above, there's still a major issue of consistency in our notions of biblical authority. The preface for that issue has been mentioned: what about all those other prohibitions? The Bible prohibits gluttony at least as many times, even calling it a form of idolatry at one point (Phil 3:19). Some 60 percent of the U.S. population is overweight, a percentage I would guess to be reflective of churchgoers. All but a tiny handful, who have biological disorders, are clearly gluttonous. Why not exclude these from our congregations? More caustic for us, especially we Baptists, is the Bible's repeated authorization for the institution of slavery. This year marks the 150th anniversary of the split among white Baptists in the U.S. over the issue of whether missionaries could also be slave holders. It's right there in the Bible, in simple language: "Slaves, obey your masters" (Eph 6:5).

The simple language of Scripture prohibits women wearing gold jewelry, braiding their hair and wearing expensive clothing (1 Peter 3:3). In other words, gold wedding bands are a sign of apostasy! And not only are women to be silent in church (1 Cor 14:34), they also are to have their heads covered and their faces veiled (11:5–6).

Fasting is everywhere a discipline in Scripture, but almost never in our churches. Paul warned the church at Corinth to "not forbid speaking in tongues." Rarely is such behavior sanctioned in our churches. In that same letter, he urges the unmarried to remain that way, judging it "better." "Do not seek marriage" is his plain advice. (Except if you can't control your passion—implying that the New Testament foundation for marriage is uncontrollable sexual appetite.) He hedged, of course, noting that "I have no command of the Lord" (1 Cor 7:25). Does that mean this part of Scripture is not divinely inspired? Taken together with Jesus' teaching that disciples will renounce biological family ties, where does this leave the "family values" movement?

The only time Jesus explicitly names the kinds of folk who are headed for eternal damnation, the ones on the list are those who did not provide food for the hungry or drink for the thirsty, did not welcome strangers or provide clothing to the naked, did not visit prisoners. Maybe the Southern Baptist Convention should indicate that question on its messenger registration cards and ask for a signed attestation. These and dozens of other plain stipulations are routinely overlooked by even the most ardent defenders of biblical authority.

The interpretive layers in these questions are as subtle as they are many. I am convinced, however, that Scripture does have within its text an insight which helps us deal with these questions, a narrative relevant to questions of sexual orientation and biblical fidelity.

THE JERUSALEM PROTOCOL

The story in Acts 10 is almost as familiar as that of Gen 19. Beginning here and moving on through chapter 15 is the narrative accounting the struggle of the early Christian community as it moved from a parochial to a universal mission. The key characters of chapter 10 are Cornelius, a God-fearing Gentile, and Peter. First, Cornelius has a vision from God telling him to locate Peter. Peter likewise has a vision, of animals descending from heaven on a sheet. He's instructed to eat them; but these are unclean and compliance would be an "abomination" according to the Bible. His refusal is met with this rebuke: "What God has made clean, you must not call common or profane."

All of this is visionary preparation for Peter's being willing to commit an abomination-to associate with Cornelius, a profane, unclean Gentile who by definition is a religious pervert-at the prompting of a "holy angel" which is identified later in the chapter as the Holy Spirit.

In subsequent chapters this theological confusion over what is and is not the divinely inspired Word of God is eclipsed by a bevy of stories about the trials of early Christian missionary work: of the journeys of Paul and Barnabas, tales of persecution and imprisonment, the martyrdom of James. Chapter 15 hints at the coming doctrinal debate in the church with a report that certain Jewish Christians from Judea were insisting on the fundamentals of the faith: circumcision for the newly-converted Gentile believers and, by implication, accountability to the law of Moses. They were insisting on the authority of the Bible.

Then comes the fight on the floor of the convention in Jerusalem. Missionary stories of revival breaking out among the (religiously perverted) Gentiles are told with jubilation. But some of the fundamentalists are upset that these converts are not being required to believe the Bible is literally true. The missionaries have gone soft on the "law of Moses."

The more conservative leaders argue that you either believe all of the Bible or none of it. Either it's authoritative or it's not. And the Bible (the "law of Moses") commands circumcision-the texts are plain, their meaning is indisputable.

Finally, Peter stood up and said, in effect: "I know what the Bible says. What I'm telling you is that I've seen indisputable evidence of the work of the Holy Spirit in the lives of these Gentile-perverts. God has cleansed their hearts by faith and has made no distinction between them and us. We don't exactly have a perfect track record when it comes to being faithful to the Bible ourselves."

Peter was on to something important. His was a precedent-setting theological argument: clear evidence of the presence of the Holy Spirit-evidence attested to in the Bible-overrules any particular regulation. The regulations, in other words, are in service to the Spirit, not the other way around. I call it the "Jerusalem Protocol." The idea is ancient and deeply biblical: "The only thing that counts is faith working through love," according to Paul (Gal 5:6). Fidelity to the Bible, to paraphrase Jesus, can be summarized in two inter-twined statements: "You shall love the Lord your God with all your heart, and with all your soul, and with all your mind" and "your neighbor as yourself" (Matt 22:37–40).

Is homosexuality compatible with Christian faith? Is hetero-sexuality compatible with Christian faith? Uncircumcised, or circumcised? Neither question, I would suggest, is relevant. To quote sacred Scripture, "We believe that we will be saved through the grace of the Lord Jesus, just as they will" (Acts 15:11).

Appendix 13

Reflections on Lynchburg II

The Return of Soulforce to "Falwell Territory"

Doug Donley

In October of 1999, I joined 200 other people from Soulforce in a journey to Lynchburg, Virginia. Having been trained in nonviolence, we went to meet 200 people from Thomas Road Baptist Church and Liberty University, both led by Jerry Falwell. The 400 of us sat around tables hearing each other's stories. We promised not to judge each other. We told our truth and took tentative steps across the chasm that often divides the gay, lesbian, bisexual and transgender (GLBT) communities and their allies from conservative evangelicals. We made lasting friendships and heard Jerry Falwell promise to scale back his rhetoric against the GLBT communities.

He did, for a while. But as the months passed, Jerry went back to his old ways. We called him on it, he repented and then again repeated his anti-gay rhetoric. So Soulforce went back to Lynchburg last October.

By that time, I had three more years of Soulforce organizing under my belt. I had seen many lives changed at national meetings of Methodists, Lutherans, Presbyterians, and even Southern Baptists. I knew that the presence of Soulforce saves lives because people see hundreds of people in the streets tirelessly working for the day when all will be welcomed at God's table. And yet, three years of continuing untruths had passed. Three years of hate crimes. Three years of sincere people doing acts of violence sincerely thinking they are following God's will. It was time to go back, to confront the untruth, to put my body, my heart, and myself in the way of the violence. I told a member of my church, as she dropped me off at the airport, that if I could save just one person from committing suicide, the time, energy, and money I spent would be worthwhile.

On October 26, 2002, we staged the first Gay Pride festival ever to be held in Lynchburg. This festival was important because the culture of Lynchburg is one of fear for the GLBT communities. Many are not able to be open about sexual orientation at their jobs, in their churches, or with their families. We offered our presence to create a place of acceptance, if even for a weekend. Under a rainbow arc of balloons in Riverside Park, we danced, sang, told our stories, and witnessed to the fact that God loves all people regardless of their sexual orientation.

We met many people who were thrilled that we were there—young and old, gay and straight, in the closet and out. Although 500 people celebrated with us, many stayed away because of fear. Closeted students from Liberty University stayed away from fear of expulsion—and for good reason. We were not the only ones there. There were about 20 counter-demonstrators, holding signs condemning the GLBT communities, berating the crowds through bullhorns, and using scare-tactics to intimidate the Pride participants.

It took all of our strength to maintain our vows of nonviolence. We were taught that love is more powerful than hate. We were taught to ignore the protestors, not to engage with them. Since we did not want them to usurp our message, we did our best to ignore them. But the more we ignored them, the more they increased their toxic rhetoric. They started making direct, personal, and explicit remarks to individuals in the crowd. It took tremendous courage not to be drawn into the desire to have our revenge.

Some of the hecklers were almost as young as my kids. They were told by their parents to say things like: "Got AIDS yet?" and "God hates fags." I got a taste of what my GLBT sisters and brothers endure all too often. We wept and prayed through it all. I took to singing hymns: "Jesus loves me this I know, for the Bible tells me so...Precious Lord, take my hand; I am weak, I am tired, I am sore . . . What a friend we have in Jesus . . ." I even found myself singing the secular songs of my childhood. "It's a beautiful day in the neighborhood . . . Would you be mine, could you be mine, won't you be my neighbor?"

Soulforce teaches us that the counter-protesters are not our enemies, they are victims of untruth, just as we have been. They are not the enemy; untruth is. If we had responded in violence, it would have escalated the problem, like adding gasoline to a fire. Eventually, the counter-demon-strators got so tired, they simply packed up and left. We had fought back, without fighting back, by taking in their verbal blows and diffusing them. This is what we call voluntary redemptive suffering.

When Sunday rolled around, we went to Thomas Road Baptist Church. Unlike last time, we did not enter the church. We did not eat a meal with Jerry Falwell and his people, nor did we expect to. Three years ago they withdrew their promise to provide us with food because a passage out of First Corinthians states that one should not eat with sinners. We stood in silent prayerful vigil outside of the church and passed out flyers and brochures to all who would accept them. The detailed booklets once again demonstrated the tragic consequences of the untruths about God's GLBT children.

Jerry Falwell didn't pay us any mind, but his son Jonathan did. He came across the street, greeted us and cordially welcomed us to Lynchburg. Two church volunteers brought us the leftover doughnut holes they had provided for people coming to worship at Thomas Road Baptist Church that morning. It was an unsanctioned, spontaneous gift of spirit. I don't think they realized the powerful theological statement that it made. But this year, people gave us doughnuts on the picket line. I have to believe that there is hope for Jerry and his people. But I am not waiting for his people to come around. I'll continue to do my work. I will relentlessly resist untruth and witness with all my might to the fact that God loves all people regardless of sexual orientation.

—*Doug Donley, a longtime member and supporter of the BPFNA, is pastor of University Baptist Church in Minneapolis, Minnesota. This article, printed in* Baptist Peacemaker, Vol 20 No 3, Summer 2000, *won the Associated Church Press Award of Merit for Editorial Courage for that year.*

"I told a member of my church, as she dropped me off at the airport, that if I could save just one person from committing suicide, then my time, energy, and money would be worthwhile."

APPENDIX 14

How Grace Gut-Punched Me in English Class

DAVID EMERSON LANE

"Bill seems somewhat agitated by the long list of people waiting to be interviewed. He stands up and walks around the small waiting room. He goes outside to smoke. He comes back in. He sits. He looks at the list. He counts heads. He goes outside to smoke. He slouches back into his chair dejectedly, looking at the floor blankly."

Editor's note: We wanted to find out how recent changes in public assistance programs were affecting people—particularly children—already living in poverty. We decided, instead of going to policy analysts and social workers, to ask the impoverished people themselves how they are faring under the new system. We sent 16-year-old David Lane to Caritas, an emergency assistance agency in Waco, Texas, to talk with recipients and get an idea from them about what it's like "out there." Here's what happened.

• • •

I DRIVE UP 5TH Street past the old cars—cars with trash bags for windows, with mufflers hanging, with ropes that keeps the doors shut, with cracked front windows, and even a car with no front windshield at all. I enter the waiting room at Caritas of Waco. Forty or fifty people sit patiently. Old church pews have been donated for the room, giving an odd sense of reverence to the room. The room is not completely silent, but the fluorescent light's hum can be heard above the quiet conversations. Heart is in the room; people are telling stories.

I'm in my grubbies, hoping I'll blend in somehow. I sit among them. I listen to the stories.

Mrs. Hernandez lives with her husband, her three children, and her mother. All other family members live in Mexico. Despite her husband's employment and governmental assistance in the form of food stamps, she cannot feed everyone all the time.

When I ask about the children she smiles. "Seven, eight, and nine. Two girls and one little boy," she said. "They don't know I come up here, but you know I think Julia, I think she guesses about where I've gotten so much groceries all of a sudden."

This is the third time she has had to come to Caritas. It is not that the Hernandez home is un-American, lazy or stupid. They have fallen through a crack in the poverty line that is widening; they are unable to eat, but don't get enough federal assistance. They come to Caritas when times are bad.

"Caritas helps me with my utility bills, so I came up here with my medical bill for the kids, thinking maybe they could help me. They said no that time. But we got by. We got by."

Last year she came up to Caritas three minutes too late to have a thanksgiving turkey. She laughs about having sliced turkey sandwiches and stuffing. "But we gave an awful lot of thanks that day, an awful lot."

• • •

Bill is a young man who lives in a halfway house. He is staying there to shake his substance abuse. On his arm are etched two gang tattoos. Although he works occasionally out in McGregor (a nearby rural town), the halfway house has advised him to apply at Caritas for assistance.

Bill is wearing jeans that have faded to nearly white. His hair is combed, and except for a hole in his shirt, he is dressed well. Bill seems somewhat agitated by the long list of people waiting to be interviewed. He stands up and walks around the small waiting room. He goes outside to smoke. He comes back in. He sits. He looks at the list. He counts heads. He goes outside to smoke. He slouches back into his chair dejectedly, looking at the floor blankly.

A small child mumbles something and turns around to Bill. The parents of the child are talking to an interviewer. Bill smiles and hands the kid a piece of candy from his pocket. The child giggles and munches it down.

"I been at this halfway house, trying to clean myself up, and this is just part of it," Bill says through the gap where his two front teeth should be.

· · ·

"I take what I can get. I have a kid at home, and it's no shame to feed him."

Danita lives in Parkside, one of Waco's housing projects, and at 24 years old is a single mother without work. I ask her how she feels about coming to Caritas for help.

She rode up in a car to Caritas with three other single mothers. Shinta is 20, recently unemployed from Church's Chicken (a fast food restaurant). The other two women are older, and don't talk. They sit with their hands folded and heads down, not sleeping, merely accustomed to the slow pace of the interview process.

Shinta asks me if I still went to school, and I reply in the negative. "I been out for six years, I did maybe two or three months at Waco High," she says with remorse. I never get the nerve to ask her why she never finished.

One of the group's friends enters the room, followed by a little pre-schooler. Bill gets up from the sofas so that the newcomer can sit on it; she is also pregnant.

They talk of boyfriends and children, of good times and hard times, of paychecks and water bills. None of them are currently fully employed. Danita takes the pregnant woman's child and bounces him on her knee. Danita talks to the child about getting good "Caritas cookies" to eat once mama gets the food she came for. [A chain of supermarkets, HEB, gives its old bread, cakes, and cookies to Caritas. It is not uncommon to get a day-old display cake along with cans of food.]

Slowly they are called and get their food, one by one. Each time they all help carry the boxes out to the trunk of the car. Each time Bill gives a helping hand. And the food seems like a lot, a whole trunk full. But, I think, I don't know how long this food has to last. I don't know how many grandmothers, I don't know how many children, I don't know how many babies . . .

There is a faction of citizens that claims that welfare creates a sub-class of Americans. In some of the more brutal portraits, they show welfare moms having more kids to receive more from the U.S. taxpayer. A cursory view of the Caritas waiting room today would lead this faction to say "Here's your proof." The pregnant woman is a "welfare mother," and she is having another child while receiving federal aid.

This young mother, is she trapped in federal programs? She is a strong-willed woman, taking her child with her on the long bus ride from her home to Caritas. She had no help in carrying her bags on the bus, not to mention herself and her young child. Could she ever become employed? I don't know. When Danita mentions that her neighbor got a job, this young mother asks where, and if they are still hiring. She writes down the address and phone number.

Did she have these children to get more money from the U.S. taxpayer? She sits and plays patty cake with her young son. Danita points to a hole in the jacket she is wearing.

"Girl, you know I haven't gotten any clothes for me in a year. But look at that jacket I got on him," pointing to her boy, "that was bought on sale. I want him looking sharp for kindergarten." She whispers nonsense syllables to the child within her. There seems to be a maternal glow about her.

Perhaps if one watched her get up slowly from her chair, with assistance from Bill, and walk out to the bus stop with her box of food and her young son trailing, then it would finally shatter the stereotype of her as a leach on the system.

Last year Caritas helped 38,922 families by giving them more than three million dollars' worth of assistance. Dr. Eugene F. Jud, Caritas of Waco's executive director, expects that number to increase even more this year because of government cutbacks.

"Say your neighbor's house burned down. Well, of course you'll let them stay at your home and have some food. But what about the poor? No one jumps out of their cars to hand food to these people. We all care, it's just that we don't fully care all the time. And the poor suffer."

The food that poured in during the agency's one-week "Food for Families" food drive is used throughout the year. Agency officials hope that it will last. Caritas clients are hurt by the changes that have occurred in legislation, and less federal aid means a greater reliance on Caritas.

"We've had to cut back in certain areas. We used to give $50 per family for utilities; now we can only give $35," said Pauline Ruiz, director of the emergency assistance program and an interviewer for Caritas since 1967. "We see a lot of people who haven't been here for a long time, because they got work, but now they've lost their jobs, and so now I see them back."

If a mother—say, Danita—doesn't go to job training, she may get cut off from certain programs. For single males there is a ticking clock on aid; you use up all your months and you are cut off. Perhaps Danita didn't check the mail when a warning came from AFDC (Aid to Families with Dependent Children), or she was sick, or she couldn't find a ride to the office. So her reapplyment is denied, and suddenly that aid she was counting on is gone. All the government sources are bound by strict regulations. She asks where she can go to feed her children. Someone says, "Caritas'll give food to anyone."

•　•　•

The children play idly in the waiting room. Some dart in and out of the cold weather. They seem happy, and most seem adequately clothed. There is a little Mexican boy, walking around the waiting room, bossing his younger brother. He holds the little brother up so that he can drink from the water fountain. The older brother's face tightens up, he clamps his teeth down, and he lifts his brother all the way up.

His mother paces the waiting room. She hears her name called. Bill lifts her boxes for her to the car.

•　•　•

I drive back to school and park in my assigned spot, beside a new 1998 Camero and a Toyota Camry. (I attend Midway Independent School District (MISD), which is carved from a conservative upper middle class suburban enclave. I walk to my all-white English class where the person beside me is wearing slacks and dress shirt. A girl in front of me, not much younger than Danita, discusses her upcoming church ski trip to Aspen.

It isn't that "welfare" is suddenly ended, but the promise of no hungry American mouths is somehow weakened by legislation. The Great Society has become the Mediocre Society, or the Fend-for-Yourself Society. The safety net is a little (or perhaps a lot) weaker. Washington has unfortunately put the responsibility of feeding widows and children to the private sector. "Go to Caritas" is the mantra of the "new welfare."

So I sit there, in a state of constant amazement, in a stupor of realization, oblivious to a worksheet on adverbs. I feel grace like one feels the cold. I woke up today and had breakfast. I had lunch. I am going home to have dinner. If I get sick, I could go to the doctor. I have my own room to sleep in.

Grace has gut-punched me during English class.

• • •

This is not my first up-close view of poverty. I have gone to Kids Club (a Christian outreach program to small children in housing developments with Saturday morning activities), the Salvation Army soup kitchen, and the Church Under the Bridge (a popular local Sunday morning service for homeless people under an interstate bridge). I've been an intern for *Seeds Magazine* for more than a year. I am not blind to poverty. Before this experience I would have told you that I *knew* poverty.

I didn't. I hadn't met Mrs. Hernandez. I hadn't spoken with Danita. I hadn't seen Bill. I hadn't spent five hours sitting with them. Once you see the faces behind the percentages and numbers, you will never forget.

At times most unexpected they visit you. I had a burrito, and it brought a memory of Shinta. I drove by Parkside Village and thought about Danita. I often wonder if Bill has found a full-time roofing job. I am reminded: I am graced.

I was given the assignment of finding and writing about the face of poverty today, in my community. I found it. But there is something else that I also found: my own personal responsibility to relieving poverty. And I am reminded of something my Sunday school teacher keeps saying, "The poor do not exist for us to save them; the poor exist for the salvation of us."

—*David Lane at this writing was a junior at Midway High School, an editorial assistant for* Seeds Magazine, *and a member of Seventh and James Baptist Church in Waco, Texas. The article is from the winter 1997 issue of* Baptist Peacemaker, *Vol 17, No 4. In 1998 the article was singled out for an Associated Church Press award. David now lives and works in New York City.*

Appendix 15

In the Valley of the Shadow

A September 11 Reflection

Ken Sehested, *with* Kyle Childress[1]

> How lonely sits the city
> that was full of people!
> How like a widow has she become,
> she that was great among the nations!
> ... She weeps bitterly in the night ... (Lam 1:1–2)

On September 11, I awoke in the home of a good friend in Nacogdoches, Texas, to the news that certain parties, unnamed at the time, had hijacked U.S. agents of affluence to attack the World Trade Center and the Pentagon, twin symbols of global economic and military dominance.

The horrific details and graphic visual images flood our ears and eyes for days—even weeks. There I sat, in the oldest city in Texas, reflecting on the oldest drama of human savagery. What might we say, dare we say, in the face of such horror? Was there any hope, any healing, any harvest of mercy to be had?

These questions led me to reminders both of pastoral insight and prophetic challenge.

PASTORAL INSIGHT: THE TASKS OF THE BODY OF CHRIST

At moment like this, the first engagement of the Body of Christ is to begin the ministry of grieving for the individuals and families whose lives have been crushed by this catastrophe. We weep with those who weep.

1. Published in *Baptist Peacemaker* 21:4 (2001) 2–3.

263

Holy grief, the practice of lament, is not a form of self-centered pity but the willingness to crouch with those forced to their knees in the face of devastation. The billowing grief rising from this trauma is very real and will not be disposed of with the power of positive thinking. We have no quick answers or explanations—or even plans of action.

Among other things, the ministry of grieving is important because it implies that the community of faith has not lost touch with the pulse of God's intent in creation, an intent confirmed in the rainbow promise of Genesis 6, ratified in the cruciform career of Jesus and dramatically broadcast in John's concluding Revelation, promising the new heaven and the new earth, when all tears will be dried and death itself shall be defeated (21:1–4).

Furthermore, the ministry of grieving reminds us that we are not engineers of the coming Reign of Peace, but witnesses, pointing to where this Promise is breaking out even in our midst (and, conversely, where it is being opposed). Grieving is also a powerful antidote to the arrogance of self-sufficiency, to confidence in wishful thinking and human control. There is a sustaining force in the universe that we can trust, which is available but not manageable.

The second engagement for the Body of Christ is to intercede in prayer for the casualties of this catastrophe. Intercessory prayer is not a form of spiritual hocus-pocus; we have no magical wand to wave to make the hurt go away. "The effective, fervent prayer of the righteous availeth much," according to the King James rendering of the Apostle Paul's advice. We may debate exactly how this is so, but this much is clear: intercessory prayer keeps us in a heightened state of readiness to intervene with compassion when the moment arises, which is the third call to the Body of Christ.

The third engagement for the church in the face of this catastrophe is to remind our congregations that the root meaning of "apocalypse" is not the advent of destruction but the occasion for uncovering. While God is certainly not the author of this pain, there is the possibility that, out of the grief, an unveiling may occur; and we must prepare to ask and respond to the question, "What is God saying to us?"

PROPHETIC CHALLENGE: CHOOSE THIS DAY
WHOM YOU WILL SERVE

Grieving and intercession make us available for the ministry of mercy and comfort. This, of course, is what U.S. President George W. Bush attempted in his speech to the nation Tuesday evening when he referenced the psalmist's affirmation of hard-won hope: "Yea, though I walk through the valley of the shadow of death, I will fear no evil; for thou art with me; thy rod and thy staff they comfort me" (Psalm 23:4). It is appropriate for the nation's leader to speak words of succor to the people. And the believing community should stand ready to echo and amplify those words whenever possible.

Nevertheless, the Body of Christ must remain alert when Caesar quotes Scripture. The text of Holy Writ is forever threatened with being co-opted, is always in danger of being robed in the garments of empire, of being mobilized to endorse injustice, of being segregated from intended conclusion. And in Tuesday night's episode, President Bush neglected to note that the text he quoted pushes forward to the point of table fellowship with enemies.

Which brings me to the parallel, if less comfortable, work of prophetic challenge to which the Body of Christ has been ordained. An essential work of Gospel proclamation is theological interrogation of political propaganda. The Body of Christ is called to ask the questions currently being disguised by newspaper headlines.

For instance: Not so long ago, following the bombing of the Murrah federal building in Oklahoma City, state authorities, news media, and common mobs alike began harassing people of Arab descent living in the U.S., only to discover that responsibility actually lay with one of our own decorated war veterans of European lineage.

The believing community, moreover, needs to recall an embarrassing bit of history about Osama bin Laden himself. It was the U.S. who originally recruited, trained, and supplied bin Laden and his colleagues for guerrilla warfare. Back then, his services were as a "hot" proxy agent in our "cold" war with the Soviet Union. He has since found a more lucrative offer on the "free market" of global political violence.

And of course there's the recent demonization of Saddam Hussein, whose original chemical weapons arsenal was supplied by the U.S. back when he was still our ally against the Iranian Ayatollah.

To our shame and peril, we have little knowledge of a millennium of Western meddling in Arab affairs—deposing this ruler, propping up that one, with no criteria other than cost/benefit calculations. Few in the U.S. realize that our nation, aided by Great Britain, has waged the longest bombing campaign in human history against Iraq. Since the formal end of the Gulf War—and without even the semblance of United Nations' authority—the U.S. has, over the past decade, continued to rain death from the skies on a weekly, sometimes daily basis.

UNICEF, the U.N.'s child-welfare agency, has indicated that at least a half-million Iraqi children have died since the end of Desert Storm from causes directly related to international economic sanctions. When former U.S. Ambassador to the U.N. Madeleine Albright was asked point-blank on national television if the death of half a million children was worth the price of opposing Hussein, she said yes. We say no. The competition of loyalty is that stark. Choose this day whom you will serve.

ELISHA'S TRANSFORMING INITIATIVE

There is another way. It is a common, though grossly unattended, melody in Gospels—repeatedly echoed by Paul—the most insistent note of which is the stress on loving enemies. For the Body of Christ, the failure to love enemies is to hedge on Jesus.

This theme is woven into the fabric of Scripture. Take for example the story of the Prophet Elisha's transforming initiative recorded in 2 Kings.

In the sixth chapter the King of Aram (Syria) is menacing Israel, sending raiding parties across the border to steal crops, livestock, even young people for sale as slaves. It was a conscious policy designed to effect Israel's submission to Aramean political, economic and military control.

Political intrigue enters the story when the king notices that Israel seems to know of all his military strategies in advance. He suspects a "mole" in his intelligence apparatus. After extensive investigation, his trusted aides return with this shocking news: No, there's no spy in our camp. The problem is that Israelite prophet, Elisha, who somehow divines the king's most highly-guarded orders.

So the king orders that Elisha be "neutralized." Troops are assembled; they undertake a cross-border raid on the prophet's home. Under the stealth of night, they surround Elisha's headquarters.

As dawn breaks, the prophet's student intern arises to fetch the newspaper. When he steps outside in the cool morning air, the sight of an Aramean army startles the residual slumber from his eyes. Panicked, he rouses his mentor.

When Elisha finally calms his protégé enough to get a coherent story, the prophet seems curiously unimpressed. "But we're surrounded by an army!" the intern exclaims. Elisha prays: "Oh, Lord, please open his eyes that he may see." After the "amen," Elisha urges the young man to take another peak out the window. He is dumbfounded by what he sees. The Aramean army is still there; yet surrounding their ranks is an even larger, encircling army of angels astride flaming chariots and horses.

At that moment the Aramean army advances on the prophet. Elisha prays again: "Close their eyes so they cannot see." And the entire army of Aram is struck blind. As the chaos ensues, Elisha steps out of the house, calls to the commanding general, saying, "I hear you're looking for the Prophet Elisha?" "Yes," comes the stuttered response from a confused and frightened voice.

"Well, he's not here," Elisha nonchalantly responds. "But I can take you to where he is." So this massive army, in stumbling formation, meekly fall in line behind Elisha. Whereupon they are led straight to Israel's capital, to the king of Israel, inside the walled city—and delivered into the waiting hands of their enemies!

The Israelite king is overjoyed and immediately sets about to order a slaughter. But Elisha has something else in mind. He prays again, this time to have the Aramean soldiers' eyesight restored. All present are then further confounded by Elisha's next directive. "There will be no killing here today. Put away your weapons; gather food and drink. Today we feast!"

So these mortal enemies sit down at common tables for a grand meal. When everyone is satisfied, Elisha instructs the Arameans to return to their home. The story ends with these brief words, "And the Arameans no longer troubled the land of Israel" (6:8–23).

Part of our prophetic calling is to insist that there are rival, realistic, and spiritually-informed alternatives to those policies which depend on superior firepower and assume the need for political domination. We lift them up and, together with all who share this common vision, recommend them to our national leaders.

THE LAMB OF GOD

For the Body of Christ, the pivotal point of the vision sustaining such alternatives is portrayed in John's Revelation. In the fifth chapter there is a picture of the end of history.

As the sacred book of life is revealed, an angel asks, "Who is worthy to open the scroll?" The text concludes that none is able, no one in heaven or on earth—neither kings nor presidents, generals nor multinational magnates. And the narrator weeps at this admission.

A member of the heavenly hosts exclaims that there is only one capable of opening the scroll: the conquering Lion of Judah. But suddenly, without explanation, the image shifts. Instead of a lion standing ready between the throne and heavenly hosts, the narrator identifies a lamb: "I saw a Lamb standing, as though it had been slain . . ."

The Lion of Judah has been transposed as the Lamb of God. The Lion of Judah has conquered by being the Lamb slain. And as the Lamb opens the book, countless creatures and angels sing: "Worthy is the Lamb who was slain, to receive power and wealth and wisdom and might and honor and glory and blessing . . . for ever and ever!"

Overcoming the world's enmity will indeed come at the cost of much blood. But in the end only the power to relinquish life, rather than take it, results in a restored community.

It is possible to fearlessly traverse the valley of the shadow of death—but not because we are the meanest S.O.B.s in sight. We have learned that only those willing to lose life, for Christ's sake—that is to say, for the sake of the promised Peaceable Reign of God—will find it.

Bibliography

"A Litany of Rededication for Use in Celebrating Dr. King's Birthday." *PeaceWork* (November-December 1987) 3.

Apel, William. *Signs of Peace. The Interfaith Letters of Thomas Merton.* Maryknoll: Orbis, 2006.

Archer, J. Douglas. "Conscientious Objectors and the Northern Baptist Convention of 1940." *Foundations* 15 (October-December 1972) 342–54.

Baker, Nicholson. *Human Smoke. The Beginnings of World War II, the End of Civilization.* New York: Simon & Schuster, 2008.

Baldridge, William E. *Be Not Afraid. Bible Studies.* Memphis: BPFNA, 1991.

———. "The Quincentenary: 500 Years and Counting." *Baptist Peacemaker* 12:1 (1991) 1.

Baldridge, William E., and Kim Mammedaty. *The Earth Is the Lord's. Sermons and Bible Studies from the 1992 Summer Conference.* Memphis: BPFNA, 1992.

Balisky, Tama Ward. "So That All May Lie Down in Safety." *Baptist Peacemaker* 25:2 (2005) 9.

Baptist Peace Fellowship of North America. "Pathways to Peacemaking: Mapping a Vision. 2004–2007."

The Baptist C.O. An Organ of the Baptist Pacifist Fellowship, September–November 1945.

Baptist Peacemaker International Spirituality Series, 1986–1988.

Baptist Peace Link, A Newsletter for Baptist Peacemakers, April 1982–February 2000.

Baptist Peacemaker, December 1980–.

Berrigan, Daniel. *Steadfastness of the Saints: A Journal of Peace and War in Central and North America.* Maryknoll: Orbis, 1985.

Berry, Wendell. *Collected Poems 1957–1982.* New York: North Point, 1985.

Bledsoe, Michael. "Robert C. Broome: A Tack 'n Hammer Peacemaker." *PeaceWork* (November–December 1985) 7.

Boulding, Elise. *Cultures of Peace: The Hidden Side of History.* Syracuse: Syracuse University Press, 2000.

Broadway, Mike. "A Report on the Self-Help Credit Union." *Baptist Peacemaker* 23:4 (2003) 4.

Broome, Robert C. "The Birth of *Baptist Peacemaker.*" *Baptist Peacemaker* 25:4 (2005) 3–4.

———, editor. *Peacemaking and a Tangled Web. Baptist Peacemaker International Spirituality Series* #1. Louisville: International Division, *Baptist Peacemaker,* 1986.

Brueggemann, Walter. "A Shalom Lectionary." *PeaceWork* (November–December 1986) 4–7.

Buckhart, Roy A. "The Church and Returning Service Men and Women." *Christian Frontiers* 1 (March 1946) 81–9.

Butler, Dawn Kirk, and Michael Butler. "Peace Mission to USSR." *Baptist Peacemaker* 5:3 (1985) 4–5.

Butterfield, Herbert. *The Whig Understanding of History.* New York: Norton, 1965.

Bibliography

Buttry, Daniel L. "BPFNA Ships 1,000 Books around the World." *Baptist Peacemaker* 20:4 (2000) 9.

———. *Christian Peacemaking: from Heritage to Hope.* Valley Forge: Judson, 1994.

———. "Ethiopians and Eritreans Vigil Together for Peace." *Baptist Peacemaker* 21:4 (2001) 8.

———. *Interfaith Heroes.* Canton, MI: Read the Spirit, 2008.

———. *Surfacing and Analyzing Conflict.* Memphis: BPFNA Pamphlet, 1997.

———. "Tears of Mutual Repentance. Eritreans and Ethiopians Pray for Peace at Michigan Conference." *Baptist Peacemaker* 20:4 (2000) 13.

Buttry, Daniel L., and Evelyn Hanneman. *Through the Year. A Peacemaker's Journal.* Charlotte: BPFNA, 2005.

Buttry, Daniel L., and Mas'ood Cajee. "Christian/Muslim Peace Training Initiative Launched." *Baptist Peacemaker* 22:2 (2002) 12.

Cain, Cliff. "Friendship Tour to the Soviet Union Stretches Hearts, Minds." *Baptist Peacemaker* 10:3–4 (1990) 16–17.

Carman, Peter J. B. "Lake Avenue Baptist Church Welcomes Karen Refugees." *Baptist Peacemaker* 28:5 (2008) 5.

Childress, Kyle C. "Always Between Places." *This Far By Faith. Celebrating Our Tenth Anniversary.* Memphis: BPFNA, 1994.

———. "How to: Preach on Peace (without Resorting to Violence)." *PeaceWork* (March–April 1986) 6–7.

Chittister, Joan. "Life, Liberty and the Pursuit of Enmity." *Baptist Peacemaker* 10:3–4 (1990) 1.

Christian Frontiers. 1946–1949.

Christman Kim and Stan Dotson. "Beyond Jackrocks and Prayer." *Baptist Peacemaker* 10:1–2 (1990) 6–7.

Claiborne, Shane. *Irresistible Revolution. Living as an Ordinary Radical.* Grand Rapids: Zondervan, 2006.

Cober, Kenneth L. "Peace Week. A Community Project." *International Journal of Religious Education* 8 (1932).

Coffin, William Sloane, Jr. *Once to Every Man: A Memoir.* New York: Scribners, 1977.

Coleman, Dee Dee M. "A Dangerous Mission. Delivering the Gospel to Those Who Have No Hope." *Baptist Peacemaker* 27:4 (2007) 7.

Collazo, Luis. "By Faith We Will Walk into the Future." *This Far By Faith. Celebrating Our Tenth Anniversary.* Memphis: BPFNA, 1994.

Committee on an Assessment of CDC Radiation Studies. *A Review of the Radiological Assessments Corporation's Fernald Dose Reconstruction Report.* Washington DC: National Academies Press, 1997.

Cook, Katie. "Ken Sehested: Journey of a Peacemaker." *Baptist Peacemaker* 22:3 (2002) 2–4.

———. "*Comunidad Evangélica Amoxcalli*: A Place of Refuge." *Baptist Peacemaker* 21:2 (2001) 4.

Cornell, Tom. "How Catholics Began to Speak Their Peace." Online: http://64.191.235.137/issues/peace/tcorn.html.

Cutten, George B. "The Intolerant Baptists." *Christian Frontiers* 1 (March 1946) 90–96.

Dahlberg, Edwin T. "Consideration on Massive Reconciliation." Hassler files, SCPC FOR DG 13, Series E, folder: 1969–1974. January 2, 1967.

Bibliography

————. "The Task before Us." Swarthmore College Peace Collection DG 13, Series D: FOR USA, 1915–1965. December 6, 1957.

Dahlberg, Keith. *Edwin T. Dahlberg. Pastor, Peacemaker, Prophet.* Valley Forge: Judson, 1998.

Damon, Allan L. "Amnesty." Accessed November 14, 2008. Online: http://www.americanheritage.com/articles/magazine/ah/1973/6/1973_6_8.shtml.

Dear, John. *A Persistent Peace. One Man's Struggle for a Nonviolent World.* Chicago: Loyola, 2008.

Dekar, Paul R. "Australia Apologizes to the Stolen Generation." *Baptist Peacemaker* 28:2 (May–June 2008) 16–17.

————. *Community of the Transfiguration. The Journey of a New Monastic Community.* Eugene, OR: Cascade, 2008.

————. *Creating the Beloved Community. A Journey with the Fellowship of Reconciliation.* Telford, PA: Cascadia, 2005.

————. "For Peace and Reconciliation in Europe and the World." *Atlantic Baptist* 26 (April 1990) 16–7.

————. *For the Healing of the Nations. Baptist Peacemakers.* Macon: Smyth and Helwys, 1993.

————. "The 'Good War' and Baptists Who Refused to Fight It." *Peace and Change* 32 (2007) 186–202.

————. "How to: Celebrate a Children's Sabbath." *Baptist Peacemaker* 15:3 (1995) 14.

————. "'I AM a Man.' Somebodyness and the Dignity of Labor in Dr. King's Last Campaign." *Memphis Theological Seminary Journal* 44 (2008) 59–69.

————. "Peacemaking in Nicaragua." *Canadian Baptist* 132:11 (1986) 7–11.

————. Review of Laura Slattery, Ken Butigan, Veronica Pelicaric, and Ken Preston-Pile. *Engage: Exploring Nonviolent Living.* Oakland: Pace e Bene, 2005. *Baptist Peacemaker* 26:3 (2006) 18.

Directory of Civilian Public Service, May 1941 to March, 1947. Washington DC: National Service Board for Religious Objectors, 1947.

Donley, Doug. "Reflections on Lynchburg II: The Return of Soulforce to 'Falwell Territory.'" *Baptist Peacemaker* 23:2 (2003) 4.

————. "Welcoming Guests: A Sister Church Delegation Experience." Model Ministries (November 2008).

Druk, Deidre. "Reflections from Nicaragua." *Baptist Peacemaker* 28:5 (2008) 14–15.

Dugan, Warren. "Faith of a Conscientious Objector." *Baptist C.O.* 3 (1945) 5.

Dussel, Enrique. Editor. *The Church in Latin America 1492–1992.* Maryknoll: Orbis, 1992.

Edelman, Marian Wright. "In Defense of Children." *PeaceWork* (May–August 1986) 8–9.

Enns, Elaine, and Ched Myers. "Seventy Times Seven: A Theology of Reconciliation." *Baptist Peacemaker* 24:2 (2004) 6–9.

Ernst, Eldon G. "Twentieth-Century Issues of War and Peace." *Foundations* 15 (October-December 1972) 298–317.

Esquivel, Julia. *Threatened With Resurrection: Prayers and Poems from an Exiled Guatemalan.* Elgin: Brethren, 1982.

Farley, Margaret A. and Serene Jones. Editors. *Liberating Eschatology. Essays in Honor of Letty M. Russell.* Louisville: Westminster John Knox Press, 1999.

Feather, Frank. "Think Globally, Act Locally." Accessed September 23, 2008. Online: http://en.wikipedia.org/wiki/Frank_Feather.

Bibliography

Finlator, William W. "Christianity in Spite of the Churches." *Christian Frontiers* 2 (February 1947) 43–4.

———. "Free the Conscientious Objectors." *Christian Frontiers* 1 (June 1946) 181.

Fosdick, Harry Emerson. *Living of These Days*. London: SCM, 1957.

Galtung, Johan and Graeme MacQueen. *Globalizing God. Religion, Spirituality and Peace*. Oslo: Kolofon, 2008.

Gates, Connie. "Jamkhed: Health and Healing with Hope and Justice." *Baptist Peacemaker* 26:4 (2006) 4–5.

Gill, Rachel. "The Heritage of the BPFNA. Presentation to the Fifth Summer Conference in Ottawa, Ontario." July 6, 1990.

Goodwin, Daniel C. Editor. *Revivals, Baptists, and George Rawlyk: A Memorial Volume*. Baptist Heritage in Atlantic Canada 17. Wolfville: Gaspereau Press, 2000.

Goosen, Rachel Waltner. *Women against the Good War. Conscientious Objection and Gender on the American Home Front, 1941–1947*. Chapel Hill: University of North Carolina, 1997.

Greene, Amy. "Cuban Baptist Women Ordained during BPFNA Women's Friendship Tour." *Baptist Peacemaker* 12:2 (1992) 16.

Gunderson, Gary. *Deeply Woven Roots. Improving the Quality of Life in Your Community*. Minneapolis: Fortress, 1997.

———. "No Simple Questions." *Seeds* 2 (January 1980) 4.

Hahn, Thich Nhat. *Being Peace*. Berkeley: Parallax, 1987.

Hammond, Steve and Daniel L. Buttry. "BPFNA Assisting Peace Project in Burma/Myanmar." *PeaceWork* (July–October 1989) 18.

Hammond, W. M., Jr. "They Serve Without Weapons." *Christian Frontiers* 1 (November 1946) 291–97.

Handy, Robert T. Editor. *The Social Gospel in America: Gladden, Ely, Rauschenbusch*. New York: Oxford University Press, 1966.

Hanneman, Evelyn. "Let Us Seek Justice: A Reflection Following the Death of Amadou Diallo." *Baptist Peacemaker* 20:1 (2000) 13.

———. "It Is Well with My Soul." *Baptist Peacemaker* 22:2 (2002) 11.

Harris, Maria. *Proclaim Jubilee! A Spirituality for the Twenty-first Century*. Louisville: Westminster John Knox, 1996.

Hassler, Alfred. *Diary of a Self-Made Convict*. Chicago: Henry Regnery, 1954.

Hayes, Paul C., "It Is Good In Our Hearts." *Baptist Peacemaker* 10:1–2 (1990) 8.

———. "Peace and the Price of Justice." *Baptist Peacemaker* 15, 1–2 (1995) 2–3.

Hinson, E. Glenn, editor. *The Doubleday Devotional Classics*. 3 Volumes. Garden City: Doubleday: 1978.

———. "Prayer in an Economy of Abundance." In *Prayer and Liberation*. Edited by M. Basil Pennington. Canfield: Alba House, 1976.

Howe, Julia Ward, "Mother's Day, 1870." *PeaceWork* (January–April 1988) 1.

Hunter, Bob and Carol Hunter. *Transforming Power. Bible Studies on Racial Reconciliation*. Lake Junaluska: BPFNA, 1997.

Jacobsen, Dennis A. *Doing Justice. Congregations and Community Organizing*. Minneapolis: Fortress, 2001.

John Paul II, *Message for the Celebration of the World Day of Peace, January 1, 2004*. Online: http://www.vatican.va/holy_father/john_paul_ii/messages/peace/documents/hf_jp-ii_mes_20031216_xxxvii-world-day-for-peace_en.html.

Jones Ellis. *The Better World Shopping Guide. Every Dollar Makes a Difference*. Philadelphia: New Society, 2008.

Bibliography

Jones, Stephen D., *Peaceteacher. Jesus' Way of Shalom.* Victoria: Trafford, 2007.

Jordan, Clarence. *The Cotton Patch Version of Paul's Epistles.* New York: Association, 1968.

Keating, Thomas. *Manifesting God.* New York: Lantern, 2005.

Kelsey, George. *Social Ethics among Southern Baptists 1917–1969.* Metuchen: Scarecrow, 1973.

Kimball, Charles. *When Religion Becomes Evil.* San Francisco: Harper, 2002.

King, Martin Luther, Jr. "The Casualties of the War in Vietnam." Accessed November 8, 2008. Online: http://www.stanford.edu/group/King/publications/speeches/unpub/670225–001_The_Casualties_of_the_War_in_Vietnam.htm.

———. *A Knock at Midnight. Inspiration from the Great Sermons of Reverend Martin Luther King, Jr.* Edited by Clayborne Carson and Peter Holloran. New York: Warner, 1998.

———. *The Papers of Martin Luther King, Jr.* Senior Editor Clayborne Carson. 6 vols. Berkeley: University of California, 1992–2007.

———. "The Quest for Peace and Justice." Accessed September 23, 2008. Online: http://nobelprize.org/nobel_prizes/peace/laureates/1964/king-lecture.html.

———. *Where Do We Go From Here: Chaos or Community?* New York: Harper & Row, 1967.

The Koran Interpreted. Translated by A. J. Arberry. New York: Macmillan, 1955.

Lane, David Emerson. "How Grace Gut-Punched Me in English Class." *Baptist Peacemaker* 17:4 (1997) 4–5.

Lee, Dallas. *The Cotton Patch Evidence.* New York: Harper & Row, 1971.

Lester, Muriel. *Training.* Nashville: Abingdon, 1940.

Lewis, John, and Michael D'Orso. *Walking with the Wind: A Memoir of the Movement.* New York: Harcourt, 2001.

Longchari, Akum. "Sowing Seeds of Peace: The Naga People's Journey for Truth, Justice, Peace and Understanding." *Baptist Peacemaker* 20:1 (2000) 14.

Loomer, Bernard M. "Dores R. Sharpe, Portrait of a Christian Rebel." *Foundations* 24:2 (1981) 99–121.

Lowder, Jim. "Imagining Our Future." *Baptist Peacemaker* 23:4 (2003) 2.

Machado, Antonio. *Selected Poems.* Translated by Alan S. Trueblood. Cambridge: Harvard University Press, 1982.

Marty, Martin E. "Foreword." In Paul R. Dekar. *For the Healing of the Nations. Baptist Peacemakers.* Macon: Smyth and Helwys, 1993.

Mashburn, Linda. "Walking the 'Way of the Cross.' Finding Faith among Guatemalan Refugees." *Baptist Peacemaker* 13:3 (1993) 15.

McKenna, Lee. "Like a Stone Cast Into Still Waters." *Baptist Peacemaker* 18:1 (1998) 13.

———. "Sudan: Never Again All over Again." *Baptist Peacemaker* 28:2 (2008) 18–19.

———. "The Seventy (More or Less)." *This Far By Faith. Celebrating Our Tenth Anniversary.* Memphis: BPFNA, 1994.

McGinnis, Jim, Gretchen Lovingood, Ken Lovingood, and Jim Vogt. *Families Creating a Circle of Peace.* St. Louis: Institute for Peace and Justice, 1996.

McGinnis, Jim, and Kathleen McGinnis. *Parenting for Peace and Justice.* Maryknoll, NY: Orbis, 1983.

McKibben, Bill. *Deep Economy: The Wealth of Communities and the Durable Future.* New York: Times, 2007.

Merrick, Bob. "Getting Rid of ROTC." *California Magazine.* Online: http://www.alumni.berkeley.edu/Alumni/Cal_Monthly/September_2004/Recalling_Cal.asp.

Bibliography

Miles, Delos. *Evangelism and Social Involvement*. Nashville: Broadman & Holman, 1986.

Minus, Paul M. *Walter Rauschenbusch: American Reformer*. New York: Macmillan, 1988.

Mixon, Rick. "Charles Z. Smith Receives Dahlberg Peace Prize at BPFNA Breakfast." *Baptist Peacemaker* 25:3 (2005) 14.

———. "Assessing the BPFNA's Statement on Homosexuality." *Baptist Peacemaker* 13:2 (1993) 15.

Morrison, Toni. *The Dancing Mind: Speech upon Acceptance of the National Book Foundation Medal for Distinguished Contribution to American Letters*. New York: Knopf, 1996.

Olive Peace Branch Initiative. *Rebirthing King, Rebirthing America: Celebrating the 80th Birthday of Reverend Dr. Martin Luther King Jr. as a New American Government Takes Office*. Washington DC: OPBI, 2008.

Palmer, G. E. H., Philip Sherrard, and Kallistos Ware. Editors. *The Philokalia. The Complete Text Compiled by St. Nikodimos of the Holy Mountain and St. Makarios of Corinth*. London: Faber and Faber, 1979.

"Patristic Retrieval and Baptist Renewal: In Honor of E. Glenn Hinson." *Review and Expositor* 101 (Fall 2004).

Paterson-Watt, Bob. "Fall and Rise of Vieques Island." *Baptist* Peacemaker 23:2 (2003) 2–3.

Percesepe, Gary. "Three Ways BPFNA Partner Congregations Can Make a Difference." *Baptist Peacemaker* 24:4 (2004) 13–19.

Pipkin, H. Wayne, editor. *Seek Peace & Pursue It. Proceedings from the 1988 International Baptist Peace Conference*. Memphis: BPFNA and Ruschlikon, Switzerland: Institute for Baptist and Anabaptist Studies, 1989.

Polaski, LeDayne McLeese. "Learning to See. A Reflection on the BPFNA Friendship Tour to Migrant Worker Camps." *Baptist Peacemaker* 18:3 (1998) 14.

Polaski, LeDayne McLeese, and Millard Eiland. *Rightly Dividing the Word of Truth. A Resource for Congregations in Dialogue on Sexual Orientation*. Charlotte: BPFNA, 1997.

Polaski, Sandra Hack. "The Southern Baptist Convention and World War II Conscientious Objectors: Defining Freedom of Conscience." *Baptist History and Heritage* 28 (April 1993) 19–33.

Powell, Stephanie Day. "Environmental Racism and Environmental Justice in New Orleans." *Baptist Peacemaker* 27:2 (2007) 14.

Practice Hospitality: Baptist Peacemakers on the Road. Memphis: BPFNA, 1990.

Pullen, Larry. "How to: Start a Human Rights Group in Your Local Congregation," *PeaceWork* (November–December 1986) 8–9.

Purchase, LeeAnn. "Caught between Hope and Horror." *Baptist Peacemaker* 12, 3 and 4 (Fall-Winter 1992) 18.

Putnam, Robert D. *Bowling Alone: The Collapse and Revival of American Community*. New York: Simon & Schuster, 2001.

Rix, Harry. "A Time for Reflection." *PeaceWork* (November–December 1989) 20–21.

Romero, Oscar. *Voice of the Voiceless. The Four Pastoral Letters and Other Statements*. Translated by Michael J. Walsh. Maryknoll, NY: Orbis , 1985.

Rutba House. Editors. *School(s) for Conversion: 12 Marks of a New Monasticism*. Eugene, OR: Cascade, 2005.

Rutenber, Culbert G. *The Dagger and the Cross: An Examination of Christian Pacifism*. New York: Fellowship, 1952.

Bibliography

Sachs, Jeffrey D. *Common Wealth. Economics for a Crowded Planet.* New York: Penguin, 2008.

Sehested, Ken. "Baptist Peacemakers in North America: A Story, a Strategy, and a Theology." *Faith and Mission* 4:1 (1986) 13–26.

———. "Character-Altered Religion. Commentary on This Issue's Special Section on Economics." *Baptist Peacemaker* 16:2 (1996) 2.

———. "Conformity and Dissent: Southern Baptists on War and Peace since 1940." *Baptist History and Heritage* 28 (April 1993) 3–17.

———. "How to: Start a Peacemaker Group in Your Local Church," *PeaceWork* (September 1985) 8–9; reprinted, *Baptist Peacemaker* 12:3 (1992) 23.

———. "How to: Start and Sustain a Sister Church Relationship," *PeaceWork* (November–December 1988) 5–7; a revised version appeared in *PeaceWork* (May–August 1990) 22–2.

———. "Inciting the Saints. The BPFNA's Commitment to Local Churches." *Baptist Peacemaker* 20:4 (2000) 3.

———. "Recipe for Peacemaking: Which Ingredient Can You Supply?" *PeaceWork* (May–June 1988) 1–12.

———. "Revive Us Again." *PeaceWork* (May–August 1986) 1–2.

———. "The Road to Rome." *Baptist Peacemaker* 28:4 (September–October 2008) 10–11.

———. "St. Peter and the Jerusalem Protocol. Commentary on Biblical Fidelity and Sexual Orientation: Why the First Matters, Why the Second Doesn't and Why Baptist Peace Fellowship Members Should Care," *Baptist Peacemaker* 15:1–2 (1995) 10–11.

———. *Trust and Obey. Notes toward a Spirituality of Justice. Baptist Peacemaker International Spirituality Series* #10. Louisville: International Division, *Baptist Peacemaker*, 1987.

———, editor. *Walk Together Children. An Ecumenical Resource for Congregations in Partnership across Racial Lines.* Lake Junaluska: BPFNA, 1997.

Sehested, Ken, and Rabia Terri Harris. *Peace Primer.* Charlotte: BPFNA, 2002.

———, with Kyle Childress, "In the Valley of the Shadow. A September 11 Reflection," *Baptist Peacemaker* 21:4 (2001) 2–3.

Sehested, Nancy Hastings. "The Heritage of the BPFNA. Presentation to the Fifth Summer Conference in Ottawa, Ontario." July 6, 1990.

Shakespeare, William. *The Tempest.* Edited by Northrop Frye. New York: Penguin, 1970.

Shaw, Susan M. *God Speaks to Us, Too: Southern Baptist Women on Church, Home, and Society.* Lexington: University Press of Kentucky, 2008.

Sibley, Mulford Q. and Philip E. Jacob. *Conscription of Conscience. The American State and the Conscientious Objector 1940–1947.* Ithaca: Cornell, 1952.

Sider, Ronald J. *Scandal of the Evangelical Conscience.* Grand Rapids: Baker, 2005.

Siler, M. Mahan, Jr. "Therefore, Love Truth and Peace." *Baptist Peacemaker* 11:2 (1991) 17.

Silko, Leslie Marmon. *Ceremony.* New York: Viking, 1977.

Smith, Andy. "Hope beyond Martyrdom." *Baptist Peacemaker* 20:2 (2000) 6–7.

Smucker, Matthew. "What Is To be Done? Assessing the Antiwar Movement," *The Indypendent.* March 14, 2008.

Staggs, Al. *A Pilgrim in Rome: Cries of Dissent.* Charlotte: BPFNA, 2008.

Stassen, Glen H. *Journey into Peacemaking.* Memphis: Brotherhood Commission, SBC, 1987.

Bibliography

———. *Just Peacemaking. Transforming Initiatives for Justice and Peace.* Louisville: Westminster John Knox, 1992.

The Story of 50 Southern Baptist Civilian Public Servicemen. Pamphlet, 1945.

This Far By Faith. Celebrating Our Tenth Anniversary. Memphis: BPFNA, 1994.

Tiller, Carl. *The Baptist Fellowship for Peace—A History.* Pamphlet, 1977.

Tiller, Olive. "Crossing the Edmund Pettus Bridge. Recollections of a Pivotal Moment in the Civil Rights Movement." *Baptist Peacemaker* 11:2 (1991) 19.

———. "How to: Organize a Public Policy Hearing in Your Church." *PeaceWork* (May 1985) 9.

Trulson, Reid S. "Baptist Pacifism: A Heritage of Nonviolence." *American Baptist Quarterly* 10 (1991) 199–217.

UNICEF. *The State of the World's Children.* New York: Oxford University Press, 1996.

Walsh, Tom. "Baptist Peace Mission to Russia." *Baptist Peacemaker* 3:4 (1983) 1.

Washington, James M. Editor. *A Testament of Hope: The Essential Writings of Martin Luther King, Jr.* San Francisco: Harper & Row, 1986.

Weber, Cindy. "Revolutionary Longings." *Baptist Peacemaker* 25, 4 (Fall 2005) 10.

Whitehead, Kim. "'. . . to bear witness to what we have seen and heard'" *PeaceWork* (May–June 1987) 7.

Wilhelm, Paul A. *Civilian Public Servants. A Report on 210 World War II Conscientious Objectors.* Washington DC: National Interreligious Service Board for Conscientious Objectors, 1990.

Williamson, George, Jr. *Be Not Afraid. Sermons.* Memphis: BPFNA, 1991.

———. "Bible Studies." *This Far By Faith. Celebrating Our Tenth Anniversary.* Memphis: BPFNA, 1994.

———. "The Coming Peace: A Vision from the Peace Conference." In Pipkin, H. Wayne, editor. *Seek Peace & Pursue It. Proceedings from the 1988 International Baptist Peace Conference,* 209–216. Memphis: BPFNA and Ruschlikon, Switzerland: Institute for Baptist and Anabaptist Studies, 1989.

———. *Holding out for a Biblical Life. Thoughts.* Baptist Peacemaker International Spirituality Series #11–12. Louisville: International Division, *Baptist Peacemaker,* 1988.

———. *Radicals: Anabaptists and the Current World Crisis. A Manifesto.* Charlotte: BPFNA, 2005.

———. "Testimonies of Struggle and Hope in Eastern Europe." *PeaceWork* (January–April 1988) 5.

———. "Twenty-five Jubilees." *Baptist Peacemaker* 29:1 (2009) 8–9.

———. *Who Is God in the Heat of War, in the Hope of Peace? Theology in the Chaos of History.* Memphis: BPFNA, 1991.

Williamson, Marianne. *A Return to Love. Reflections on the Principles of A Course in Miracles.* New York: HarperCollins, 1992.

Wilson, Jonathan R. *Living Faithfully in a Fragmented World: Lessons for the Church from MacIntyre's After Virtue.* Harrisburg, VA: Trinity, 1997.

Wilson-Hartgrove, Jonathan. *New Monasticism; What It Has to Say to Today's Church.* Grand Rapids: Brazos, 3008.

Womack, Paula. "Baptist Pen Pals for Peace." *Baptist Peacemaker* 11:4 (1991) 5.

———. "Beyond the 'Aunt and Uncle' Syndrome." *PeaceWork* (May–August 1990) 18–9.

Bibliography

Worldwatch Institute. *State of the World 2009. Into a Warming World. A Worldwatch Institute Report on Progress Toward a Sustainable Society.* New York: W. W. Norton & Company, 2009.

Yoder, John Howard, translator and editor. *The Schleitheim Confession.* Scottdale, PA: Herald, 1977.

Young, Marion Marshall. *Journey of Discovery. An Autobiography 1914–.* Chattanooga: PIP, 1992.

Yurke, Jeanne. Reaping Where Others Have Sown." *PeaceWork* (May–June 1989) 3–5.

Zahn, Gordon Charles. "A Descriptive Study of the Social Backgrounds of Conscientious Objectors in Civilian Public Service during World War II." PhD diss., Catholic University of America. 1953.